ACTION RESEARCH IN EDUCATION

SECOND EDITION

ERNIE STRINGER

Curtin University of Technology

PEARSON

Merrill
Prentice Hall

Upper Saddle River, New Jersey
Columbus, Ohio

Library of Congress Cataloging-in-Publication Data

Stringer, Ernest T.
  Action research in education / Ernie Stringer.
    p. cm.
  Includes bibliographical references and index.
  ISBN 978-0-13-225518-9
  1. Action research in education. I. Title.
  LB1028.24.S86 2008
  370.7′2—dc22   2007016425

Vice President and Executive Publisher: Jeffery W. Johnston
Publisher: Kevin M. Davis
Editorial Assistant: Sarah N. Kenoyer
Production Editor: Mary Harlan
Production Coordinator: Norine Strang, Carlisle Publishing Services
Design Coordinator: Diane C. Lorenzo
Text Design and Illustrations: Carlisle Publishing Services
Cover Design: Jeff Vanik
Cover Image: SuperStock
Production Manager: Laura Messerly
Director of Marketing: David Gesell
Marketing Manager: Autumn Purdy
Marketing Coordinator: Brian Mounts

This book was set in Berkeley Book by Carlisle Publishing Services. It was printed and bound by R.R. Donnelley & Sons Company. The cover was printed by R.R. Donnelley & Sons Company.

Pearson Prentice Hall™ is a trademark of Pearson Education, Inc.
Pearson® is a registered trademark of Pearson plc
Prentice Hall® is a registered trademark of Pearson Education, Inc.
Merrill® is a registered trademark of Pearson Education, Inc.

Pearson Education Ltd.   Pearson Education Australia Pty. Limited
Pearson Education Singapore Pte. Ltd.   Pearson Education North Asia Ltd.
Pearson Education Canada, Ltd.   Pearson Educación de Mexico, S.A. de C. V.
Pearson Education–Japan   Pearson Education Malaysia Pte. Ltd.

1 0 9 8 7 6 5
ISBN-13: 978-0-13-225518-9
ISBN-10:   0-13-225518-9

PREFACE

INTRODUCTION

In the past few years action research has achieved bandwagon status in education. In an era driven by high-stakes testing, where teachers are expected to achieve increased test scores within dramatically short time intervals, action research is often the chosen instrument of accountability. "Try out this approach to instruction, test the students, and see if you get increased scores," seems to be a rather standard modus operandi in many quarters. This "try it and see if it works" approach to research, a misapplication of a plan-act-reflect-evaluate process, is not only simplistic but has little chance of providing the desired outcomes. Poor educational performance is not merely a reflection of inadequate teaching strategies but the consequence of a wide range of possible factors that include classroom, school, family, and community effects. Quick-fix, spray-on solutions that try to identify the "silver bullet" teaching technique are not only unlikely to succeed but have the added deficiency of failing to provide the means to adequately identify the sources of poor performance and appropriate remedial action.

Action research, applied systematically to the issue of poor academic performance, provides a high likelihood of improving student outcomes, but only if all issues likely to have an effect are taken into account. The research processes described in this book are honed by many years of successful application, and provide teachers, educational leaders, families, and community members with a set of tools for engaging significant problems in classroom and school. The stories embedded in each chapter are but a small sample of many highly successful projects in schools in the United States, Australia, East Timor, and other locations. They are based on projects implemented by teachers, students, parents, principals, and university faculty, and cover a wide range of school-related problems, from classroom learning through student behavioral issues to parent and family participation.

While the processes, as they are presented herein, may seem laborious and time consuming, they may be applied expediently and judiciously in ways that integrate easily with regular school activities. It is possible to apply action research as a process of inquiry learning in a single lesson lasting 30 to 40 minutes. Novice researchers should therefore limit trials of the methodology to relatively small problems to learn how to move through the processes of investigation easily and productively. As they become more experienced they will acquire increased levels of skill and understanding, eventually moving easily through an action research routine as part of their regular teaching or leadership activities. Action research, to some extent, is a state of mind—an attitude of inquiry that is an integral part of the habits of a reflective practitioner.

But action research is not just a technical routine. It provides the basis for developing strong and productive relationships with people, enlivening their work together and producing sometimes dramatic and creative outcomes that enhance their classrooms and schools. Action research, in these terms, provides high levels of motivation that highlight the potentials that lie in the heart of any educational setting. Research can truly become "the search for truth in the company of friends," and provide deep levels of satisfaction for teachers wishing to make a difference in the lives of their students.

ACTION RESEARCH ON THE RUN

One reviewer of a draft version of this book commented, "My students would never have time to do all this." The text is necessarily detailed, providing specific guidance for many of the skills that may be required for the different contexts and problems to which action research can be applied. Conceptual frameworks provide a "compass" or "roadmap" that enables practitioners to keep track of action research processes applied to their work. The look-think-act routine included in Chapter 1, for instance, has been used in planning or problem-solving sessions covering a period of only two hours. Teachers and educational leaders therefore can apply action research processes simply and flexibly for routine issues, though complex and endemic problems may require more extensive and detailed work. For simpler issues, however, practitioners may apply a simple research routine "on the run," as an integral part of their daily work activities.

STRUCTURE OF THE BOOK

The purpose of this book is to provide teachers and educational leaders with an understanding of the nature of action research (Chapters 1 and 2) and the procedures and applications of action research (Chapters 3 through 7). In addition, it provides practical resources that add to the fund of knowledge available to action researchers (Chapters 8 and 9).

Chapter 1 presents an overview of action research, describing its characteristics and accentuating the research relationships that are an integral part of this methodology.

Chapter 2 provides readers with a deeper understanding of the epistemology (system of meaning) that drives action research. It describes the theoretical positions that inform the practice of action research, focusing on the analytic processes that are now an integral part of much professional and social scientific research.

Chapters 3 through 7 describe in detail the stages of one cycle of an action research process—research design, data gathering, data analysis, reporting, and taking action. Each of these chapters features both the process and skills, providing readers with clear guidance for enacting action research routines.

Chapter 8 presents a number of case studies that are indicative of the broad range of ways that action research can be applied in classroom and school settings. Stories and reports drawn from diverse environments describe ways that teachers, educational leaders, and community groups have enhanced their work by the use of action research.

Finally, Chapter 9 presents a small sample of the proliferating resources now available on websites throughout the world, providing a rich resource for any action research project.

ACKNOWLEDGMENTS

This book could not have been written without the input and support of many people. I would particularly like to acknowledge the influence and support of many of my colleagues and friends who over the years have provided us with the benefit of their wisdom. I am particularly indebted to my partner, Rosalie Dwyer, who continues to support me through the long process of writing entailed in completing this book.

I also am grateful to the staff of Pearson Merrill/Prentice Hall who consistently provided support during the development and production stages of this text—Kevin Davis, Mary Harlan, and Sarah Kenoyer, and to Norine Strang, Carlisle Publishing Services. I thank the reviewers: Harry S. Boguzewski, Bowling Green State University; Nola Butler Byrd, San Diego State University; and Suzanne Medina, California State University, Dominquez Hills. Their many useful comments and their keen insights ensured that this book has gained greatly in clarity and usability.

RESEARCH NAVIGATOR:
RESEARCH MADE SIMPLE!

www.ResearchNavigator.com

Merrill Education is pleased to introduce Research Navigator—a one-stop research solution for students that simplifies and streamlines the entire research process. At www.research-navigator.com, students will find extensive resources to enhance their understanding of the research process so they can effectively complete research assignments. In addition, Research Navigator has three exclusive databases of credible and reliable source content to help students focus their research efforts and begin the research process.

HOW WILL RESEARCH NAVIGATOR ENHANCE YOUR COURSE?

- Extensive content helps students understand the research process, including writing, internet research, and citing sources.
- Step-by-step tutorial guides students through the entire research process from selecting a topic to revising a rough draft.
- Research Writing in the Disciplines section details the differences in research across disciplines.
- Three exclusive databases—EBSCO's ContentSelect Academic Journal Database, The New York Times Search by Subject Archive and "Best of the Web" Link Library—allow students to easily find journal articles and sources.

WHAT'S THE COST?

A subscription to Research Navigator is $7.50 but is free when used in conjunction with this textbook. To obtain free passcodes for your students, simply contact your local Merrill/Prentice Hall sales representative, and your representative will send you the Evaluating Online Resource Guide, which contains the code to access Research Navigator as well as tips on how to use Research Navigator and how to evaluate research. To preview the value of this website to your students, please go to www.educatorlearningcenter.com and use the Login Name "Research" and the password "Demo."

BRIEF CONTENTS

CONTENTS

8 Case Studies: Action Research Reports, Presentations, and Performances   176

9 Online Resources   224

NOTE: Every effort has been made to provide accurate and current Internet information in this book. However, the Internet and information posted on it are constantly changing, so it is inevitable that some of the Internet addresses listed in this textbook will change.

The Purposes of Action Research

ACTION RESEARCH IN CLASSROOMS AND SCHOOLS

When teachers are asked to do action research in their classrooms, their response is likely to be a combination of surprise, disbelief, and/or wariness. Their responses are linked to images of research involving highly technical routines of investigation engaging sophisticated research instruments and complex statistical analysis. They cannot imagine that they would have the time or the inclination to engage in the highly technical research processes or to use the complex statistical analysis they imagine to be associated with research activities. They are also horrified at the prospect of adding more work to their already busy classroom routines, and can't imagine that "research" would serve any useful purpose in their teaching. The research studies they have read about in teacher preparation programs seem highly theoretical, and a considerable distance from the demanding realities of their daily classroom life.

Action research, however, is a distinctive approach to inquiry that is directly relevant to classroom instruction and learning and provides the means for teachers to enhance their teaching and improve student learning. Far from an "extra" that teachers must somehow cram into an already challenging work schedule, action research can be integrated into regular classroom activities to assist them to enhance student learning and improve their professional practice. The flexibility of action research, however, also provides others involved in schools—administrators, students, parents, school boards, and so on—with the means to solve many of the significant problems that are part of the complex life of a school.

In a recent research class I asked participants, all experienced teachers, to tell me why doing research was important for them. Some were concerned about the impact of current school practices on children and teachers, many of which they perceived as either damaging or inequitable. They wished to learn an approach to research that empowered teachers and children and enabled them to take control of their own teaching and learning, rather than being driven by the sometimes inappropriate dictates of a bureaucracy, or the lack of practical relevance of academic theory.

One class member, focusing on the administrative, organizational context of her work, talked of "the need to learn to think outside the hierarchy," making the familiar ways of organizing school life "strange." Her words echoed the sentiments of another class member who, speaking as a Hispanic person, realized how damaging research sometimes could be when information derived from generalized studies was applied inappropriately in particular classroom settings. She expressed that situation as "using research as a vehicle of oppression." Another, mindful of ways in which experts and administrators had impinged on his own professional life, expressed a concern that he might himself be guilty of the same crime. "How do I leave my own baggage behind in order to see the world [as it really is]?"

This was a common sentiment, expressed variously by individuals as the need to "change my mind-set," to be more alert, more sensitive, and to see more clearly what was happening to the children and colleagues with whom they worked. Others spoke of the need to be sensitive to their position as researchers, expressing a desire to "be a game-player with the people I'm working with," or "to sit with children and talk with them." All were concerned that their research work should have some practical outcome. As one indicated passionately, "I want to do research that will make a difference!" and another concurred, saying, "I want to have a positive effect for children." All saw action research, therefore, as a way of furthering their professional lines, enabling them to improve the educational experience of children in schools and having a beneficial impact on the lives of those with whom they worked.

Although there are limits on the time and resources available to engage research in everyday classroom and school life, by building their research capabilities teachers enhance their professional capabilities as they acquire and extend the skills and experience to engage in systematic investigation of significant issues. Action research is designed for practical purposes having direct and effective outcomes in the settings in which it is engaged. At the heart of the process, however, are teachers with the intent to investigate issues, which helps them to more effectively and efficiently engage the complex world of the classroom.

Action research is not just a formal process of inquiry, but may be applied systematically as a tool for learning in classrooms and schools. Sometimes referred to as inquiry learning, it is particularly relevant to those who engage in constructivist approaches to pedagogy. From an administrator's perspective, it is also a management tool, providing the means for developing effective plans, policies, programs, and procedures at classroom, school, or regional levels. Chapter 7 provides specific procedures, with relevant examples, of the ways action research processes assist educators to accomplish these types of activities. Although the application of systematic research processes sometimes requires a significant investment of time and resources, the pay-offs are considerable. Improved educational outcomes, highly engaged students, enthusiastic parents, and effective programs emerge that not only enhance the quality of student achievement, but also the quality of the educational life of all those who attend the school.

RESEARCH CONCEPTUALIZED

The Meriam-Webster Online Dictionary (2001) provides the following common ways of using the term "research":

1. the collecting of information about a particular subject
2. careful or diligent search

3. studious inquiry or examination
4. investigation or experimentation aimed at the discovery and interpretation of facts
5. revision of accepted theories or laws in the light of new facts
6. practical application of such new or revised theories or laws

Thus, when we research a particular topic for a school project, we are doing so in terms indicated by definition 1, collecting information in a general sense. Traditionally, research performed by scientists and scholars tended to be that related to definitions 4 and 5, though in recent times a broader use includes a more general sense of systematic inquiry inferred by definitions 2 and 3. When practitioners engage in *action* research, however, they add another dimension to the definition. They engage in careful, diligent inquiry, not for purposes of discovering new facts or revising accepted laws or theories, but to acquire information having practical application to the solution of specific problems related to their work. This book focuses on the latter use of the term, though its intent is to demonstrate how some of the tools of scientists and scholars may assist professionals to solve significant problems and to enhance their educational practices.

The deeper purpose of research is to extend people's knowledge and understanding, enabling them to make more informed choices and judgments about the complex issues embedded in their professional lives. Research increases the "stock of knowledge" that provides people with the means to expand their expertise and improve their professional capabilities. Understandings derived from research can provide people with new concepts, ideas, explanations, or interpretations that enable them to see the world in a different way and therefore approach situations in a new, hopefully better, way.

Though any type of learning may provide people with feelings of satisfaction, research provides the possibility of understandings that are truly transformational, requiring people to change the way they see the world. The physical sciences have many easily identified epiphanies, from Copernicus through Newton to Einstein and beyond, where scientific investigations transformed people's understanding of the nature of the physical universe. Though the human sciences have less definitive landmarks, the rigorous and systematic investigation of researchers has transformed the way people think about the social world. Rigorous studies by Kinsey, for instance, dramatically changed people's perception of human sexuality, and within education an emerging body of knowledge struggles to overcome the prejudices and preconceived notions of "common sense" often deeply embedded in the social consciousness of education. Research is a process of inquiry that refuses to accept the taken-for-granted, commonsense assumptions often enshrined in the fabric of any society, and holds them up for scrutiny, asking for observable and trustworthy evidence of "what is going on here."

> Good research can be truly transformative, having the capacity to enable people to see the world in a different way—the effect of a truly "ah-haaa!" experience, when "the light bulb went on." It can thus be a epiphanic experience, and I have seen the excitement in people's eyes, heard the wonder in their voices, felt the sense of awe that sometimes comes with a new way of seeing, and occasionally, a new way of being. It encapsulates the old saying "the truth shall make you free!"

Research, more formally, may be defined as a process of systematic investigation leading to increased understanding of a phenomenon or issue of interest. Though research ultimately is quite an ordinary activity, a process for looking again at an existing situation (re-searching it) and seeing it in a different way, systematic processes of investigation provide the means for ensuring strong and effective processes of inquiry. Within the academic and professional worlds, however, two major systems of inquiry—paradigms—provide distinctly different ways in which to investigate phenomena in the physical and human universe. **Quantitative research**, or **scientific positivism** as it is more correctly known, and **naturalistic inquiry**—often referred to as **qualitative research**—provide powerful but different approaches to research. For purposes of clarity, Chapter 2 explores the differences between the two paradigms, to provide researchers with clearer understandings about the nature of the investigations in which they are involved in their own classrooms and schools. As following sections indicate, action research has a history and tradition that differs significantly from other forms of research that have been commonly used to investigate educational issues.

AN ACTION RESEARCH ROUTINE: SYSTEMATIC PROCESSES OF INQUIRY

Although action research has much in common with the regular problem-solving and planning processes used by educators in the course of their daily classroom routine and school-work, its strength lies in its systematic execution of carefully articulated processes of inquiry. A simple "look-think-act" routine encapsulates the basic action research processes. As researchers implement a study they focus on a specific issue and then:

> **Look:** *Gathering information* (data) by careful observation that includes looking, listening, and recording.
> **Think:** *Analyzing* the information to identify significant features and elements.
> **Act:** Using that newly formulated information to *devise solutions* to the issue investigated.

This simple routine is enacted repeatedly, so that solutions are enacted, observed, analyzed, and reformulated until a successful outcome is achieved. An action research routine is therefore often depicted as a helix (Figure 1.1).

More complex problems and issues require more sophisticated formulations of this simple process, so that a fully articulated action research cycle incorporates the following processes:

- *Design the study*, carefully refining the issue to be investigated, planning systematic processes of inquiry, and checking the ethics and validity of the work.

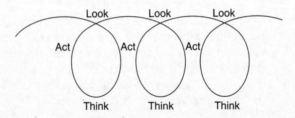

Figure 1.1
Action Research Helix

Figure 1.2
Action Research Cycle

- **Gather data,** including information from a variety of sources.
- **Analyze the data** to identify key features of the issue investigated.
- **Communicate** the outcomes of the study to relevant audiences.
- **Use** the outcomes of the study to work toward resolution of the issue investigated.

The cyclical nature of these processes may usefully be depicted as shown in Figure 1.2. For clarity of detail, however, steps in the action research cycle may also be presented as a sequence, as in Figure 1.3. As the figure illustrates, action research is distinguished from basic research by an "action" phase of inquiry. Although basic research provides information not necessarily used in the research context, action research always has an immediate practical or applied purpose.

USING ACTION RESEARCH

Action research has a wide range of applications in classroom, school, and community contexts. Action research provides the basis for formulating effective solutions to highly significant classroom and school problems—such as classes that are particularly fractious, exceptionally problematic groups of students, underachieving students, multiple external demands, and so on. Action research also provides a useful tool for day-to-day planning in classrooms, such as in lesson planning, formulation of teaching strategies, and student assessment, or more extensive tasks such as syllabus planning, curriculum construction, and evaluation. For the school administrator, action research is also a management tool, providing the means to systematically resolve difficult situations, to engage in program development and evaluation, or to develop strategic initiatives with families and the community.

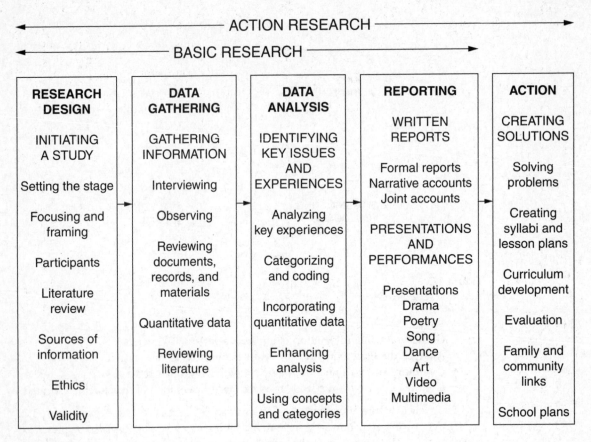

Figure 1.3
Action Research Sequence

A small sample of action research projects in schools, universities, and community contexts includes the following:

- A young teacher, concerned by the disciplinary problems she experienced with a group of "at-risk" boys in her classroom, engaged in an action research process that revealed to her a very different understanding of these children. The knowledge she gained changed her view of the problems she was experiencing, leading to dramatic changes in the way she approached her teaching.
- A grade 3 teacher, concerned that the district was cutting funds for art in schools, investigated with her students the part art played in their classroom lives. They produced an illustrated booklet and a mural for presentation to the district superintendent.
- A teacher engaged in action research processes with his students to construct and implement class syllabi, achieving high levels of student engagement and exciting learning outcomes.
- A neighborhood group engaged in participatory action research with principals, teachers, and parents to investigate ways of increasing parental involvement in local schools. Between them they produced a highly useful list of actions to be taken by teachers and parents.

- A school hired a consultant to assist faculty in evaluating the school's programs. Using action research, the consultant worked with teachers, administrators, and students to highlight positive features of the school's operation and to reveal issues and challenges needing to be addressed.
- A university department used action research processes to plan the implementation of a large, new program to integrate technology into educational areas. The project was highly successful in terms of the levels of engagement of participants and the outcomes achieved.
- A school used action research to resolve racial problems that threatened the stability of school life. A teacher assisted a group of students to investigate related issues in their school and community, leading to a new program aimed at ameliorating problems the school had experienced.
- Two middle school teachers used action research processes to investigate issues of harassment and prejudice with middle school students. Following processes of exploration, students in both groups identified key features of these issues and used them as the basis for producing and staging highly informative plays.

Case Study: Teacher Action Research

The following story and the examples contained in subsequent chapters provide some indication of the potential rewards to be attained as educators become sophisticated researchers in their own right. The stories illustrate how classroom teachers have added to their repertoire of professional skills, and in the process made their work more productive, successful, and enjoyable.

Student Apathy: A Teacher Studies Her Classroom

By Lorise Dorry

A month into a new school year I was puzzled by my inability to engage the students in my year 6 elementary class in a poorer suburb of a large city. In my fifth year of teaching, I felt myself to be a competent and experienced teacher, now well able to handle the rigorous daily routines of working with a large group of children. Despite careful creative planning, however, the students seemed to lack the life and vitality I had experienced in other classes. While they were not badly behaved children, they seemed to be merely "going through the motions," were apt to be a little cynical about the work I prescribed, and "smart" comments intruded into their classroom discussions with some degree of regularity. Despite instituting a number of classroom management techniques and attempting to find interesting ways to present the work, I found them decidedly apathetic. Nothing I tried, it seemed, had any impact on the dull listlessness with which they greeted each new learning activity, or enticed them to improve the rather mediocre work they consistently produced.

Six weeks into the semester, experiencing some degree of frustration and increasing levels of anxiety about my capabilities as a teacher, I decided the time had come to investigate the situation more thoroughly. Using an action research routine I had learned at college, I systematically planned how I would seek to gain greater understanding about how and why it was that my students were so apathetic in class. I began to observe my class more carefully, noting the ways different students went about their work; when, where, and how they engaged in the different classroom activities; their responses to different events occurring within the classroom; and the ways in which different individuals and groups interacted. In doing so I gained greater insights into the social dynamics of my classroom, noting those students who tended to "hang" together, individuals who seemed to be the natural leaders, and those who were isolates—the informal social groups and leaders that are part of any social situation. Over the following weeks I also found opportunities to meet informally with a number of students—leaders and members from the different informal groups—chatting with them in the schoolyard, corridors, and in "downtimes" in the classroom. I gradually accumulated information that enabled me to understand my classroom from the children's perspective and gained much deeper insights into what was affecting my children's classroom life.

Wishing to take advantage of the new insights into my students' experience, I decided to engage the class in a research project as part of the literacy objectives of my class syllabus. I explained to them my concerns about their apparent lack of interest in their schoolwork and my desire to have them assist me in exploring the issue. Using small focus groups, I provided time for students to talk about this issue and list the major features of their experience. As the list of issues emerged I noticed how negative the comments seemed:

- The work we do in class is boring.
- We don't like the reading we have to do each day.
- Math is too difficult.
- Its embarrassing when Mrs. Dorry comments on our work.
- We have the comments some students make about us.

And so on.

A little perturbed by the negative tone of their comments, I asked students to return to their groups to discuss whether there was anything they liked about the class. Feedback sessions revealed a number of aspects of their class experience they enjoyed:

- The computer lab is cool.
- The last social studies project was awesome.
- We like it when we can work in groups.
- We really like Mrs. Dorry.

And so on.

The following day I returned to the issues with the whole class, asking them to talk about those they considered most important. Gradually a consensus emerged that "boring class work" was a major issue. Further group discussions identified the areas of work and the type of activities they found boring. In the process, some children started to spontaneously suggest ways they could make their work more interesting. At that stage I suggested that students form work groups to investigate ways they could make work in those areas more interesting. Different groups focused on reading and literature, social studies, math, and science worked excitedly as they came up with "bright ideas" drawn from their previous classroom experiences, from ideas they'd heard other students or family talk of, or from their own creative imagination.

Sessions in following days provided opportunities for each group to present their ideas to the whole class, and for other students to provide suggestions for extending or enhancing *the learning content or activities being presented. The process was not straightforward for all groups. The math group, for instance, required considerable attention, and I discovered I needed to provide a simple explanation of the purposes and content of the math syllabus to the work group. I discovered, however, that this provided them with a much deeper under-standing of math as an area of study, an understanding that was passed on to the rest of the class in feedback sessions.*

In the following weeks, I was able to work with the class, providing simple descriptions of the syllabus for each of the content areas and having the students assist me to show how they could attain the objectives through learning activities they were largely able to define themselves. As they engaged the process, I noticed increasing levels of engagement, as students not only became absorbed in the learning activities they had helped devise, but also became excited about their achievements. They also, in the process, dealt with some of the behavioral problems that had been noted in their initial discussions, devising a "code of con-duct" that, amongst other things, prohibited "putting down" remarks or comments likely to embarrass individuals.

Within a few weeks of starting the process, I was able to reflect on what the class had accomplished under my guidance. Most of the students were engaged in their work most of the time, they appeared happy with and interested in the work they were doing, and the qual-ity of their work had risen dramatically. Eventually I started getting positive comments from parents indicating they were aware of the differences in their children's responses to school. "I don't know what you've done," said one parent with a laugh, "But I have to stop Clyde from coming to school at daybreak!" My principal and fellow teachers also noted the differ-ence. One commented, "That class has been difficult to work with for years. You've certainly made a difference. What are you doing?"

By the end of the year, comparing results on tests from previous years, I was able to take satisfaction in noting the gains accomplished in many areas by many of the students, and the excitement and enthusiasm that permeated my class for much of the day. By having the class assist me to systematically investigate the problem I had identified, I was not only able to un-derstand more clearly the nature of the problem, but to engage my students in helping plan solutions to the problems that emerged during our research.

Characteristics of Action Research

Action research has a long history, one often associated with the work of Kurt Lewin, who viewed action research as a cyclical, dynamic, and collaborative process in which people addressed social issues affecting their lives. Through cycles of planning, acting, observing, and reflecting, participants sought changes in practices leading to social action for im-provement. A form of action research was used to address problems of assimilation, seg-regation, and discrimination, assisting people to resolve issues, initiate change, and study the impact of those changes (Lewin, 1938, 1946, 1948; Lewin & Lewin, 1942). His ap-proach to action research is reflected in the definition given by Bogdan and Biklen (1992), "the systematic collection of information that is designed to bring about social change."

Noffke (1997), however, suggests that action research is best thought of as a large family, one in which beliefs and relationships vary greatly (p. 306).

Kemmis and McTaggart (1988) suggest that action research is a "form of collective, self-reflective enquiry undertaken by participants in social situations in order to improve the rationality and justice of their own social or educational practices, as well as their understanding of these practices and the situations in which these practices are carried out" (p. 6). For Kemmis and McTaggart, research is carried out by any group with a shared concern, and is only action research when it is collaborative.

Reason and Bradbury (2001, p.10) extend this vision by describing action research as "a participatory, democratic process concerned with developing practical knowing in the pursuit of worthwhile human purposes, grounded in a participatory worldview which we believe is emerging at this historical moment. It seeks to bring together action and reflection, theory and practice, in participation with others, in the pursuit of practical solutions to issues of pressing concern to people, and more generally the flourishing of individual persons and their communities." For them, action research requires skills and methods to enable researchers to foster an inquiring approach to their own practices, to engage in face-to-face work with others to address issues of mutual concern, and to create a wider community of inquiry involving whole organizations.

The relevance of action research to education is signaled in the recent proliferation of texts in this area. They cover a diverse range of orientations and methodologies that reflect the different purposes and theoretical orientations of the authors, and lead to quite different sets of practices. Much action research in education is teacher-centered, focusing on teacher reflection, instructional practices, and evaluation of student outcomes. More sophisticated forms of action research engage collaborative practices that may include any combination of students, colleagues, administrators, parents, and the community.

Texts that focus on the use of action research to improve teacher practices and/or student outcomes include those by Johnson (2002); Johnson (2007); Koshy (2005); Mertler (2005); Calhoun (1994); Brown and Dowling (1998); and Burnaford, Fischer, and Hobson (2000). Literature that provides a broader orientation to the use of action research in school settings—such as applications to broader curriculum and ethical and legal issues—includes Holly, Arhar, and Kasten (2004); Armstrong (2004); Bray, Lee, Smith, and Yorks (2000); Tomai (2003); Mills (2007); Anderson, Herr, and Nihlen (2007); and Somekh (2005). In the same vein, Meyers and Rust (2003) and McNiff and Whitehead (2006) describe how teachers can use action research to tackle basic classroom issues, design their own professional development, and reshape instructional practices. Kalmbach, Phillips, and Carr (2006) describe how action research can serve as a vehicle for assuming a professional identity for students seeking initial teaching licensure. McClean, Herman, and Herman (2005) reveal the way teachers and administrators adopt action research as a strategy for taking a more active role in determining the best solutions to problems in schools.

Literature that focuses more broadly on school improvement or change and development includes Sagor (2000), who provides a seven-step process for improving teaching and learning, and Glanz (2003), who focuses on improvements to the work community within a school. Some of the literature is more clearly directed to educational change, sometimes incorporating social change as an essential element of an action research process (Atweh, Kemmis, & Weeks, 2005; Berge & Ve, 2000; Brown & Jones, 2002; Christiansen,

Goulet, Krentz, & Maeers, 1997; Fals-Borda & Rahman, 1991; O'Hanlon, 2003). Pedraza and Rivera (2005) likewise focus on school reform through educational research with and for Latino communities.

Other texts focus on specific areas of educational life. Burns (1999) presents action research as a collaborative process emerging from the common concerns of English language teachers; Wallace (1998) shows how language teachers can develop their expertise; and Sykes (2002) shows how media specialists can convince their constituents of the importance of school libraries as technology drastically transforms the way information is stored, accessed, and used.

International perspectives are presented by Hollingsworth (1997), who demonstrates how practioners are influencing policy by conducting research, and McTaggart (1997), who describes the development of democratic research practice in quite different institutional and cultural contexts.

Though many authors incorporate quantitative data into an action research process, most recognize it as a naturalistic approach to research that engages teachers in reflective processes that illuminate significant features of their classroom practice. The approach to action research presented in this book differs from much of the literature on teacher research or practitioner research in that it does not focus solely on the teacher, though teachers are central participants in the process. The orientation to action research described herein focuses on:

1. **Change:** Improving practices and behaviors by changing them.
2. **Reflection:** People thinking, reflecting, and/or theorizing about their own practices, behaviors, and situations.
3. **Participation:** People changing their own practices and behaviors, not those of others.
4. **Inclusion:** Starting with the agendas and perspectives of the least powerful, widening the circle to include all those affected by the problem.
5. **Sharing:** People sharing their perspectives with others.
6. **Understanding:** Achieving clarity of understanding of the different perspectives and experiences of all involved.
7. **Repetition:** Repeating cycles of research activity leading toward the solution to a problem.
8. **Practice:** Testing emerging understandings by using them as the basis for changing practices or constructing new practices.
9. **Community:** Working toward the development/construction of a learning community.

WORKING DEVELOPMENTALLY: ENLARGING THE CIRCLE OF INQUIRY

Although action research works effectively for discrete problems and issues within classrooms, it has the potential for more extended applications across classrooms, within schools, or within a community. As participants cycle through a research process, increasing understandings reveal related issues going beyond the immediate focus of investigation, pointing to productive possibilities that might emerge by increasing the scope and power of inquiry. Investigation of specific problems often reveals the multiple dimensions of the situation requiring attention, and investigation of each of those dimensions further illuminates the situation, revealing further possibilities for action.

The process of "starting small" and increasing the breadth and complexity of activity, I call "working developmentally." This is very different from developmental psychology or child development, which is an integral part of most education programs, though conceptually there are some similarities. In each, it is important to engage learners at the level they are capable of comprehending and achieving, according to their stage of "development." In participatory action research, a study may start with limited objectives but the scope of the study may be extended as understanding and awareness increase. The potential for positive change and development increases exponentially as increasing numbers of people and issues are included.

When Shelia Baldwin's group (Baldwin, 1997) investigated the problem of racial disharmony in their school, for instance, they discovered the need to increase the scope of their investigation to include their homes and neighborhoods. The understandings emerging from these investigations greatly increased the power of their investigation and provided the basis for schoolwide action.

In similar fashion, girls involved in the sexual harassment study (see Chapter 9) first increased the number of girls involved, then discovered the need to include boys as part of the group. Investigation of group members' own experiences eventually revealed the need to communicate with other people, including school administrators and security officers. Eventually, they were able to take actions that enabled them to inform all people within the school of the outcomes of their investigation, and to see quite dramatic changes emerge from their efforts.

A key feature of the developmental process is to start with limited objectives. Although many problems within schools, such as high drop-out rates or low student achievement, are complex and multidimensional in scope, it is best to focus initial inquiries on some tangible and achievable objectives. Small initial gains provide people with the stimulus of success and inspire them to take further action. By engaging in continuous cycles of the "look-think-act" process they are able to encompass more dimensions of the problem and increased levels of engagement. Eventually they may be able to incorporate other stakeholders—teachers, administrators, family, and community—thus marshalling increased levels of support and resources that extend the power of the actions they take (See Figure 1.4).

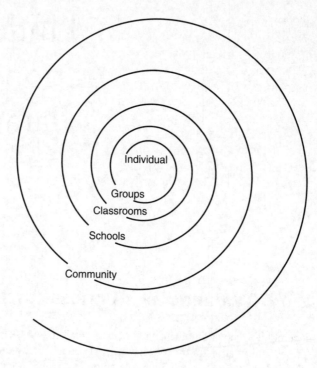

Figure 1.4
Action Research Spiral

SUMMARY

The Purposes of Action Research

Action research is a process of systematic inquiry.

The purpose of action research is to provide educational practitioners with new knowledge and understanding, enabling them to improve educational practices or resolve significant problems in classrooms and schools.

Action research derives from a research tradition emphasizing cyclical, dynamic, and collaborative approaches to investigation.

A common process of inquiry includes:

- Design of the study
- Data gathering
- Data analysis
- Communicating outcomes
- Taking action

Action research may be engaged as a developmental process that systematically increases the scope of the investigation.

Understanding Action Research: Paradigms and Methods

INTRODUCTION: TEACHING AS A PROCESS OF INQUIRY

The public perception of teaching is that it is a simple task, merely requiring the teacher to present information to students, have them learn it, and test them to see that they have learned it. As teachers know, teaching and learning is a much more complex task requiring an extended body of professional knowledge that can be applied to the formulation of effective learning processes for students. Teachers are confronted by a diversity of students who differ markedly in what they bring to the classroom in terms of their ability levels, gender, personalities, family environment, socioeconomic status, and ethnic and cultural backgrounds.

There is no "one-size-fits-all" formula that teachers can apply to their teaching in all situations. Thus, the first task of a teacher—one that becomes an ongoing part of classroom life—is to engage in systematic processes of inquiry and planning. Some of the basic questions that teachers must ask are:

- Who are these children?
- How old are they?
- What are the attributes of the children I will need to take into account in planning a program of learning for them? Age? Ability levels? Gender? Ethnicity? Family background? Health? And so on.

The nature of the curriculum itself also will be subject to conscious processes of inquiry. Teachers will plan a program of learning and devise strategies of teaching and learning according to the content areas to be taught, specified state standards, the age/grade level of the class, and the appropriate strategies of teaching and accompanying learning activities. Their initial inquiries into teaching a class will be based on questions such as the following:

- What is to be taught (to these children, at this level)?
- How can it be taught?

- Which teaching strategies will be appropriate?
- Which learning activities will be effective?

Teachers therefore must engage in systematic processes of inquiry as an ongoing feature of their classroom life in order to enable their students to attain effective learning outcomes. Action research therefore provides them with a framework of activities that enables them to systematically accomplish these tasks. It provides the means for them, over a period of time, to build a body of knowledge about the students in their care, and to incorporate it into an effective program of teaching and learning.

The need for action research applies not only to classroom teachers, but also to administrators who, like teachers, confront complex problems in planning the ongoing organization and operation of a school. They must deal with the diverse attributes of the children in the school, the teachers that comprise their staff, the parents of the children, and the particular communities in which their school is located. Systematic processes of inquiry will, over time, provide them with a wealth of information that contributes to the operation of a harmonious and highly productive educational environment.

Action research as an approach to inquiry provides information that is very specific to the particular situations that confront teachers or administrators, and provides the means to devise actions that are effective in that context. This context-relevant information stands alongside of the more generalized body of knowledge within the research literature that is incorporated into their professional preparation and development.

Because of the diversity of approaches to research now associated with education, this chapter will clarify the distinction between the major paradigms—research systems—that now comprise the literature. The action research enacted by teachers and principals, although having some of the major attributes of a good research process, differs in purpose and outcomes from that embodied in the research literature. While the former is designed to produce practical outcomes relevant to a specific classroom or school, the research literature provides a more general body of knowledge that can be applied across a wide spectrum of locations and contexts. As becomes clear when we learn more about action research, one of its functions is to provide teachers and principals with the means to test the relevance of the research literature to the particular contexts in which they work.

The body of professional knowledge contained within the research literature largely is the product of two different *paradigms* that signal distinctively different approaches to investigation. One, often called *quantitative research,* but more properly known as objective science or scientific positivism, is a hallmark of the modern world. The other paradigm, often called *qualitative research,* though more correctly labeled naturalistic inquiry, is a more recent addition to the research arena. Action research, although it often makes use of quantitative or statistical information, is more clearly associated with the latter paradigm. As we engage in any form of research we need to keep clear the different intentions of our research to ensure that we enact appropriate procedures that enable us to attain the purposes we seek to accomplish.

OBJECTIVE SCIENCE AND EXPERIMENTAL RESEARCH

A large body of educational research based on the application of the procedures of objective science provides an enduring and powerful base of professional knowledge for teachers, administrators, and others with interests in education. It results from one of the enduring legacies of the modern world that is bestowed by science—the application of the scientific method to the solution of problems. So successful has science been at providing miraculous material benefits to human life that billions of dollars are now routinely invested in scientific research, and education has benefited greatly from this systematic investigation of problems and issues related to teaching and learning.

This body of "scientific" knowledge derives from a philosophical perspective that is technically known as scientific positivism. Scientific positivism operates according to a particular set of underlying assumptions and beliefs about the way knowledge can be acquired. It assumes a fixed universe—that events occur in stable and predictable ways according fundamental laws that govern the operation of all things. Scientific positivism assumes that ultimately, in principle, everything in the universe can be measured with precision, and the relationship between things can be described accurately. Continuing scientific efforts to refine and extend our understanding of the universe are carried out in the disciplinary spheres of physics, chemistry, biology, and so on. Each has a distinctive focus, providing scientifically verified information that extends our understanding of the physical universe. Physiology and human biology focus on those aspects of the universe dealing with the human body, but generally stop short of involvement of the "mind," that aspect of the universe that is peculiar to human beings.

The purpose of scientific inquiry, therefore, is to describe with precision the features of the universe in which we live, and the stable relationships that hold between those features. Scientific work is therefore often associated with accurate definition and measurement of "variables"—the features that comprise the universe. The ultimate goal of such work is to establish causal connections that enable us to say that "If x occurs, then y will follow (in all places, at all times)"—for example, if you heat a metal it will expand at a particular rate; if you cool water to a certain temperature it will turn into a solid. Our ability to describe the universe in these terms is responsible for the miraculous transformation of the material environment—aircraft, computers, motor vehicles, fabrics, construction materials, household goods—as well as huge improvements in health and longevity. Many diseases that once ravaged whole regions of the world have now been eradicated, and medications provide the means to alleviate a host of ailments to which humans are susceptible. All result from the careful application of the scientific method to the description of the laws governing the physical universe.

The outcome of the application of scientific principles to the development of explanation and understanding is a highly sophisticated and rigorous stock of scientific knowledge resulting in many advances in policies, practices, and technologies across all areas of human life. The knowledge emerging from positivistic science continues to have the potential to dramatically enhance people's lives.

The primary method for establishing scientific explanations is the experimental method. Experiments are carefully designed so that random assignment of subjects to experimental groups and the controlled application of experimental treatments or interventions allows researchers to state with high degrees of certainty that the effects observed were related to the treatments or interventions. Many studies, for instance, have observed the effect of different teaching strategies on student learning, with researchers carefully controlling the conditions under which these strategies were applied in classrooms to carefully selected groups of students, and the experiments operating in carefully controlled classroom conditions. The intent of such designs is to attempt to eliminate rival explanations for the results obtained. Controlling extraneous variables is thus an important aspect of experimental design, since the potential influences on learning are many and varied, including such variables as class size, student learning styles, ethnicity, race, gender, social class, type of school, parenting style experienced by students, motivation, personality, illness, drug use, intelligence, aptitude, school size, exposure to media, and so on. Researchers want to be sure that any result they obtain from experimentally manipulating teaching strategies may not, in fact, be attributable to one or more of these or any other factors. The body of knowledge derived from these studies enables educational practitioners to analyze problems occurring in a classroom, to identify the factors likely to be their cause, and to formulate actions that will provide a remedy.

Quasi-experiments, or nonexperiments as they are sometimes called (Johnson, 2001), are used where it is not possible to manipulate variables experimentally, either for ethical or pragmatic reasons. It would be difficult, for instance, to imagine setting up a study in which students were subject to intense pain to see whether that factor increased their performance on tests. What is possible, in these situations, is to engage in studies where variables are controlled or manipulated statistically rather than experimentally, establishing the nature of the relationship between variables by carefully contrived statistical manipulation. Researchers are able to employ statistical methods that control for a wide range of variables and, in the process, minimize the plausibility of rival explanations for the effects observed.

McEwan (2000) provides a clear description of quasi-experimental studies of school voucher programs, showing how in conditions where it is not possible to control who enters private and public schools, researchers are able to employ statistical methods that control for the background of families and students. In this manner it is possible to minimize the possibility of plausible rival explanations for the effects of school voucher programs and to control for the effect of variables such as parental education, family income, gender, race, and ethnicity.

Both experimental and quasi-experimental research are subject to forms of quality control to ensure rigor in procedure and stability of results. For these reasons, experiments are evaluated according to their reliability, internal validity, and external validity—the extent to which similar results may be obtained from different settings, samples, and times (reliability); the extent to which results might be attributed to the experimental variables (internal validity); and the extent to which results apply to the broader population from which the sample was drawn (external validity or generalizability).

Experimental and quasi-experimental research have provided a large array of information having the potential to dramatically improve people's social health and well-being. As will become evident in the following discussion, however, health problems continue to proliferate, despite the huge array of scientifically validated knowledge now at our disposal. Although scientific positivism has provided a powerful body of knowledge about the operation of the nature of the physical environment and the human body, the operation of the physical environment and the human body, it is clear that this approach to research is limited in its ability to explain human conduct, as will become evident in the sections that follow.

The application of scientific principles through experimental and quasi-experimental studies has obvious implications for education. If we can scientifically measure and describe the precise nature of the learning process, then we should, in theory, be able to control all of the factors likely to influence a student's learning and therefore produce a highly effective education for each and every person. Armed with scientific knowledge, we should be able to predict with precision the conditions required for any child to acquire the knowledge necessary to achieve success in education, irrespective of his or her gender, class, ethnicity, or any other factor likely to impinge on learning. As the following section reveals, however, understanding human social and cultural behavior has proven much more elusive, and other research strategies have emerged to provide different but effective ways of understanding educational issues and problems.

UNDERSTANDING HUMAN SOCIAL LIFE: NATURALISTIC INQUIRY

The problem with applying science to human affairs lies in the nature of humanity. We are at once physical, biological, and sociocultural beings, and attempts to understand our behavior need to take into account each of those facets. While the methods of positivistic science are powerful ways of understanding our physical being, and provide deep insights into our biologic nature, they come up short as vehicles for providing explanations for the sociocultural aspects of human life. Although experimentation still assists us to understand certain features of human social and cultural life, positivistic explanations, ultimately, must fail to encompass some of the fundamental features of human life—the creative construction of meaning that is at the center of every social activity. It is the need to investigate meaning that is at the heart of naturalistic inquiry—in classroom terms, the different ways that teachers and students experience classroom events, and the meaning they attach to them.

While experimental science, therefore, has provided much useful information, the reality of this knowledge, however, is that any theory of human behavior can only be a tentative, partial explanation of any individual's or group's actions or behaviors. Two things intervene in attempts to describe scientific laws of human behavior. One is the nature of human beings themselves. As cross-cultural studies have demonstrated convincingly, people perceive the world and respond to it in many different ways. Given the same sets of "facts," people will interpret both what they are seeing and what that means in many different ways. No amount of explanation or clarification can provide an ultimate truth about the way people should behave, since behavior is predicated on sets of beliefs that are not, in principle, verifiable. Any "truth" of human experience is true only within a given framework of meanings.

This becomes increasingly clear if we consider some of the fundamental conditions of human social life and the way they impact the lives of individuals. The concept of the life-world comes to us from the work of sociologists such as Peter Berger (Berger, Berger, & Kellner, 1973; Berger & Luckmann, 1967) who engage research from the perspective that people construct reality as an ongoing social process in their everyday lives. The life-world refers to the consciousness of everyday life carried by every individual that provides coherence and order to our existence. The life-world is not a genetically inherited view of the world, but is learned by individuals as they experience everyday events and interactions within the environments of their families and communities. The life-world is therefore socially constructed, so that individuals learn to live in a social world according to sets of meaning, deeply embedded in their everyday conduct, that are shared by others living in that particular place and time.

The life-world is not a random set of events, but is given order and coherence by a patterned, structured organization of meaning that is so "ordinary" that people literally do not see, or usually do not consciously realize, the depth and complexity of the worlds they inhabit. A child learns to associate with parents and siblings in particular ways, to communicate using a particular language, to act in particular ways, and to participate in events such as meals, conversation, play, work, and so on using appropriate behaviors and routine ways of accomplishing his or her tasks of everyday life. Like a fish in the sea, people cannot see the "water" of this patterned, structured everyday life, but live in a taken-for-granted social world providing order and coherence for every aspect of their everyday lives—the interactions, acts, activities, events, purposes, feelings, and productions that comprise their lives.

We get some idea of what this means when we visit a new place for the first time, especially if it is in a foreign country. We feel uncomfortable to varying degrees until we learn the "rules" that enable us to operate in the new setting—the appropriate words to use, how sit or stand, how to eat, how to dress appropriately, and so on. We become aware of a myriad of small behaviors that those living in the context take for granted because it is so much an ordinary part of their life-world.

I remember people's consternation when I visited an Aboriginal community for the first time and sat with my wife in church, not realizing that the sexes had been strictly segregated and that I was sitting with the women. I've also entered a school staffroom and felt the embarrassed silence when I inadvertently sat in "Mr Jeffries's chair." Small and apparently inconsequential behaviors can sometimes have quite a dramatic impact on our ability to interact comfortably with people.

Anthropologist Goodenough (1971) conceptualized this life-world in terms of the concept of culture, which he defines as the socially learned rules and boundaries that enable a person to know what *is* (how the world is *defined*, structured, made up), what *can be* (what is *possible* in the world, whether it be ancestral ghosts, the existence of God, or faster-than-light travel), what *should be* (the system of values enabling the individual to distinguish between good and bad, appropriate and inappropriate), *what to do* (what acts or behaviors are required to accomplish a purpose), and *how to do it* (the steps required to accomplish that purpose). Individuals, therefore, inhabit a life-world comprised of taken-for-granted rules and boundaries giving order and coherence to their lives. Without these patterns and structures of meaning, people would live in a bewildering, chaotic world of sensation and events that would make human life as we know it impossible. It is this cultural cradle that enables us to live together in harmony, to accomplish day-to-day tasks such as eating meals, dressing, communicating through talk and discussion, working, resolving disputes, and mowing the lawn.

The distinctive aspect of our cultural life-world is that we share it with people who have learned similar sets of meanings and who act according to the patterns and structures of meaning with those who have had similar life experiences. But beneath the apparent order and coherence of the social life-world is a deeply chaotic system of meanings that continually threatens the possibility of an ordered and productive daily life. For each person has had somewhat different experiences, and each has built a system of meanings that works superficially to accomplish ordinary tasks, but has slightly different nuances and interpretations that at any one time can be magnified and distorted, causing confusion or conflict as people try to accomplish their everyday lives.

This is readily apparent when people get married and discover that a person with whom they thought they shared deeply consonant views of the world evinces actions and behaviors not in accord with their own. Small acts, the dropping of a sock or tissue, the use of a word, can trigger discomfort, discordance, and even conflict. The art of marriage requires people to learn new sets of meaning, to negotiate actions and behaviors consonant with a partner's existing habits and values, in order to accomplish a life together. It is something that is sometimes astonishingly difficult, even for people closely committed to each other.

Teachers, likewise, interact with students who often come from significantly different social and cultural backgrounds, and who define and respond to events in the classroom according to a wide range of expectations, beliefs, and perceptions. Finding a way of building a repetoire of classroom activities and rules to govern a well-ordered classroom requires a sensitive understanding of these diverse sets of meanings. One of a teacher's major tasks is to uncover the meanings implicit in the acts and behaviors of students, and through that increased understanding to seek ways of enacting classroom activities that will "make sense" to them.

This is not just a technical task, but involves deeply held feelings associated with the meanings implicit in a person's life-world. Not only are people attached to their particular life-worlds emotionally, they also react unfavorably when their life-world is threatened. A denial of the veracity or validity of any aspect of a person's life-world is likely to create negative feelings that inhibit the possibility of productivity. The world of human life is meaningful, interactional, emotional, and constructive, and accomplishing productive and harmonious human activity requires all these aspects of experience to be taken into account. It is this understanding that is at the heart of action research—the need to clarify and understand the meaning implicit in the actions and behaviors of all people involved in events on which research is focused, and to use those extended understandings as the basis for devising effective and productive classroom and school routines and activities.

This lesson is deeply inscribed in my consciousness. As a young teacher I worked with the children of Australian Aboriginal people who lived a very traditional hunter-gatherer lifestyle. It soon became evident to me that they literally lived in a different universe—that the way they viewed the world, the way they acted toward each other, and their aspirations and responses were so dramatically different from my own that my teaching made absolutely no "sense" to their everyday world. I became aware of the need to come to know something of that world in order to provide a bridge of understanding between their world and the curriculum that I was teaching.

Even the simplest aspects of the syllabus entailed elements that were deeply engaged with the different visions of the world and the lifestyles attached. As I watched the people engaged in the simple act of gathering seeds and fruit from the plants in the desert to provide for their immediate needs, I became aware of how deeply embedded I was in the world of technological production when I cut a slice of bread for my lunch. Behind that simple act lay the mining and production of metals needed for the knife, as well as that required for the production of the machinery needed to grow and process the wheat, and to fabricate the ovens and other machinery needed to make the bread. What I had seen as a simple loaf of bread became a complex technological production.

My eyes began to see a different world when I asked the question, "What do I need to know in order to understand where this bread came from?" A very different order of understanding came to mind when I asked, "What do Aboriginal people need to know when they ask a similar question about their own foodstuffs?" Not only does the actual world of technological production intrude, but the web of work and economic relationships enabling me to acquire that loaf of bread is likewise complex, and very different from the web of relationships surrounding Aboriginal meals.

This experience changed forever the way I see teaching. I now realize the need to find ways of making connections between what my students know—how they perceive and understand the world from the standpoint of their own history of experience—what they need to learn, and how they can learn it. That fundamental perception has been recently reinforced as I've worked in schools in the United States, where the experiences and perspectives of Hispanic and African American students and community people has enriched and challenged my educational endeavors. As I worked in the South Valley in Albuquerque and the poorer suburbs of Columbia and Richmond, I had learning work to do before I could frame my knowledge in ways that made sense to people in those places. As a teacher I had to do some on-the-spot research to enable me to do my work effectively.

Differences in cultural perspective do not relate to ethnic differences alone, however. We have only to look at the differences in the way teenagers and their parents interpret events to realize the extent to which their age differences create differences in cultural experience and perspective in everyday life. Parents listening to their children's music often shake their heads in wonder that *anyone* could find the experience pleasurable—a response shared by teenagers listening to their parent's music. They all are hearing the same music, in terms of the sounds emanating from the instrument or recording, but they have very different experiences of the sounds, and associate very different meanings with them.

OBJECTIVE SCIENCE AND NATURALISTIC INQUIRY: A COMPARISON

Objective science and **naturalistic inquiry** provide quite different approaches to research. Both provide the means for teachers and other educational practitioners to acquire knowledge and understanding that assists them to accomplish their complex professional duties. As the previous discussion has indicated, however, they have quite different purposes, processes, and outcomes, the first being to acquire objective, factual information about a limited number of variables, and the second to understand more clearly the multiple dimensions of socially constructed human behavior. Theses attributes are summarized in Figure 2.1.

We need to be wary of setting up boundaries that make too fixed the distinctions between the two paradigms. Qualitative research does, for instance, sometimes make use of statistical data to extend or clarify information emerging in the research process. Conversely, quantitative researchers sometimes engage in preliminary qualitative studies to identify the variables to be included in their research. Neither paradigm is right or wrong, better or worse. Each seeks to attain different purposes, using different processes to attain

OBJECTIVE SCIENCE	NATURALISTIC INQUIRY
Purposes	Purposes
Studies events and behaviors *objectively*.	Studies people's *subjective* experience.
Hypothesizes a relationship between variables of interest.	*Explores perspectives* on an issue or problem.
Processes	Processes
Precisely *measures* quantities of variables.	*Describes* people's experience and perspective of the issue/problem.
Carefully *controls* events and conditions within the study.	Allows events to unfold *naturally*.
Uses *statistical analysis* of data.	Uses *interpretive methods* to analyze the data.
Outcomes	Outcomes
Seeks *explanations* for events and behaviors.	Seeks to *understand* events and behaviors.
Describes *causes* of events and behaviors.	Constructs *detailed descriptions* of events and behaviors.
Generalizes findings to sites and people not included in the study.	Findings are *setting and person specific*.

Figure 2.1
Objective Science and Naturalistic Inquiry

different types of outcome.[1] Each is evaluated by different sets of criteria to determine the strength, quality, or rigor of the research (see the section on validity in Chapter 3).

To ensure that their research does not become caught in the muddy waters between the paradigms, however, researchers need to frequently ask themselves "What is the purpose or

---

[1]Distinguishing between different research paradigms is not always straightforward. The problem partially relates to the rather loose use of associated terminology, where the literature often refers to *quantitative* and *qualitative* methods as equivalent to the distinction between objective science and naturalistic inquiry and fails to differentiate between the research *paradigm* and the research *methods*. There is a difference, for instance, between qualitative *research* and qualitative *methods*. It is possible to use qualitative methods to acquire and partially analyze data in experimental science—to use qualitative data objectively. Conversely, it is possible to use numerical or quantitative data within a naturalistic study to clarify emerging perspectives.

objective of this part of the research? How can I attain that purpose, and what type of methods should I use to achieve my purposes?" Answers to these questions help us assess the nature of the information we require, and the appropriate research tools we therefore apply.

GAINING INSIGHT: MEANING, INTERPRETATION, AND QUALITATIVE RESEARCH

The purposeful move for teachers to understand the experience and perspective of their students is informed by a philosophical standpoint called *phenomenology* that explores the subjective dimensions of human experience. Van Manen's perspective on the study of teaching is quite different from the objective, detached viewpoints that dominate much of the research literature. Through a continuing body of work, Van Manen (1979, 1982, 1984, 1988, 1990) focuses on phenomenological approaches to research and teaching that put us subjectively in touch with *people's everyday experience*. He suggests that a phenomenological perspective offers plausible insights that bring us in more direct contact with the world of our students (Van Manen, 1984).

The purpose of research and teaching, according to Van Manen, is not to put us in *command* of our students, but to put us in *touch* with them. The emphasis is on "seeing" or "insight" rather than explanation—revealing the meanings people attach to events they experience, and the way they are connected to their general life-world. To gain phenomenological insight we do not ask "How do these children learn this material?" but rather "What is the nature of the children's experience of learning?" with the intent of better understanding what the learning experience is like for the children (Van Manen, 1984).

Van Manen's perspective should not be taken as a prescription for the totality of all classroom interaction or all research, since it will sometimes be appropriate for teachers and researchers to stand back and observe the situation objectively, assessing and evaluating events in an unemotional and disengaged manner. At other times educators need to enter the life-world of students to understand how to construct educational activities that are truly meaningful and worthwhile within their everyday lives. Naturalistic inquiry, or qualitative research, provides the tools for these tasks.

A central feature of naturalistic inquiry is that it provides the means for researchers to gain these types of insight by viewing events through a lens of understanding quite different from their personal ways of seeing the world. According to Denzin (1989a, 1989b), research requires an act of interpretation that enables a researcher to view social

---

The use of qualitative data does not necessarily constitute qualitative research; nor does the use of quantitative data constitute a quantitative study. The way the data are manipulated and applied to research outcomes provides an indication of the appropriate use of the terminology. Objective studies seeking causal explanations and generalizable results are appropriately named quantitative or positivistic research, while interpretive studies resulting in detailed and descriptive accounts of people's subjective experience are appropriately identified as naturalistic or qualitative research.

While we can mix methods and data, it is difficult to mix research paradigms within the same study without damaging the utility and integrity of the research. Studies without a random sample, for instance, cannot generalize results. Similarly, qualitative studies that measure fixed variables limit the extent of experiential insight that emerges from naturalistic inquiry.

life from the perspective of another person. This interpretive approach to investigation provides the means to understand how others construct their lives in an ongoing way according to meanings and taken-for-granted procedures that are embedded in the everyday practices of the worlds in which they live.

Denzin suggests that the problem with many human services is that programs, policies, and practices are based on interpretations and judgments of people responsible for their development and delivery. In schools, for instance, faulty or incorrect understandings arise when teachers mistake their own experiences and perspectives for their students' experiences and perspectives. A consequence of this dynamic, then, is that teaching doesn't work adequately because the teaching/learning strategies bear little relationship to the students' meanings, interpretations, and experiences.

Denzin's take on interpretation suggests that far more is involved than "theorizing" about another person's experience. It is an essentially phenomenological[2] process, requiring one to enter into or take the point of view of another's experience; in Mead's (1934) words, "taking the attitude of the other," or in Berger and Luckmann's (1967) terms, entering their "consciousness of everyday life." Understanding, in an interpretive sense, enables us to project ourselves (enter) into the experience of "the other," to understand what they think and feel about particular acts and events. As Denzin says (1989b), "the goal of interpretation is to build true, authentic understandings of the phenomena under investigation" (p. 123). More particularly, though, it seeks to reveal how significant experiences are embedded in the taken-for-granted world of everyday life. Interpretive investigation records the agonies, pains, tragedies, triumphs, and deeply felt emotions—love, pride, dignity, honor, hate, and envy—that influence people's lives.

This perspective has direct implications for teaching. If we consider teaching to be the transmission of objective knowledge, then knowing something of a student's life-world will be peripherally relevant to the task of teaching. Where it is engaged as a process of socially constructed knowledge, it becomes a process of assisting learners to make sense of the material being learned from within their own frames of reference. If we cannot frame our teaching/learning processes in ways enabling diverse learners to understand what they are learning in ways that are meaningful within their own social and cultural life-worlds, then we run the risk of engaging in a series of mechanistic or ritualistic acts that we impose on our students by means of systems of rewards and punishments.

The need to understand the world of classroom and school in these ways has resulted in a proliferation of naturalistic investigation, so that the literature on qualitative research is now both extensive and diverse. Some recent useful contributions, largely focusing on education, include Creswell (2002), De Marrais (1998), Weis and Fine (2000), De Laine (2000), Merchant and Willis (2001), Marshall and Rossman (1999), Silverman (2000), Connelly and Clandinin (1999), and Bogdan and Biklen (1992).

Qualitative, interpretive approaches to inquiry, therefore, provide the principal means for enabling teachers to engage action research to devise teaching and learning strategies more attuned to the realities of students' lives. While it is useful in some contexts to think of students in objective terms, to plan strategies and interventions that enable good learning processes to occur, there will be times when the collaborative construction of learning

---

[2]Phenomenology is the study of phenomena, or ordinary occurrences.

processes or the formulation of socially and culturally appropriate curricula will be enhanced by the processes explored in the coming chapters.

When I first entered teaching I was the sole arbiter of the content and processes of teaching in my classroom. I formulated the syllabus from a preordained state curriculum, establishing teaching/learning processes that I had learned in my professional preparation as providing the greatest likelihood of successful learning, and ensured that I maintained sound classroom management processes in order to ensure that students in my class worked systematically.

As a result of my experiences in many different cultural contexts, my preparation for classes and my teaching is much more flexible and participatory. I engage my students in the process of assisting me to formulate a syllabus and, in the process, try to accommodate the diverse backgrounds and learning styles with which they come to my classes. That doesn't mean that I do not prepare thoroughly, or that classroom management is never an issue, but preparation and management have necessarily become a collaborative process. At first, as I learned how to do this, it seemed like extra work, but having become more skilled I can now accomplish it easily. Further, I've learned that by engaging students in these processes they not only become more interested and enthusiastic about their learning, but have some wonderful ideas about both the content and the processes of learning.

While I still appreciate and make use of the information acquired from my studies of educational psychology, sociology, and anthropology—much of it gained through experimental or quasi-experimental research—I am able to place that alongside the knowledge I acquire of my students' experience using naturalistic techniques of inquiry. Each has its place. Each provides tools for acquiring knowledge.

RESEARCH RELATIONSHIPS IN CLASSROOMS AND SCHOOLS

Traditional approaches to experimental research place a strong emphasis on the need for researchers to remain objective, working at an emotional distance and interacting as little as possible with research subjects and the context. In technical terms, action research participants are *positioned* quite differently, taking different roles and having different sets of responsibility within the research act. Teacher researchers are no longer seen as having sole responsibility for enacting the routines of investigation, but act more like team leaders, coordinators, or facilitators. Their role is not to engage in research, but to assist students and other participants to carry out an investigation. In the most ideal version of action research, teachers and students together, sometimes in conjunction with other participants, do the work of clarifying the issue, acquiring information, analyzing the data, constructing reports, and formulating actions.

The importance of this issue, broadly speaking, is that a set of *relationships* has been built into professional life that sometimes needs to be modified in order to carry out an effective action research process. A common assumption built into interactions between professionals and their client groups says, in effect, "I'm the expert here. I know what needs to be done." The assumption here is that training and experience have provided professionals with special knowledge enabling them to make definitive judgments about the nature of the problem experienced and to formulate appropriate solutions to the problem. While this works in some instances, or in instances where the clients are culturally and socially similar to the professional, there are many, many instances where the "expert" knowledge of the professional does not provide the basis for an effective solution to the problem.

Interpretive action research, therefore, starts from quite a different position. It says, in effect, "Although I have professional knowledge that may be useful in exploring the issue or problem facing us, my knowledge is incomplete. We will need to investigate the issue further to reveal other relevant (cultural) knowledge that may extend our understanding of the issue." The teacher's expert knowledge, in this case, becomes another resource to be applied to the issue investigated, and complements the knowledge and understandings of students and parents, whose extended understanding of their own circumstances provides knowledge resources that might usefully be applied to the solution of classroom problems. As anthropologist George Marcus (1998) indicated "[social] affiliations and identities give [research participants] an immense advantage in shaping research. . . . There is . . . a well of life experience that are great assets for achieving the sort of depth [of understanding] that anthropologists have always hoped for from one- to two-year fieldwork projects."

Shelia Baldwin describes the change in relationships that occurred when she, as teacher, became facilitator of her high school students' ethnographic research. "Throughout our time together, I likened our project to a journey we were taking together to discover our community and school culture." One student commented, "I really like that word 'ethnographer.' It makes me feel special." As Shelia indicates, there is some uncertainty at the beginning of the project as students learn that there is not one "correct" answer to the research question. She was eventually surprised, however, at the level of commitment of her students, and realized that she could have established higher degrees of trust and lesser degrees of control from the earliest stages of the study. Her students demonstrated their commitment by attending meetings outside of class hours, turning up at 7:00 A.M. and staying with the project to the end. She ends by saying "They have given me the confidence I needed to be a facilitator [of research]. Now I can allow my students to take ownership."

Many teachers have had similar experiences. One group (Stringer & colleagues, 1997) spoke of the ways in which a participatory approach to research had enhanced their understanding of teaching. "We discovered that teaching is a complex art that requires teachers to facilitate learning, to enact or model what is to be learned, and to create appropriate organizational and social conditions that enable learning to occur . . . engaging students in learning processes that not only enable them to acquire discrete pieces of information, but also to engage in active inquiry and discovery that lead [them] to see and understand their real-life experiences in new ways." The end product is students who take ownership and responsibility for their own learning, and teachers who are able to engender these feelings. One teacher wrote of her experience doing research with other teachers and some of her students (Petty, 1997):

We're much more aware. We're not so definite or absolute anymore in who we are—in a productive way. We're able to absorb so much more when we don't deflect what comes our way. We went through a process of evolution . . . went in with preconceived notions of school, but became aware of different life perspectives and realities. We started from one point, became different people, and have continued to evolve as we tried to recreate the learning experience. We're different teachers for it.

THE SOCIAL PRINCIPLES OF ACTION RESEARCH: NOT JUST A TECHNICAL ROUTINE

There are, however, deeper issues to be considered in engaging participatory action research as a mode of inquiry. Modern social life, with its tendency toward centralized, bureaucratic forms of organization, too easily slides into a form of autocratic operation at odds with the democratic intent of its institutions. Too often, powerful figures in school contexts take on the manner and style of a dictator, imposing their perspectives and agendas on others, and disregarding the needs and views of others. Though this sometimes "works"—the father-figure principal who keeps an iron hand on the reins of the school, or the demanding, disciplinary teacher who will not accept poor behavior or performance—it provides poor socialization for life in a democratic society. Too often people accept the unacceptable, are passive contributors to processes that inhibit or sometimes damage their lives or the lives of their children.

Participatory action research therefore enacts systematic inquiry in ways that are:

- Democratic
- Participatory
- Empowering
- Life-enhancing

These changes highlight the nature and exciting potentials of action research, providing opportunities for teachers, principals, students, and parents to engage in exciting and sometimes exhilarating work together. Processes of investigation, therefore, not only provide information and understanding as key outcomes of a process of inquiry, but provide the possibility of enabling people to develop a sense of togetherness, providing the basis for effective and productive relationships spilling over into all aspects of their lives together. As they participate in action research, people develop high degrees of motivation and are often empowered to act in ways they never thought possible. Action research is not only empowering, therefore, but provides the basis for building democratic learning communities that enhance the environments of schools and institutions.

Recently I engaged in an action research process in a school in a poorer part of town. When debriefing parent participants in the latter stages of the process, I was struck by the excitement evident in their lively talk, shining eyes, and the enthusiasm with which they reviewed their experience. "You know, Ernie," said one, "It was such an empowering experience for us." Asked how it had been empowering, she responded, "Because we were able to do it ourselves, instead of having experts come and do it and tell us. We learned so much in the process, and now we know how to do research." She and another woman who participated in the project indicated a desire to extend their understanding of research processes and to extend their skills. Enrolled as extension students, they sat in on my graduate research class, participating actively and providing class participants with great insight into effective ways of practicing action research in community contexts.

This is not an isolated instance, as I've shared the excitement and experienced the feelings of accomplishment of young children, teenagers, teachers, principals, parents, student teachers, graduate students, and professors in large cities, small country towns, and remote communities. My experience encompasses a wide range of social and cultural contexts on two continents, and the power of participatory processes to engage enthusiasm and excitement still excites me. For me, action research is not a dreary, objective, mechanistic process, but a vital, energizing process that engages the mind, enhances the spirit, and creates the unity that enables people to accomplish highly significant goals. At its best, it is a transformational experience enabling people to see the world anew, and in some cases, to literally change their lives.

There is another side to action research, however, that continues to sustain me professionally: the ability to provide the means to accomplish exciting work in the most difficult of circumstances. In a world made increasingly by the forces of economic rationalism and accountability, where every activity must be justified in terms of a pre-specified "benchmark" and justified in dollar terms, the spiritual and artistic side of education can easily be lost in a maze of technical, mechanistic, and clinical procedures that too easily dulls and nullifies the creative, life-enhancing outcomes of a truly educational experience. The energy and excitement generated by collaborative accomplishment not only provides the means to accomplish the technical, clinical goals of our work, but to do so in ways that are truly meaningful and enriching.

The process of collaboratively working toward that goal not only provides a wide range of expertise, both professional and cultural, but also generates positive working relationships. By including students and parents in the search for solutions to these types of problems we open the possibility of making use of their wisdom, and acknowledging the concrete realities affecting student behavior and performance. Moreover, by engaging them in processes of inquiry that recognize their competence and worth, we provide the basis for developing productive relationships that engender trust and understanding. Even the poorest communities have a store of experience and local knowledge that can be incorporated into exciting and meaningful activities that have the power to transform the education of people and children.

This participatory approach to research therefore accomplishes both a sense of community and a living democracy. It provides the means to bring people together in dialogic and productive relationships, enabling the development of a sense of community through the sharing of perspectives, the negotiation of meaning, and the production of collaboratively produced activities, programs, and projects. The search for harmony, peace, caring, and joy can be integrated with technical efficiency in ways that create truly democratic and humane classrooms and schools.

CONCLUSION

Research texts quite often work on an unspoken assumption that applications of the technical routines of scientific research provide the basis for enlightened and improved professional practice. This chapter has suggested the need to broaden ideas about the nature and function of research to ensure that they acknowledge and take into account the social and human dimensions of educational life. While scientifically validated knowledge truly has the potential to increase understanding of significant features of our social life and educational practice, to the extent that it fails to acknowledge or take into account the social, cultural, ethical, and political nature of social life, it fails to provide the means to improve people's educational endeavors.

The participatory and interpretive approach to action research found in this text seeks to provide a more balanced approach to inquiry, providing research procedures that are conducive of democratic and humane social processes within classrooms and schools. The intent is to provide a rigorous approach to inquiry that legitimizes the perspectives and experiences of all people involved, takes account of scientifically validated information in the processes, and encompasses the means for accomplishing sustainable and effective educational practices that really make a difference in people's lives.

In the chapters that follow, therefore, the technical routines of research are accomplished within a set of principles that values the human dimensions of educational life. These principles are expressed more clearly in the next chapter, as a precursor to the detailed articulation of action research processes.

SUMMARY

Understanding Action Research: Exploring Issues of Paradigm and Method

The chapter distinguishes between two major research paradigms: *Objective science*, sometimes called scientific positivism, and *naturalistic inquiry*, often referred to as qualitative or interpretive research.

Objective science assumes a fixed universe that can be observed and explained with precision. Through the experimental method it seeks generalizable information with high degrees of reliability that can be applied across diverse settings. It seeks high degrees of predictability and control of events.

Naturalistic inquiry focuses on understanding the way people interpret events in their everyday lives. It makes use of qualitative methods that use both qualitative and quantitative information to gain insight and understanding of issues and events.

Action research requires a different set of relationships than those often engaged by professionals. It seeks to make use of the deep-seated and extended understandings people have of their own situations and their own experiences.

Action research embodies a set of social principles that are both democratic and ethical. It seeks to engage processes of inquiry that are democratic, participatory, empowering, and life enhancing.

Initiating a Study: Research Design

RESEARCH DESIGN	DATA GATHERING	DATA ANALYSIS	REPORTING	ACTION
INITIATING A STUDY	GATHERING INFORMATION	IDENTIFYING KEY ISSUES AND EXPERIENCES	WRITTEN REPORTS	CREATING SOLUTIONS
Setting the stage	Interviewing		Formal reports	Solving problems
		Analyzing key experiences	Narrative accounts	
Focusing and framing	Observing		Joint accounts	Creating syllabi and lesson plans
	Reviewing documents, records, and materials	Categorizing and coding	PRESENTATIONS AND PERFORMANCES	
Participants				Curriculum development
Literature review		Incorporating quantitative data	Presentations	
	Quantitative data		Drama	Evaluation
Sources of information			Poetry	
	Reviewing literature	Enhancing analysis	Song	Family and community links
			Dance	
Ethics			Art	
		Using concepts and categories	Video	
Validity			Multimedia	School plans

Contents of the Chapter

This chapter presents ways of initiating a research study. It describes procedures for:

1. creating a productive research environment.
2. *designing* the study, that is, formulating an action plan for the research processes.
3. *focusing* the study and stating it in researchable terms.
4. *framing* the scope of the inquiry.
5. engaging in a preliminary *review of the literature.*
6. identifying *sources of data.*
7. describing methods of *data analysis.*
8. taking account of *ethical* considerations.
9. establishing the validity of the study.

SETTING THE STAGE: CREATING A PRODUCTIVE RESEARCH ENVIRONMENT

As indicated in previous chapters, action research provides the means for teachers and administrators to use systematic processes of inquiry to enrich and enhance the planning and operation of the routine tasks of schooling—planning, evaluation, problem solving, and so on. This chapter sets out the preliminary processes that enable you to incorporate a clear plan to integrate a process of inquiry into regular school teaching and administrative practices.

Technical routines, however, are only part of the picture, and to the extent that they have an effect on other people—students, colleagues, administrators, parents—they must necessarily be enacted with the dignity and kindness that befits any civilized social activity. In the sections that follow, therefore, the technical features of designing an effective action research process are presented, and are complemented by working principles that focus on the human dimensions of classroom and school life. Effective action research is a holistic process that takes into account *all* features and elements of a situation likely to have an effect on the issue investigated. Since the process is as important as the product, we start by focusing on features of the research context that need to be taken into account in developing positive working environments that form the basis for effective action.

WITH HEAD, HEART, AND HAND: THE HUMAN DIMENSIONS OF ACTION RESEARCH

When we can work with head, heart and hand, we begin to shape a kind of community that is responsive to many different communities, in different places and in different times, and one that opens many ways forward. (Kelly & Sewell, 1988)

Too often students move through routinized reading and writing tasks, engaging their hands, and to some extent their heads, but without having their hearts in it. Teachers may likewise move mechanically through a teaching routine, maintaining order in their classes as they "keep the kids quiet" and "cover the content of the curriculum," their hearts likewise disengaged. In such circumstances classroom life threatens to become tedious, boring, and irrelevant, to be endured by students to gain a class credit, certificate, or diploma. Good teaching provides learning experiences that excite students and provide knowledge and skills that enhance their lives. One of the very productive aspects of both teaching and research is the ability to fully engage all dimensions of experience, to employ the heads, hands, and hearts of the people who participate in classroom and school.

This is not always an easy task, as teachers often face groups of students who are disinterested, fractious, or rebellious. One of the enduring tasks of teaching is to develop and sustain student interest, and experienced teachers engage a broad repertoire of strategies with this end in mind. We speak of the need to "motivate" students as part of the language of instruction, often attributing student disinterest to personality factors such as poor self-concept or poor concentration, or to a student's home or community background. Motivation is often seen as extrinsic to the content of learning, so that grades, assessments, or reward systems become primary means for encouraging students to maintain their focus and/or interest in their work. Motivation, however, may be more broadly conceived as engaging the *heart*, or the *spirit*, of the students and others with whom we work, so they do not just "go through the motions," but take ownership for their work and engage it joyously, enthusiastically, and creatively. The same is true for teachers themselves, who must constantly find ways to develop and sustain the creative energy required for their demanding day-to-day work with children in schools.

Teachers sometimes have difficulty imagining that research could make such a difference in their classroom lives. As a teacher myself, I discovered the energy emerging from participatory processes of inquiry. Over the past decades, however, I have been humbled by the sometimes impassioned comments of ordinary teachers who have embraced these tenets. Often working in the most difficult of situations, they have been able to transform their classroom and teaching lives, engaging creative energies of students, families, and community people. One preschool teacher, engaging this form of research for the first time, commented "It has been a long time since I have had a paradigmatic shift like this in such a profound way. [It] is like a small earthquake or miniature shock of lightening arousing me from my day-to-day, automatic pilot semi-slumber." These types of responses from people with whom I work in school and community settings continue to sustain my excitement and enthusiasm. The technical routines I learn and teach are important, but the process by which they become instilled in people's experience is a central ingredient of a truly educational experience. When I teach I still aspire to a productive and enjoyable classroom experience for my students and myself. After decades in the classroom I can still accomplish this, most times, in most places.

One of the problems of engaging the "heart" of our students, however, lies in the complexity teachers face in their daily class lives. My work alongside Australian Aboriginal people, whose needs are often quite different from the mainstream population, has sensitized me to this facet of school life. These experiences have been reinforced by my work in American schools and universities, where African American, Hispanic, Native American, and other groups of students provide a rich tapestry of humanity that not only holds a fertile cultural resource, but challenges teachers to accommodate the diversity that exists in their classrooms. Often the complexity of these situations encourages us to ignore the implicit differences in students, speaking of them in technical or objectifying language—"organisms," "the learner," or "the student," and characterizing their failure to accomplish learning objectives in terms of "deviance" or other personal inadequacies. We often focus on "interventions" or "strategies" to repair their inappropriate or inadequate performances without acknowledging the possibility of engaging the resourcefulness of the students with whom we work.

The approach to action research presented in this book works on the assumption that people, even very young people, have deep and extended understandings of their lives, enabling them to negotiate their ways through an often bewildering and unpredictable lifeworld. It is our willingness to acknowledge the legitimacy of their worldviews, and the wisdom that enables them to survive and sometimes thrive in difficult circumstances, that is at the heart of the participatory processes described in this book. The use of interviews as a central component of action research enables us to listen carefully to what people say, to record and represent events in their own terms, and to use their perceptions and interpretations in formulating plans and activities. The task is not to convince them of the inadequacies of their perspective, but to find ways of enabling them, through sharing each other's perspectives, to formulate more productive understandings of their own situation.

This orientation to research therefore seeks to enhance people's feelings of competence and worth, engaging them in processes that provide an affirmation of themselves, their friends, their families, and their communities. Our work with others—students, colleagues, parents, and administrators—enables them to maintain a constructive vision of themselves, anchoring them in a productive perspective of their worlds and enabling them to work easily and comfortably with those around them. Engaging the heart means caring, in an ongoing way, about those facets of human experience that make a difference in the quality of their day-to-day lives. When we talk of the "heart" of the matter, or engaging the heart of the people, we are talking of their feelings of pride, dignity, identity, responsibility, and locatedness (see Figure 3.1).

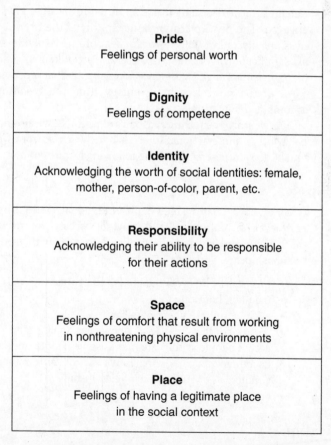

Figure 3.1
The Human Dimensions of Action Research

The energy and joy emerging from research processes that hear the voices of the people, engage their knowledge and skills, and enable them to actively participate in the construction of activities, events, projects, programs, and services have been an integral part of my professional experience for many years. When I see people talk with shining eyes of their accomplishments, when I see them deeply engaged in work affecting their lives, when I see them moved to upgrade and extend their education, and continue to move in often-difficult terrain over extended periods, I know that their hearts have been engaged. They rarely do so in isolation, however; the work they accomplish is enhanced by the common unity they share with those with whom they have worked.

WORKING PRINCIPLES OF ACTION RESEARCH

In another publication (Stringer, 2007a), I present a group of key concepts holding the principles of action research. The first key principle is that of *relationship*, for when relationships are wrong, it is hard to accomplish the desired outcomes of any project. *Communication* also is a central feature of action research, enabling all participants to remain informed of and in harmony with the different activities in which people are engaged. The principle of *inclusion* speaks to the need to ensure that all people whose lives are affected or who have an effect on the issue investigated are included, and that all significant factors having an effect are taken into account. Finally, the principle of *participation* signals the need to ensure that people are actively engaged in the work of the project, gaining energy from the resulting feelings of ownership and accomplishment.

As we learn the technical aspects of research, we also need to encompass and integrate behaviors and interactional styles that facilitate the work we wish to accomplish. We need to take account, therefore, of the following features of our work in all that we do.

Relationships

Good working relationships enable individuals and groups to trust each other, provide high levels of motivation, and provide the basis for continuing research activities over the sometimes long periods required to deal with significant issues. Good working relationships:

- promote feelings of equality for all people involved.
- maintain harmony.
- avoid conflicts, where possible.
- resolve conflicts that arise, openly and dialogically.
- accept people as they are, not as some people think they ought to be.
- encourage personal, cooperative relationships, rather than impersonal, competitive, conflictual, or authoritarian relationships.
- are sensitive to people's feelings.

Communication

Maintaining good relationships depends, to a significant extent, on the ability of people to communicate effectively. The quality, consistency, and correctness of communication have a vital effect on interactions between individuals and groups. Their work together is likely to be short-lived or ineffectual if people talk to each other in disparaging or demeaning ways, if they fail to provide information about their activities, or if they distort or selectively communicate information.

Effective communication occurs when all participants:

- listen attentively to each other.
- accept and act upon what is said.
- can understand what has been said.
- are truthful and sincere.
- act in socially and culturally appropriate ways.
- regularly advise others about what is happening.

Participation

It is normal practice for professional practitioners to take responsibility for all that needs to be done in their sphere of operation. They either do things themselves or engage someone to do it for them. While this is quite necessary for many activities related to schooling and other professional areas, one of the purposes of action research is to engage the natural expertise and experience of all participants. When people are able to see that their worth is acknowledged by the activities in which they are able to engage, high levels of personal investment—of resources, time, and emotion—often result. Active participation is very empowering, especially for people who have a poor self-image. Another of the key features of action research, therefore, is for facilitators to provide opportunities for people to demonstrate their competence by engaging in research-related activities themselves. Sometimes people may commence with quite simple tasks, taking on increasingly complex activities as their confidence increases. Although this sometimes requires more time and considerable patience on the part of research facilitators, the long-term benefits easily outweigh the initial outlay of time and effort.

Participation is most effective when it:

- enables significant levels of active involvement.
- enables people to perform significant tasks.
- provides support for people as they learn to act for themselves.
- encourages plans and activities that people are able to accomplish themselves.
- deals personally with people rather than with their representatives or agents.

Inclusion

Often people are tempted to carve out a piece of "territory," or to "take charge" of an issue. In professional life, teachers and administrators almost automatically take responsibility for any actions required to deal with issues within their professional realm. Further, there is often pressure to find short-term solutions to complex problems with a long history, providing teachers and/or administrators with the temptation to take immediate action themselves. Usually, these actions fail to take into account many of the factors contributing to the problem or to include people who are an integral part of the context or whose lives are substantially affected by the problem.

Inclusion requires participants to:

- involve all relevant groups and individuals whose lives are affected by the issue investigated.
- take account of all relevant issues affecting the research question.
- cooperate with related groups, agencies, and organizations where necessary.
- ensure all relevant groups benefit from activities.

RESEARCH DESIGN

As teacher researchers engage in action research, they need to have a clear view of the details of the investigation in which they will be engaged. Initially they will construct a preliminary picture of the project, but will work with other stakeholders to refine this picture and incorporate more details of research activities.

As they commence the work of inquiry they will design the research, detailing an action plan listing the steps to be taken. The design will include:

- **Building a preliminary picture:** Identifying the research problem and the people affected by or having an effect on the problem.
- **Focusing:** Refining the statement of the research problem, the research question, and the research objectives.
- **Framing:** Establishing the scope of the inquiry.
- **Sampling:** Determining procedures for identifying project participants.
- **Sources of information/data:** Identifying stakeholding groups, sites and settings, statistical records, and other sources of documentary information providing input to the study.
- **Form of the information/data:** Determining the type of information that will inform the inquiry—interview transcripts, observational records, review summaries, televisual documentaries, formal research reports, school records, and so on.
- **Data gathering procedures:** Determining how information will be gathered—including interviews, focus groups, observations, review of materials and equipment, and so on.
- **Data analysis procedures:** Selecting methods of distilling information to identify key features, concepts, or meanings—for example, event analysis, categorizing, and coding.
- **Ethics:** Taking steps to ensure that no harm is done to people through their inclusion in the research.
- **Validity:** Establishing procedures used to enhance the strength of the research.

BUILDING A PRELIMINARY PICTURE: THE REFLECTIVE PRACTITIONER

One of the first difficulties confronting researchers is to acquire clarity about the nature and purposes of the research. In their day-to-day work, teachers deal with a vast array of interrelated issues and problems that have a continuing impact on their students' learning. The initial processes of designing an action research study can be assisted by implementing a simple process of reflection—depicted here as a "look-think-act" sequence—that enables the teacher researcher to build a clear picture of the issue on which the research is focused, and the context in which it will be played out. In the first research cycle, teacher researchers carefully observe relevant classroom or school settings and then reflect on their observations to clarify the nature of the research problem. They identify the people who will be involved and formulate the research question upon which the study will initially focus. Continuing cycles of the look-think-act process enable the teacher researcher and other participants to further refine these details as they explore the issue.

For example, a teacher may not be happy with what her students are accomplishing in an area of study, and thus may ask the question "How can I improve student learning of [content area] in my classroom?" To answer this question effectively she will need to reflect on the range of issues that may be influencing her students' performance. She will "look" at the students in her classroom, the classroom itself, and the way she has organized learning in this area. As she does so, she will "think," reflecting on the means by which she can identify the source of the problem—poor student performance. Finally, she will "act," planning a process of systematic inquiry that will lead to more effective teaching/learning processes that accomplish her desired end.

In general terms, the look-think-act routine mirrors a traditional research process— look = gathering data; think = analyzing data; act = reporting results (see Figure 3.2). In the first phase of action research:

Look entails gathering information to build a preliminary picture of the situation, enabling the researcher to describe *who* is involved; *what* is happening; and *how, where,* and *when* events and activities occur. Information is acquired by observing participants, the context, and identifying factors influencing the issue to be investigated.

Think requires researchers to reflect on the emerging picture. It is essentially preliminary analysis of the situation that enables researchers to develop a clearer understanding of

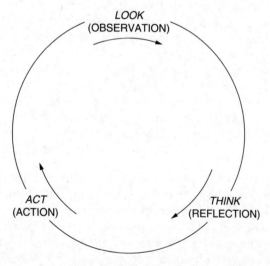

Figure 3.2
The Look-Think-Act Research Cycle

what is happening, how it is happening, and the stakeholding groups affected by or affecting the issue.

Act defines the actions emerging from reflection. It requires people to *plan* their next steps and *implement* appropriate activity. *Evaluation* of these steps requires another cycle of the look-think-act process.

FOCUSING THE STUDY

In the everyday world of the classroom, teachers are confronted with an ongoing series of small crises and problems that they solve using a repertoire of skills and knowledge acquired through their professional training and school experience. More systematic research becomes necessary when they find themselves unable to find an effective solution to a persistent or serious problem. Identifying the point of entry is sometimes not easy, since any problems tend to occur as an interrelated or intertwined series of events or features of a situation. Behavioral problems are often associated with poor academic performance, negative attitudes, lack of engagement, and so on. Trying to define what *the problem* is can easily become a "chicken-and-egg" process having no particular beginning or end, or no clearly defined cause-and-effect relationships.

Sometimes our first analysis of a situation focuses on related events that prove to be peripheral to the problem about which we are concerned. A recent meeting of a school board I attended focused on the "problem" of lack of parent participation, with members discussing ways of increasing parent participation. Eventually I asked board members whether, in fact, parent participation was the "real" problem, and asked them to consider "the problem behind the problem." They spoke of a number of issues about which they were concerned, including the failure of parents to engage in required actions to remediate their children's poor academic performance or inappropriate behavior. In this case, the "problem" upon which the school board initially focused turned out to be multidimensional, parent participation being one facet of more deep-seated educational problems. Once the underlying problems were identified, the board was able to reflect more broadly on the issues about which they were concerned. The "problem" of parent participation turned out to be a suggested solution that was not working. In the first stages of research, therefore, research participants need to carefully reflect on the nature of "the problem" about which they are concerned.

One of the major strengths of qualitative research is its ability to allow researchers to tentatively state the problem, then refine and reframe the study by continuing iterations of the look-think-act research cycle. In one study, for instance, researchers focused initially on afterschool vandalism in the local district and attributed it to poor parental supervision. Preliminary investigations revealed, however, that youth from their school suffered from boredom and frustration because of the lack of activities or facilities in their small town. The investigation took a markedly different turn at this point, focusing more clearly on exactly what facilities were available, and what might be developed. In another investigation, preliminary inquiries indicated to a classroom teacher that an apparent lack of interest in reading in her class could be attributed more clearly to her teaching methods and the reading material she used. She refocused her research at this point from her students to her own syllabus.

At this stage the research is essentially a reflective process, requiring research participants to think carefully through all dimensions of the issue causing concern. The first step is to reflect carefully on what is happening that is problematic and what issues and events are related to that problem. To focus the research more clearly, the issue or problem is stated in the form of a researchable question, and the objective of studying that issue is identified. The following should be clearly stated:[1]

- The **issue or topic** to be studied: Define which issues or events are causing concern.
- The **research problem:** State the issue as a problem.
- The **research question:** Reframe that problem as a question—asking, in effect, "What is happening here?"
- The **research objective:** Describe what we would hope to achieve by studying this question.[2]

The preliminary reflective process for developing the focus of the study is assisted by dialogue with both potential participants and colleagues. While it is possible that the research focus may later change as other participants pose their own particular questions, the initiator of the project should be clear about his or her own research questions and their significance.

The initial development of the research question should focus on *how* participants and other stakeholders experience the problematic issue and *how* they interpret events and other information. How is it that these problems occur? How do students perceive that they manage to complete their assignments? How do students describe learning processes that

---

Shelley Jones's study of reading in her class was defined in the following terms:

Issue: Students are consistently failing to complete their reading homework, are listless in reading lessons, and score poorly on reading proficiency tests.
Problem: The students are uninterested in reading.
Question: How do students experience reading?
Objective: To understand what the experience of reading means to students.

---

[1]Since this is a qualitative research study, a research hypothesis—a suggested answer to the research question—is not part of the design. Qualitative or interpretive inquiry is hypothesis generating, rather than hypothesis testing. "Testing" of the "answers" generated by an action research process is accomplished through continual cycling through the look-think-act routine, so that actions put into place as a result of the first cycle of investigation are subject to evaluative processes through further observation and analysis—looking and thinking.

[2]Qualitative studies usually focus on *understanding* people's experience and perspectives as a common outcome of the research process. Quantitative or experimental studies, on the other hand, more often focus on *causal explanations* that explain how one group of variables is "caused" by the effect of preceding variables.

are stimulating? In action research the focus is largely on events and their interpretation, rather than factual information or strongly developed causal connections explaining "why" events occur.

By developing a clear, precise, and focused research question, researchers add an essential reference point into their inquiry. Once investigations have commenced, they are able to evaluate the emerging data according to its reference to the research question. The initial research question should be shared by all participants and reiterated consistently throughout the research cycles as a constant guide to investigation.

FRAMING THE STUDY: DELIMITING THE SCOPE OF THE INQUIRY

As research participants identify and clarify the research issues and questions, they will also need to define the broad parameters of the study, determining whether it will be limited in scope, involving a small number of people over a small time period, or whether more extended study is required. Sometimes it is a relatively simple matter to work with students within a classroom to formulate successful strategies to solve the problem studied. At other times it may be necessary to work in conjunction with teachers from other classes, with the school administration, and/or with families. Before commencing research, therefore, participants will make decisions about the sample of people to be included in the study, the sites or settings in which the research will take place, and the times the research activities will take place. Decisions will also be made about the extent of participation by those involved in the study, defining who will be involved in the various research activities and who will monitor and support people in their research work.

These considerations run hand-in-hand with the need to consider the breadth of issues to be incorporated into the study. Including too many issues is likely to make the study complex and unwieldy, but delimiting the study too closely may neglect issues that have an important bearing on the problem. In the Barrios Juntos study, for instance (see pages 192–196), participants concerned with ways of improving parent participation in the school decided to focus their study on parent–teacher conferences, rather than investigating the other possible forums and vehicles of parent participation. In this instance, the research revealed ways in which parent–teacher conferences could be improved, but also identified a range of related issues that would need to be addressed. Researchers therefore will initially broadly identify:

- **What:** What is the problem requiring investigation? What is my central research question?
- **Participants:** *Who* are the stakeholders? Which people are affected by or have an effect on the issue being studied? Students? Teachers? Administrators? Parents or other family members? Others?
- **Place:** *Where* will the research take place? Which sites or settings will be included in the study? Classrooms? Schoolyard? Offices? Homes? Other locations?
- **Time:** *When* will the research begin? How long might it take?
- **Scope:** What is the likely scope of the issues to be investigated? Student academic experience? Student reading experience? Reading comprehension experience?

Student experiences of the curriculum, classroom, or learning? Student and teacher experiences of school organization? Student, teacher, and parent perspectives on student experiences?

Once the research participants have clarified the focus, frame, and scope of the research, they will undertake a preliminary review of the literature to identify other perspectives on the issue embedded in the literature. This may assist them to further clarify the nature and extent of their investigations.

Preliminary Literature Review

As Creswell (2002) points out, literature reviews for qualitative research have different purposes than those in quantitative research. While substantial use of the literature provides the basis for formulating a quantitative study, qualitative studies use the literature review quite minimally in the earlier phases of a study. Since the latter focuses on stakeholder experiences and perspectives, preformulation of the issue according to concepts and analyses in the literature is deemed inappropriate at this point. Because of the nature of qualitative research, initial conceptions of the research are always assumed to be provisional, thus limiting the possibility of an exhaustive review of the literature.

Understandings and information emerging from the literature, however, may augment, complement, or challenge stakeholder perspectives as the study progresses. Since classroom and school life have been subjects of study for many decades, research participants may increase the power of their investigation by reviewing literature that speaks to emerging concepts and issues. In some cases they may identify potential solutions to the problem that have been successfully enacted in other contexts, or acquire information that clarifies issues emerging in the study. Frequently, salient issues emerging in the data collection phase influence the direction of the investigation, causing participants to pursue different but related questions. Hence the literature search will evolve as an ongoing feature of the research process, emerging in accordance with the directions and agendas indicated by participant-constructed descriptions of the situation.

Literature Search The first phase of a search requires researchers to identify relevant literature. This task is greatly enhanced by the capabilities of computer-assisted search engines available in most libraries. It will be necessary to identify three or four key concepts related to the issue to feed into the search routine. Where large numbers of items are identified, it may be necessary to delineate further key concepts to narrow the search to the most relevant sources of information. Perusing annotated collections, such as ERIC, which provide a brief description of the content of the reading, may enhance this process.

An increasing body of material is available on the web, providing researchers with useful resources for their study. Sole reliance on the web, however, is not recommended, as the information available from web sources tends to be incomplete and patchy. As in library searches, researchers will need to identify key concepts to feed into the search process.

Researchers often distinguish between:

- **Primary sources** that provide direct reports of original research
- **Secondary sources** that report on or summarize primary source material
- **Professional literature** based on the perspectives of experienced professionals

- **Institutional reports** from government or institutional authorities
- **Practice literature** that presents or advocates particular approaches to professional practice

University and professional libraries provide a wide variety of relevant literature, including theses and dissertations, journals, books, handbooks, abstracts, and encyclopedias. Library staff can often assist in identifying initial reading pertinent to the problem being investigated, but review of any material will identify other sources of information, so that a review of the literature becomes an ever-expanding search. Researchers should note sources cited in journal articles, research reports, and texts, then review those for further information.

Identifying Different Perspectives in the Literature The preliminary literature review extends the think/reflect part of the research cycle, providing new possibilities for conceptualizing or interpreting the issue. The preliminary search therefore should be sufficiently broad to provide researchers with an understanding of the different perspectives and types of information presented within the literature. These will not only differ according to the disciplines of the authors—psychology, sociology, cultural studies, and so on—but also according to different theoretical positions from within each discipline. The literature may also vary according to the formal and informal reports from a variety of educational sources, including school, district, state, and national documents. It may include video/television documentaries, as well as information on projects and activities available on the web.

As the project progresses, participants will select, review, and evaluate relevant literature as part of the processes of data collection, identifying pertinent information to enhance the understandings emerging from other sources (see Chapter 4). Studies by other people within the literature become other perspectives (or stakeholders) to be incorporated into the process of data collection and analysis. The preliminary review of the literature within the first iteration of the action research cycle is conducted through the lens of the initial research question, alerting participants to other findings about similar problems, assisting with the refinement of the research question, and/or providing insight into research methods.

Sampling: Selecting Participants

In most studies limits on time and resources make it impossible to include all people who might potentially inform the research process, so it is necessary to select a smaller group to provide the information (data) on which the research is grounded. A technique called *purposive*, or *purposeful*, *sampling* seeks to ensure that the diverse perspectives of people likely to affect the issue are included in the study. Creswell (2002) suggests that purposive sampling seeks to select participants for a variety of purposes. These include:

- people who represent the diverse perspectives found in any social context (maximal variation sampling)
- particularly troublesome or enlightening cases (extreme case sampling)
- participants who are "typical" of people in the setting (typical sampling)
- participants who have particular knowledge related to the issue studied (theory or concept sampling)

In all cases, researchers need to purposively select a sample of participants that represents the variation of perspectives and experiences across all groups and subgroups who affect or are affected by the issue under investigation—the stakeholders in the study.[3]

The first task is to identify the primary stakeholding groups[4]—that is, the groups most centrally involved or affected by the issue studied. If a study is concerned about poorly performing boys in a classroom, the poorly performing boys would be the primary stakeholding group, while a study of parent participation in school would have parents as the primary stakeholders. Sometimes the primary stakeholding groups are complementary groups. A study of a classroom issue might include teachers and students as primary stakeholders, while a study of parent participation might include parents, teachers, and students.

Sometimes the primary stakeholders are able to resolve the problem themselves and there is no need to extend their study further. Where the problem persists, however, research participants need to identify other stakeholders—other people likely to have an effect on the issue studied. Parents, other teachers, or school administrators may need to be included, depending on the nature of the problem investigated. They need to ensure that all relevant groups are included—that girls and boys are represented in their sample, and that students from poorer families as well as those from more middle-class homes are an integral part of the study. Each racial, ethnic, or cultural group should also be included. Depending on the context, it may be necessary for researchers to include members of different social cliques, religious affiliations, sporting groups, or other types of groups represented in the social setting.

While it is not always possible to include people from *all* groups in any setting, those selected should include participants from groups likely to have a significant impact on the issue studied, or to be impacted by that issue. To fail to include participants because it is not convenient, because they show little interest, or because they are noncommunicative is to put the effectiveness of the study at risk. The previous chapter talked of the need to establish research relationships to maximize the possibility of including everyone likely to affect the issue studied.

It is not always possible for researchers to nominate in advance those who need to be included in a study. A technique called *snowballing* enables researchers to ask participants who they think needs to be included, or to ask someone they might nominate who has quite a different perspective or set of experiences related to the issue studied. In this way, researchers commence by defining likely participants, but extend their sample to be more inclusive of the diverse and significant perspectives included in the study.

Any group, however, is likely to include people who are natural leaders, or who in some way are able to sway the opinions or perspectives of others in their group—sometimes referred to as opinion leaders. Researchers should try to ensure that the sample selected includes both natural leaders and opinion leaders. A general rule of thumb in this process is to ask "Who can speak for this group? Whose word will group members acknowledge as representing their perspective?"

---

[3]Purposive sampling differs in nature and purpose from the random sampling used for experimental studies. A random sample drawn from a larger population enables experimental researchers to use statistical procedures to generalize from that sample to a larger population. Rather than seeking to generalize, action research seeks solutions to problems and questions that are quite context specific.

[4]In some literature the *primary stakeholding group* is referred to as the *critical reference group*. The intent, however, is similar—to focus on those primarily affected by the issue studied.

The research design may not specify a particular sample, therefore, but will describe the procedures for identifying those who will be active participants in the study.

Sources and Forms of Information (Data Gathering)

In planning the study researchers also need to identify the type of information that will be gathered, and the source of that information. Sources may include interviews with stakeholders—the "sample" described earlier—observation of people, places, events, or activities; materials and equipment; work samples; documents, records, and reports; relevant literature; and so on (see Chapter 4).

The research design should stipulate the methods employed to access these types of information, including interviews, focus groups, observations, literature and document reviews, photographs, and video and audio recording. Because of the nature of qualitative research it is not possible to signal precisely all sources of information, but the design should provide participants with guidance about where, when, how, and from whom initial information will be acquired. Later iterations of the research may include structured questionnaires, surveys, or other data gathering instruments.

Distilling the Information (Data Analysis)

The research design should inform participants and those reading research proposals of the type of data analysis to be used in the study. The research design should clearly signal the type of data analysis employed and the way in which analyzed data will be used to formulate actions (see Chapter 5).

RESEARCH DESIGN

A qualitative action research design provides a description of:

1. **Focus:** A statement of the issue, the research problem, the research question, and research objectives.
2. **Framing the scope of inquiry:** The place, the time, the stakeholding groups, and the scope of the issues included in the study.
3. **Preliminary literature review:** Processes for reviewing the literature.
4. **Sources of information/data:** The stakeholders, sites and settings, and literature from which information will be acquired.
5. **Data gathering processes:** Ways information will be gathered—interviews, observation, review of materials and equipment, and so on.
6. **Data analysis processes:** Procedures used for distilling information.

RESEARCH ETHICS

The research design also includes ethical considerations that protect the well-being and interests of research participants. Punch (1994) suggests that "the view that science is intrinsically neutral and essentially beneficial disappeared with the revelations at the

Nuremberg trials." Some well-known studies have shown that researchers are not always aware of potential harm that may come to those who participate in research studies (e.g., Horowitz, 1970; Milgram, 1963). Most public institutions and professional organizations have formal procedures to ensure that researchers do not knowingly or unknowingly put research participants at risk. The research design includes procedures for ensuring the safety of the participants. As Sieber (1992) indicates, sound ethics and sound methodology go hand in hand.

Universities have Internal Review Boards (IRB) to ensure the ethical conduct of research engaged in by students and faculty. Usually such boards require a copy of the proposal, and an indication of the procedures that will ensure the safety of research participants, including the confidentiality of research processes. Although each university will have its own set of rules, the following procedures provide a general means to satisfy most IRB regulations.

Confidentiality, Care, and Sensitivity

When people talk for extended periods they often speak of very private matters, revealing highly problematic events or even potentially harmful information. A prime directive of social research is to protect the anonymity of participants. In practice it is best to assume that *all* information acquired is highly confidential. Where we require information to be shared with other participants or audiences, we must first ask relevant participants for permission to do so. When I read back my field notes, or share analyzed information with participants, I ask "Is there anything here you would not like to reveal to other people in this project?" If they appear unsure, I inform them that it may be possible to present the information, but to disguise its source. We can do this by using fictitious names, or by reporting it generally—"Some people suggest that . . ." or "Other participants provide a different perspective on . . ."

Aligned with confidentiality is the duty of care we have to participants. We need to ensure that information is stored securely so that others do not inadvertently see it. We certainly should not share recorded information with others without permission of the persons concerned, even if that information points to apparently harmful events in a person's life—drug abuse, physical abuse, and so on. This points to another possibility occasionally arising in the processes of extended interview—the recall of distressing events sometimes creates a deep emotional response. Duty of care requires researchers to provide sufficient time for the person to "debrief" by talking through issues or events to a point of comfort, or by putting the individual in contact with a family member or counselor who can assist in resolving the situation.

Permissions

Permission is not usually required when teachers engage in research directly related to their ongoing work in the classroom. Where they engage in more extended studies involving other school staff, children from other classes, or parents, then they may need to obtain formal permission prior to commencing the project. To the extent that the research becomes a public process, therefore, where people's privacy or personal well-being is "at risk," written permission from a person in a position of authority is warranted—a principal, school district superintendent, or other relevant authority. In these circumstances it is necessary to provide information about the nature of the research, the significance of the study, and the ways in which ethical considerations will be taken into account. It is useful to attach a copy of the research design to the request for permission to pursue the study.

Where research is associated with a university course or program, the institution itself will usually have processes for reviewing research through an ethics committee. A similar system operates in school districts. Though the procedures are sometimes unwieldy and time consuming, they provide a means of ensuring that people's privacy is not violated and that research processes do not interfere with their well-being.

Informed Consent

In many contexts, protocols require those facilitating research to engage processes of informed consent. This requires the research facilitator and others engaged in data gathering to:

- Inform each participant of the purpose and nature of the study.
- Ask whether they wish to participate.
- Ask permission to record information they provide.
- Assure them of the confidentiality of that information.
- Advise them that they may withdraw at any stage and have their recorded information returned.
- Ask them to sign a short document affirming their permission.

The following document provides an example of how these processes are presented to participants and documented. A consent form not only provides information, but is a record of consent, so that copies should be provided to each signatory.

YOUTH RECREATIONAL FACILITIES IN LEDDINGHALL

Mrs. Miles' ninth-grade class at Leddinghall High School is concerned that no recreational facilities for young people are available in the district. They are now engaged in reviewing the services, facilities, and resources available to young people in the community and will invite young people who live there to tell of their experiences. On the basis of this study, the class will write a report on recreation for young people in the Leddinghall community to be presented to the town council.

Consent Form

I, _____ have read the above information and been informed of the nature of the study. I consent to being interviewed by a class member for this study. I understand that:

- All information will be kept confidential
- I may withdraw from the study at any time and have information I have given returned to me at that time
- I will not be identified in any way in reports arising from this study without my written permission

Signed: _____

Date: _____

RESEARCH ETHICS

Ethical procedures are established by:

1. **Confidentiality:** Privacy is protected by ensuring confidentiality of information.
2. **Permissions:** Permission is obtained to carry out the research from people in positions of responsibility.
3. **Informed consent:** Participants are informed of the nature of the study and provide formal consent to be included.

VALIDITY IN ACTION RESEARCH: EVALUATING QUALITY

When teachers engage in research in their own classrooms, they are usually able to ascertain the worth of research according to its usefulness in helping them accomplish their teaching objectives. Studies wider in scope, however, involving official approval or requests for funding, often need to satisfy more stringent requirements. People want assurance that sloppy, poorly devised, or unbalanced research is not likely to result in inadequate or potentially damaging outcomes. In these circumstances they often require an examination of the rigor or strength of the procedures to be included in the research design sections of a proposal, or in the methodology section of a research report.

Action research, being essentially qualitative or naturalistic, seeks to construct holistic understandings of the dynamic and complex social world of classroom and school. It reveals people's subjective experience and the ways they meaningfully construct and interpret events, activities, behaviors, responses, and problems. Although these types of studies provide powerful understandings that enable the development of effective practices and activities, they are mostly specific to particular contexts and lack stability over time—what is true at one time may vary as policies and procedures shift and the actors in the setting change. When a new principal arrives at a school, or staff changes occur, for instance, then the life of the school is likely to change in significant ways. The truths emerging from naturalistic inquiry therefore are always contingent; that is, they are "true" only for the people, the time, and the setting of that particular study. We are not looking for "the truth" or "the causes," but "truths-in-context."

Procedures for evaluating the rigor of experimental or survey research evolve around well-formulated processes for testing reliability[5] and establishing the validity[6] of a study. Traditional experimental criteria for establishing validity, however, are inappropriate for

---

[5]Reliability is estimated by measures of the extent to which similar results may be expected from similar samples within the population studied, across different contexts and at different times. Reliability focuses on the stability of results across time, settings, and samples.

[6]Experimental validity is defined in two ways—external validity and internal validity. Measures of external validity estimate the probability that results obtained from the sample differ significantly from results we would expect. Internal validity focuses on the extent to which results obtained might be attributed to the dependent variables included in the study, and not some other cause. Researchers ask "Do our instruments actually measure what we wish them to measure?" and "Are the results attributal to the dependent variables we have stipulated, or to some other related variable?" Internal validity focuses on careful research design and instrumentation. Both reliability and validity are verified by statistical and other techniques.

qualitative action research, and debate continues about a broadly acceptable set of criteria to use for this purpose. Some researchers have approached this task by seeking to identify the foundational assumptions underlying the term *validity*. "What does it mean," they ask, "when we seek to establish the 'validity' of a study?" Two highly respected scholars, Denzin and Lincoln (1998b, p. 414), interpret validity to mean:

> . . . a text's call to authority and truth . . .is established through recourse to a set of rules concerning knowledge, its production, and representation. The rules, as Scheurich (1992, p. 1) notes, if properly followed, establish validity. Without validity there is not truth, and without truth there can be no trust in a text's claims to validity. . . . Validity becomes a boundary line that "divides good research from bad, separates acceptable (to a particular research community) research from unacceptable research . . ." (Scheurich, 1992, p. 5).

Because qualitative methods are essentially subjective in nature and local in scope, procedures for assessing the validity of research are quite different than those used for experimental study. As the previous quote suggests, a new set of criteria is required to provide people with trust that the research is acceptable. A common set of criteria for establishing the validity of research has been provided by Lincoln and Guba (1985). They suggest that because there can be no objective measures of validity, the underlying issue is to identify ways of establishing *trustworthiness*, the extent to which we can trust the truthfulness or adequacy of a research project. They propose that means for establishing trustworthiness involve procedures for attaining:

- **Credibility:** The plausibility and integrity of a study.
- **Transferability:** Whether results might be applied to other contexts than the research setting.
- **Dependability:** Research processes are clearly defined and open to scrutiny.
- **Confirmability:** The outcomes of the study are demonstrably drawn from the data.

Trustworthiness, therefore, is established by recording and reviewing the research procedures themselves to establish the extent to which they ensure that the phenomena studied are accurately and adequately represented. The following procedures are adapted from those suggested by Guba and Lincoln.

Credibility

Qualitative research is easily open to sloppy, biased processes that merely reinscribe the biases and perspectives of those in control of the research process. Careful adherence to the following processes assists researchers in minimizing the extent to which their own viewpoints intrude. They may also review and record the following features of the research process to provide evidence of rigorous procedure, which enhances the plausibility of their findings (Lincoln & Guba, 1985).

Prolonged Engagement Brief visits to a research site provide only superficial understandings of events. A rigorous study requires researchers to invest sufficient time to achieve a relatively sophisticated understanding of a context: to learn the intricacies of cultural knowledge and meaning that sustain people's actions and activities in a setting. Prolonged engagement in a setting also enables researchers to establish relationships of trust with participants, allowing them to gain greater access to "insider" knowledge rather than the often superficial or purposeful information given to strangers. Researchers therefore add to the credibility of a study by extending and recording the time spent in the research context.

Persistent Observation Being present in the research context for an extended time period is not a sufficient condition to establish credibility, however. Sometimes researchers mistake their presence in the field for engagement in research. In a recent study one investigator indicated he had worked with a group of teachers for months. He had, however, not engaged in systematic research at that time and his "observations" were undirected, unfocused, and unrecorded. Participants need to consciously engage in data collection activities to provide depth to their inquiries. This is essential to interviewing processes, as a single interview lasting 15 to 20 minutes provides very superficial understandings that lack both detail and adequacy. Prolonged engagement signals the need for repeated, extended interviews to establish the adequacy, accuracy, and appropriateness of research materials. Researchers therefore need to record the number and duration of observations and interviews.

Triangulation Triangulation involves the use of multiple and different sources, methods, and perspectives to corroborate, elaborate, or illuminate the research problem and its outcomes. It enables the inquirer to clarify meaning by identifying different ways the phenomenon is being perceived (Stake, 2005). In action research we include all stakeholders relevant to the issue investigated, observe multiple sites and events relevant to the stakeholders and issue investigated, and review all relevant materials, including resources, reports, records, research literature, and so on. These multiple sources and methods provide rich resources for building adequate and appropriate accounts and understandings that form the base for working toward the resolution of research problems.

Participant Debriefing This process is similar to *peer debriefing* as proposed by Lincoln and Guba (1985), but differs because of the change in the status of the researcher in an action research process. It is not solely the research facilitator who is in need of debriefing, but other participants in the process as well. Debriefing is a process of exposing oneself to a disinterested person for the purpose of exploring and challenging aspects of the inquiry that might otherwise remain implicit only within the participant's mind (Lincoln & Guba, 1985). The purposes of debriefing are to review the appropriateness of research procedures and to clarify the participant's ways of describing and interpreting events. Debriefing also provides participants with an opportunity for catharsis, enabling them to deal with emotions and feelings that might cloud their vision or prevent relevant information from emerging. Researcher facilitators often provide debriefing sessions with research participants, but may also require an interested colleague to engage in debriefing them on the processes of research they are guiding. The credibility of a study is enhanced when researchers record debriefing opportunities given to participants.

Diverse Case Analysis In all research it is necessary to ensure that other interpretations of the data are fully explored. Sometimes there is a temptation to include in a research process only those people who are positively inclined toward the issue under study, or to interpret the information in particular ways. Diverse case analysis seeks to ensure that all possible perspectives are taken into account, and that the interpretations of important, significant, or powerful people do not overwhelm others. Diverse case analysis enables participants to constantly refine interpretations so that all participant perspectives are included in the final report, and all issues are dealt with. The credibility of a study is enhanced if researchers can demonstrate that all perspectives affecting the study have been included. A clear statement of sampling procedures assists in this process.

Referential Adequacy Referential adequacy refers to the need for concepts and structures of meaning within the study to clearly reflect the perspectives, perceptions, and language of participants. When participants' experiences and perspectives are reinterpreted through the lenses of other existing reports or theories, or in terms derived from existing practices, procedures, or policies, research outcomes are likely to be distorted. One of the key features of qualitative research is the need to ensure that interpretations are "experience-near," grounded in the language and terminology used by participants to frame and describe their experience. Where it is necessary to use more general terms to refer to a number of phenomena, those terms should adequately apply to the specific details to which they refer. The credibility of a study is enhanced to the extent that researchers can demonstrate that outcomes of the study have a direct relationship to the terminology and language used by participants.

Member Checks In experimental inquiry, research subjects rarely have the opportunity to question or review the information gathered and the outcomes of the study. The practical nature of action research, however, requires that participants be given frequent opportunity to review the raw data, the analyzed data, and reports that are produced. This process of review is called *member checking* and provides the means for ensuring that the research adequately and accurately represents the perspectives and experiences of participants. Member checking is one of the key procedures required to establish the credibility of a study.

Transferability

Unlike quantitative research that assumes the need to generalize the results of the study, qualitative research by its very nature can only apply results directly to the context of the study. Nevertheless, researchers seek to provide the possibility that results might be transferred to other settings to enable people to take advantage of the knowledge acquired in the course of the study. Whether such application is possible, it is assumed, can be assessed according to the likelihood that another context is sufficiently similar to allow results to be applicable. A study from rural Australia, for instance, may or may not have importance for suburban Holland. Qualitative research reports seek to provide sufficiently detailed descriptions of the context and the participants to enable others to assess the likely applicability of the research to their own situation. Thickly detailed descriptions therefore contribute to the trustworthiness of a study by enabling other audiences to clearly understand the nature of the context and the people participating in the study.

Dependability

Trustworthiness also depends on the extent to which observers are able to ascertain whether research procedures are adequate for the purposes of the study. Where insufficient information is available, or available information indicates the likelihood of superficial and/or limited inquiry, observers will not feel the study is dependable. The dependability of research is achieved through an *inquiry audit* whereby details of the research process—including processes for defining the research problem, collecting and analyzing data, and constructing reports—are made available to participants and other audiences.

Confirmability

Confirmability is achieved through an audit trail, the inquirer having retained recorded information that can be made available for review. This information includes raw data such as field notes, photographs, diary entries, original and annotated documents, copies of letters and materials generated at meetings, and so on. Data reduction and analysis products are also included, as well as plans and reports derived from the study. This information enables participants or other observers to be able to confirm that research accurately and adequately represents the perspectives presented in the study. By this means they enhance the trustworthiness of the study.

Validity and Participation

The strength of qualitative research derives from the methodological intent to build accounts that more clearly represent the experience, perspective, and voice of those studied. The credibility of accounts, to some extent, is derived from the extent to which researchers are able to enact the procedures delineated in the previous section. Throughout the process, however, researchers constantly run the risk of observing and interpreting events through the lens of their own history of experience, thus putting the validity of the study at risk (Stringer & Genat, 1998).

A much greater degree of credibility, however, is gained through the use of participatory processes. When research participants engage in the processes of collecting and analyzing data, they are in a position to constantly check and extend the veracity of the material with which they are working. As they read the data of their interviews, they not only "see themselves" more clearly (the looking-glass-self), but are drawn to extend and clarify the events they describe. As they engage in data analysis, they are able to identify more clearly and correctly the significant experiences and features as well as the elements of which they are comprised. As they assist in the construction of reports they help formulate accounts that more clearly use familiar language to represent their experience and perspective.

Participatory processes respond to recent developments in qualitative research (Altheide & Johnson, 1998) that point to the multiple means now used to establish validity, according to the nature and purposes of the study and the theoretical frames of reference upon which the research rests. In a very direct way, engaging people as direct participants in the research also enables a study to take into account such issues as emotionality, caring, subjective understanding, and relationships in research (Haraway, 1988; Lather, 1993; Oleson, 1998, 2005), which are important features of feminist research. They are incorporated as a means of ensuring the validity/trustworthiness of a study, but also enhance the possibility of effective change.

Validity and Utility

One of the greatest sources of validity in action research is the utility of the outcomes of research. Where participants are able to construct ways of describing and interpreting events that enable them to take effective action on the issue they have investigated, they demonstrate the validity of the research. The power of the processes is nowhere more evident than in effective actions emerging from the research, clearly demonstrating the success in identifying appropriate perspectives and meanings. High degrees of credibility are evident, since the understandings that emerge from the processes of inquiry are successfully applied to actions within the research setting. It becomes immediately evident that the features on which the research has focused are adequate to account for the phenomena investigated.

SUMMARY

Establishing Validity

The validity of action research is verified through procedures establishing credibility, transferability, dependability, confirmability, degrees of participation, and utility. These are attained through:

1. *Prolonged engagement:* The duration of the research processes.
2. *Persistent observation:* The number and duration of observations and interviews.
3. *Triangulation:* All sources of data, including the settings observed, the stakeholders interviewed, and materials reviewed.
4. *Participant debriefing:* Processes for reviewing research procedures.
5. *Negative case analysis:* Processes for ensuring that a diversity of interpretations is explored.
6. *Referential adequacy:* How terminology within the study is drawn from participant language and concepts.
7. *Member checks:* Procedures for checking the accuracy of data, and the appropriateness of data analysis and reporting.
8. *Transferability:* The inclusion of detailed descriptions of the participants and the research context.
9. *Dependability:* Detailed description of the research process.
10. *Confirmability:* The data available for review.
11. *Participation:* The extent of stakeholder participation in the research process.
12. *Utility:* Practical outcomes of the research process.

Gathering Data: Sources of Information

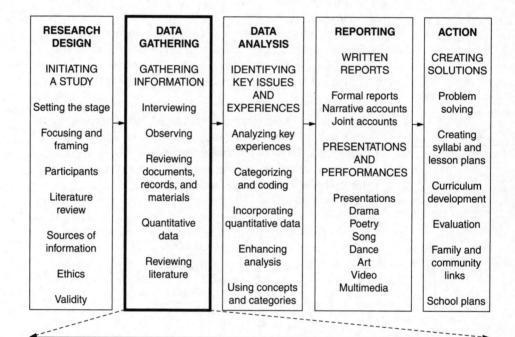

RESEARCH DESIGN	DATA GATHERING	DATA ANALYSIS	REPORTING	ACTION
INITIATING A STUDY	GATHERING INFORMATION	IDENTIFYING KEY ISSUES AND EXPERIENCES	WRITTEN REPORTS	CREATING SOLUTIONS
Setting the stage	Interviewing	Analyzing key experiences	Formal reports Narrative accounts Joint accounts	Problem solving
Focusing and framing	Observing		PRESENTATIONS AND PERFORMANCES	Creating syllabi and lesson plans
Participants	Reviewing documents, records, and materials	Categorizing and coding		Curriculum development
Literature review		Incorporating quantitative data	Presentations Drama	
Sources of information	Quantitative data		Poetry Song	Evaluation
		Enhancing analysis	Dance Art	Family and community links
Ethics	Reviewing literature		Video Multimedia	
Validity		Using concepts and categories		School plans

Contents of the Chapter

The previous chapter described the first phase of inquiry, in which participants focus their investigation and design a valid and ethical research process. This chapter presents the first steps of that investigation, describing procedures for systematically accumulating information that will contribute to extended understandings of the issue investigated. It provides details of:

- the *purposes* for gathering information.
- procedures for *interviewing* participants.
- procedures for *observing* settings and events.
- procedures for reviewing *artifacts*—records, documents, and materials.
- procedures for incorporating *quantitative data*, including those obtained from *surveys*.
- procedures for reviewing the *literature*.

Later chapters reveal how participants distill this body of information to crystallize and clarify their understandings of the issue investigated.

Building a Picture: Gathering Information

Chapter 3 described a basic research routine—*look*: gathering information; *think*: analyzing the information; *act*: taking action on the basis of that analysis (see Figure 4.1). The routine was used to clarify the issue being investigated, to build a preliminary picture of the people and the context, and to design a research plan.

This chapter focuses on the first phase of that research plan—gathering information relevant to the research question that emerged as part of the research plan. It is, in effect, the "look" phase of research, in which research participants gather information from a variety of sources that might shed light on the issue investigated. They are, in effect, extending the picture that emerged from preliminary planning activities.

Information can come from a variety of sources, and the sources used will be determined by the nature of the issue investigated. If a teacher is not satisfied with the level or quality of student learning, for instance, he or she would need to ask "Why are my students not learning at a level I might expect of them?" To answer this question he or she needs to consider information from a variety of sources. The teacher might:

- **Observe** students at work.
- Have students **talk** about their learning/classroom experience.
- **Talk** with colleagues, school administrators, and/or parents.
- **Read** research or professional literature.
- Review **records and documentation** of past student performance.
- Identify available **materials and resources**.

Figure 4.1
Look: Gathering Information

The teacher would select from these sources according to the level of difficulty he or she is experiencing. Simpler, routine planning processes may require minimal inputs from only some of these sources. More complex or longstanding problems that fail to respond to routine teaching processes may require more extended exploration and may include any or all of the resources just listed.

The following sections therefore provide guidance for systematically acquiring relevant information. They include procedures for:

- Interviewing
- Focus groups
- Participant observation
- Reviewing artifacts—documents, records, materials, and equipment
- Conducting a survey
- Gathering numerical and statistical information
- Reviewing literature

Each of these types of information has the potential to increase the power and scope of the research process. If we not only listen to people describe and interpret their experience, but observe and participate in events, and read reports of those or similar events, then we enrich the research process. The use of multiple sources diminishes the possibility that one perspective alone will shape the course or determine the outcomes of investigation, and provides a diversity of materials from which to fashion effective solutions to the problem. This **triangulation** of data adds depth and rigor to the research process.

INTERVIEWING: GUIDED CONVERSATIONS

One of the major purposes of this phase of inquiry is to understand how students are experiencing classroom and school events and activities. When we work with children who are disengaged, disinterested, or misbehaving, for instance, we ask "What is happening for this child? What aspect of the child's experience is creating these responses to the situation?" This approach differs from the detached, clinical perspective of the psychologist, another useful viewpoint, who may explain those behaviors in terms of behavioral or personality disorders—depression, anxiety, attention deficit disorder, and so on. In action research, however, we seek to understand the natural world of the child, and to understand it in the child's terms.

I've heard many stories of children refusing to go to school or misbehaving badly and subsequent investigations revealing reasons for their behavior—a child who feared the departure of her mother after a parental argument; another scared to go school because he didn't have the right pens; one who was scared of a bully; another whose brother had been sent to prison. In many cases this became apparent only when the child was asked to talk at length about his or her experience and provided the basis for effective actions to deal with the issue. Children are like adults in many ways. We can't assume that we all understand ourselves perfectly, but what knowledge and understanding we have needs to be taken seriously when actions are taken that affect our lives.

The same is true for other research participants—colleagues, parents, administrators, and so on. Interviews enable them to describe the situation from their own perspective and to interpret events in their own terms. They enable other participants to "enter the world" of the person interviewed and to understand events from their perspective (Denzin, 1997; Spradley, 1979a, Spradley & McCurdy, 1972). Interviews not only provide a record of their views and perspectives, but also symbolically recognize the legitimacy of their points of view. The interview process, however, also provides opportunities for participants to revisit and reflect on events in their lives, and in the process, to extend their understanding of their own experience. This double hermeneutic—or meaning-making process—serves as the principal powerhouse of the research process, enabling all participants to extend their understanding of their own and other's experience. In classroom terms, the teacher has a greater understanding of the experience and perspective of the student, and vice versa.

Interviewing is best accomplished as a sociable series of events, not unlike a conversation between friends, where the easy exchange of information takes place in a comfortable, friendly environment. Although some people envisage interviewing as a form of authentic dialogue, we need to be wary of the way this "dialogue" emerges. When interviewers engage in exchanges of information or experience, as in a normal conversation, they unwittingly inscribe their own sets of meanings into the research process, constructing descriptions and interpretations that easily distort the experience or perspective of the participant interviewed. Authentic dialogue can only occur when a research facilitator is a natural participant in the setting, and when other participants have had opportunities to explore their own experience prior to engaging in dialogue. The following protocols provide ways to engage the interview process comfortably, ethically, and productively.

A wide range of literature provides information about interviewing (e.g., Chirban, 1996; Holstein & Gubrium, 1995; Kvale, 1996; McCracken, 1988; Rubin & Rubin 1995). Researchers should use these materials selectively, however, since some interview techniques are used for clinical or hypothesis-testing processes not suited to the purposes of action research. The key issue guiding the selection of a technique is whether it is used to reveal the perspective of the participant or whether it focuses on revealing specified types of information.

Although interviewing can be very time consuming, the processes are very productive, enabling research participants to explore an issue in some depth and, in the process, to develop understanding, trust, and good working relationships. In teaching terms, interviews provide the means to accomplish a wide range of student learning outcomes. Where time does not permit widespread use of interviews, focus groups provide a similar means for accomplishing the data gathering potential of interviews. By using group activities in the classroom teachers can provide stimulating and informative exploration of issues that enables students to enter an action research process (see following discussion).

Initiating Interviews: Establishing Relationships of Trust

Initial stages of the interview process can be a little uncomfortable for both interviewer and interviewee, and the interviewer must establish a relationship of trust in order to enable interviewees to feel comfortable in revealing their experiences, either to a stranger or a colleague. Chapter 3 suggests using initial contacts with people to inform them of the issue being studied and explore the possibility of their participation. The researcher:

- identifies him- or herself.
- identifies the issue of interest.
- asks permission to talk about that issue.
- negotiates a convenient time and place to meet.

The actual conversation might sound something like the following:

> "Hi! I'm Ernie Stringer. The principal says he's informed staff I'd be working here. I've been asked to assist staff to explore ways of improving parent–teacher conferences. I'd like to hear your views about that. Could we set up a time to talk? I'd need about half an hour of your time."

The prime directive in interviewing is for the interviewee to feel comfortable and safe when talking with the interviewer. The pertinent information should be presented in ways appropriate to the people and the setting, and that enable people to feel in control of the situation—to make them feel they're not being "put upon." Provide them with opportunities to determine the time and place of interviews, and ask them to suggest places to meet where they are comfortable. A classroom or school office may not be the best place to interview children or parents—the site itself might put them into a particular role or frame of mind. Behavior and talk are greatly influenced by the environment in which they occur. Research is a sociable process and should be treated as such. According to the circumstances, people may be comfortable in their own homes, in cafes or fast food outlets, or in a park or other public place. A meeting over coffee enables interviewer and interviewee to chat about general events and establish a conversational tone in their interactions. This provides a context to move easily to the issue of interest.

Initiating interviews is sometimes a sensitive issue. You might manage, initially, short chats in hallways and lounges, which open possibilities for more extended "conversations" (interviews). It's important to keep these initial occasions low key and informal, so people feel they aren't being imposed upon. After an initial interaction, you might indicate your desire to have them speak at greater length about issues arising in your conversation. Let them know of the focus of your interests and that you're interested in their perspective. "This has been interesting, Jack. I'd like to be able to explore this issue further. Could we meet somewhere and continue this conversation?" This provides a context for commencing more in-depth "conversations" that provide the basis for a continuing research relationship.

Questioning Techniques

Spradley (1979a) provides a useful framework of questions derived from his attempts to elicit natural structures of meaning used by people to describe and organize their social worlds. His essentially ethnographic methodology seeks neutral, nonleading questions that minimize the extent to which participant responses will be governed by frameworks of meaning inadvertently imposed by the researcher. A modified form of this framework provides the means to engage research participants in extended interviews revealing detailed descriptions of events and interactions in their lives and providing opportunities to explore significant issues in depth on their own terms.

A major problem with the interview process is that researcher perceptions, perspectives, interests, and agendas easily flavor questions, but the central purpose of the process is to obtain *interviewee* perspectives. Common approaches to interviewing based on extended lists of predefined questions are therefore inappropriate for the purpose of this type of research. Ethnographic interviews are quite different from questionnaires that frame the issue in terms making sense to the researcher, often focusing on technical/professional concepts, agendas, procedures, or practices. This detracts from the ability of participants to define, describe, and interpret experiences in their own terms, and can sometimes alienate audiences central to the study. Questionnaires, therefore, usually are inappropriate in the early stages of action research. At later stages of the process they may be used to gather data from a broader audience but care must be taken to frame them in terms derived from participants' concepts and terminology (see discussion on page 77).

First Phase: Grand Tour Questions An action research interview begins with one general "grand tour" question taking the form:

"Tell me about . . ." For example, "Tell me about your work." "Tell me about your school."

Though there are many extensions from this fundamental query, the simple framing enables respondents to describe, frame, and interpret events, issues, and other phenomena in their own terms. The question is not asked in bald isolation, but emerges contextually when sufficient rapport between participants has been established. It is also necessary to *frame* or contextualize the question:

"There are a number of people in this school concerned about [students dropping out of school]. Last time we talked you spoke briefly about this issue. Could you *tell me about* [students dropping out of your school]?"

Often it is best to contextualize the issue by starting with a more general question:

"Last time we spoke of [students dropping out of your school]. I'm not very familiar with your school. Could you *tell me about* your school?"

In most cases people are able to talk at length on an issue about which they are concerned. It merely requires a listener with an attentive attitude to enable them to engage in an extended discourse, sometimes encouraged by prompts (described next) to extend their descriptions. In some instances, however, participants may be unable to answer such a general question, tempting the researcher to insert more specific questions that destroy the intent of the research process. Spradley (1979a) suggests alternative ways of asking grand tour questions when respondents are able only to give limited responses to the more general question:

- **Typical** grand tour questions, enabling respondents to talk of ways events usually occur (e.g., How does your group usually work? Describe a typical day in your school.).
- **Specific** grand tour questions, which focus on particular events or times (e.g., Can you tell me about yesterday's meeting? Describe what happened the last time.).
- **A guided tour** question is a request for an actual tour that allows participants to show researchers (and, where possible, other stakeholders) around their offices, schools, classrooms, centers, or agencies (e.g., Could you show me around your

classroom/school?). As they walk around the school or classroom, participants may explain details about the people and activities involved in each part of the setting.

- **A task-related** grand tour question aids in description (e.g., Could you draw me a map of the school/classroom?). Maps are often very instructive and provide opportunities for extensive description and questioning. You can also ask participants to demonstrate how things are done (e.g., Can you show me how you write up your syllabus? Can you show me how the children do this work?).

Grand tour questions comprise ways of initiating participant descriptions of their experience. Information acquired in this way provides the basis for more extended descriptions, elicited by similar types of questions but emerging from ideas and agendas within the respondent's own descriptions.

Novice researchers sometimes find interviewing an uncomfortable experience—working through structured questioning processes seems awkward and unnatural. It seems impossible that such a discomfiting process would enable people to speak freely, and they tend to fall back on "conversation" as a means of engaging participants. Practice and experience, however, show how it is possible for interview questions to freely and easily construct a conversation. In their best formulation, questions should emerge in a fashion similar to the streetwise informality inherent in media presentations of urban youth: "What's happenin', man? What's goin' down? What's up?"

Novice researchers should prepare for interviewing processes by memorizing the forms of questioning described next and practicing mock interviews with friends and colleagues until they are able to translate the rather formal interview structures suggested in this book into the common language of the contexts they engage. Like any set of skills, practice may not make perfect, but it certainly increases effectiveness.

An interesting outcome of the acquisition of these questioning skills is their application to educational contexts. Teachers will find them wonderful tools for classroom questioning procedures, and administrators will find them useful in defining their managerial work—consultation, planning, leadership, and organization. A teacher wrote of this work in a message to a colleague:

> Spradley's format is very helpful when I apply it for interviewing my kids. I use the visual cues, have them write stuff out on paper, make drawings, maps of the school. The work is shared. We physically walk the area—a guided tour. I first thought the idea was dumb, but it's a great success. It's engaged, it's shared, we are walking together. The movement stops the tape in the head. The experience is shared. It's generative.

Second Phase: Extending the Interview—Mini-Tour Questions Interviews emerge and expand from responses to the initial grand tour questions. As people respond to the initial grand tour questions, a number of details begin to emerge, revealing events, activities, issues, and so on that comprise their experience and perspective. Sometimes the information is limited and interviewers need to probe further to enable the respondent to "dig deeper" into his or her experience. At this stage, the source of further questions emerges

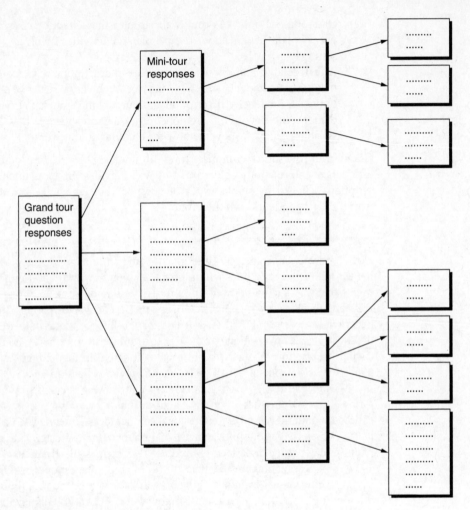

Figure 4.2
Mini-Tour Questioning Processes

from concepts, issues, and ideas embedded in respondent answers to the first questions. The interviewer asks *mini-tour* questions that enable interviewees to extend their responses (see Figure 4.2).

Mini-tour questions are similar in form to the general, typical, specific, guided, and task-related grand tour questions, but the focus of the questions is derived from information revealed in initial responses. They take forms such as the following:

"You talked of the way students start their work in the morning. *Tell me more about* students starting their work."
"Tell me how your students *usually* start their work."
"Tell me how your students started their work *this morning*."

"Can we *sit in your room* and have you tell me what's happening as students start their work?"

"Can you *show me* how students start their work?"

Responses to these questions may lead to other mini-tour questions that eventually provide extended, detailed descriptions of the issues and contexts investigated.

Extending Participant Responses: Prompt Questions Further information may be acquired through the skillful use of "prompts," which enable participants to reveal more details of the phenomena they are discussing. For example:

- **Extension** questions (e.g., "Tell me more about . . .," "Is there anything else you can tell me about . . .," "What else can you tell me about . . .?"
- **Encouragement** comments/questions (e.g., "Go on." "Yes?" "Uh-huh?")
- **Example** questions (e.g., "Can you give me an example of how children start their work?")

Prompt questions are not designed to elicit particular types of information the interviewer might see as desirable, but merely to enable the interviewee to think more closely about the events or perspectives described.

As interviews progress, research facilitators may be presented with viewpoints that appear limited, biased, wrong, or potentially harmful. They should not, however, attempt to extend the participant's responses by suggesting appropriate responses—such as "Don't you think that . . ."—and definitely must avoid discussion or debate about information presented. They should certainly avoid criticizing the perspective presented or suggesting alternative acceptable viewpoints. Acceptance of diverse viewpoints is a prime directive in action research, even where those perspectives conflict dramatically with those of other research participants. Challenges to particular viewpoints will occur naturally as differing perspectives are presented in more public arenas. The task at this stage, to employ the words of a well-known anthropologist, is "to grasp the natives' point of view, to realize their vision of their world" (Malinowski, 1922/1961, p. 5).

In the course of work with senior government department managers, my Aboriginal colleagues and I sometimes faced people whose perspectives were fundamentally racist. I would converse with them with barely controlled rage, fuming at the insensitive nature of their remarks. On one occasion an Aboriginal colleague later said "Take it easy, Stringer. He doesn't understand," to which I responded, "How do you stand it?" He looked at me quizzically and said, "You just get used to it." In many of these situations we were able to engage in productive work with these departments that, in the longer term, sensitized the people with whom we had been speaking to their inappropriate behavior and/or perspectives. I learned at that time that immediate confrontation is not always an appropriate response to inappropriate speech or behavior.

Prolonged Engagement The intent of action research is to assist people to develop new understandings of issues or problems. Asking them to "explain" superficially why and how the issue affects them often tends merely to elicit taken-for-granted responses or perspectives that reproduce existing understandings and provide little basis for revealing underlying features of their experience. Interview processes should give people the opportunity to carefully explore their experience, examining how events and issues are embedded in the complex features of their everyday lives.

The questioning techniques previously described help facilitate this descriptive process, but can usually only be effective if sufficient time is allocated to enable participants to explore the issue in depth. While simple problems or issues may require relatively small investments of time, larger or long-standing issues require prolonged periods of reflection and analysis. While a single 15- to 20-minute interview may suffice for a simple issue, significant issues require more than a superficial exploration. Multiple interviews of 30 to 60 minutes' duration enable participants to explore issues in depth, engaging the multiple dimensions of their experience and, in the process, extending their understanding of the complexity of the issues they face.

Except for in simple research processes, repeat interviews are therefore an essential feature of good qualitative research. Repeat interviews not only enable participants to reflect on issues more extensively, but provide opportunities to review and extend information previously acquired. Extended engagement therefore suggests the need for a significant time commitment, and repeated interaction with or between research participants. Merely being in the context is not sufficient—one must be engaged in systematic inquiry required to *re-search* an issue within a context.

When I queried the extent of the engagement of one researcher, she replied, "Oh, I was working with these teachers for months." Unfortunately, the intensive nature of the project work in which teachers and researchers were engaged provided little opportunity for them to discuss the nature of their experience, most of their attention being focused on the technical issues related to the project. The single 15-minute interview for each teacher was an inadequate vehicle for revealing the complex nature of their experience, providing only superficial comments that were uninformative and uninspiring.

Recording Information

Although action research processes often are informal, especially in small-scale or localized projects, it is important to keep a record of information acquired. This is especially important when different groups are involved, when personality differences are likely to create discord, or when sensitive issues are investigated. Participants acquire a degree of safety in knowing their perspectives are not forgotten or distorted over time. For reasons of accuracy and harmony, an ongoing record of information is a central feature of research. Field notes and tape recordings provide the two major forms of recording, of information, though increasing use is being made of video recording.

Field Notes
Verbatim Record Wherever possible, interviewees should make an immediate record of responses. You should ask permission for this before the interview, or in some cases, after the first few minutes, when the person has commenced talking. "This is very interesting. Do

On numerous occasions I have been engaged in action research projects that threatened to be disrupted by disputes about things people had said or decisions that had been made. Referring back to the recorded data and reading the actual words people had used usually restores order when disputes threaten to erupt. In numerous instances a mollified participant has acknowledged his or her error by saying "Did I say that?" or "I forgot that we'd decided that."

you mind if I take notes as you talk?" Handwritten field notes are a common form of recording, wherein researchers write a verbatim record of people's actual words. This requires researchers to be constantly aware of the need to record what is actually *said* by the person being interviewed, rather than a condensed or "tidied up" version. It is a "warts and all" procedure, where colloquialisms, incorrect grammar, or even blatantly incorrect information are precisely recorded. This all goes into the mix to ensure an accurate and authentic account of the person's perspective. At later stages of the interview (see the following "Member Checking" discussion) the interviewee will have opportunities to correct or add to the information given.

The following example is a record of an interview with a middle school teacher:

Interviewer: Some teachers say they'd like greater parent participation in this school. Can you tell me what you think of the idea of greater parent participation?

Teacher: Well, parents should feel they are part of the school. . . . We could provide, like, inservices for parents on things like handling children, using computers . . . you know, inspiration, web searches.

It would help parents to have skills to assist their kids, especially those who are struggling. Parents could be offered stuff at low cost, no cost—like study skills, how to develop study habits with children. It'd be low pressure, low key. You could have staff volunteers with special skills, special expertise.

It helps establish good relationships with parents. Give them greater ability to communicate results. They'd be able to talk more easily about their children.

Interviewer: Are there other ways to increase parent participation?

Teacher: I like having parents in class who can guide and help a child, but not do the work for the kids. Some parents help, but they end up doing the work for the kids. That's not on. But if they help the kids with their work, it's a great help to me.

One school had a parent scheduled to help a child. They'd have that child each time they came to the classroom, helping with, like, reading, if the child was having difficulty with reading. . . .

This type of handwritten record requires practice in writing at speed and the concomitant development of personal "shorthand" writing protocols—"&" for "and," "w/" for "with," "t" for "the," "g" for "-ing," missing consonants (e.g., *writg*, or *wrtg* for *writing*), and so on. It takes practice, but is essential if researchers are to record the respondent's actual words. Those responsible for recording information need to be wary of paraphrasing or abstracting, since this defeats the purpose of interviewing, which is to capture the voice of participants, describing things as they would describe them. Sometimes it may be necessary to ask the person interviewed to repeat information, or to pause momentarily so the interviewee can "catch up" on note taking.

Member Checking Once an interview has finished, the interviewer should read back the notes, giving the respondent an opportunity to confirm the accuracy of the notes, or to extend or clarify information given. In some cases it may also be possible to identify the key features of the interview to use in data analysis (see Chapter 5). Some people type their notes and have the respondent read them to check for accuracy. It may also be appropriate, in some instances, to provide a copy of the field notes to the respondent for his or her own information.

Tape Recorders Using a tape recorder has the advantage of allowing the researcher to acquire a detailed and accurate account of an interview. Researchers acquire large quantities of information from multiple sources, so they should keep a careful record of their tapes, noting on each tape the person, place, time, and date of the interview. Tapes should be transcribed as soon as possible after the interview, and the accuracy of the resulting text should be verified by the person interviewed.

Tape recordings have a number of disadvantages, however, and researchers should carefully weigh the merits of this technology. Technical difficulties with equipment may damage rapport with respondents, and people sometimes find it difficult to talk freely in the presence of a recording device, especially when sensitive issues are discussed. A researcher may need to wait until a reasonable degree of rapport has been established before introducing the possibility of using a tape recorder. When using a recorder, the researcher should be prepared to stop the tape to allow respondents to speak "off the record" if they show signs of discomfort.

The sheer volume of material obtained through tape recording also may inhibit the steady progress of a research process. If tape recordings are used, they should be transcribed immediately so the relevant information becomes available to participants. This is particularly useful when contentious or sensitive issues are explored, since a person's own words may help resolve potentially inflammatory situations. Researchers should be wary of accumulating tapes for later transcribing—transcription is a lengthy and tedious process that may detract from the power of the research.

Interviewing Children

Action research works on the premise that children are active constructors of their own knowledge. By talking, listening, and reflecting on events within a system of mutually supportive relations, children are able to extend their understanding of events and experiences. An extensive literature has revealed the possibilities of engaging children in research processes related to their own learning environments.

Some researchers, however, initially find interviews with children to be somewhat problematic. Young children, especially, sometimes have difficulty engaging in the forms of discourse common to adults, and tend to respond or react to events in immediate rather than abstract terms. Asking children a grand tour question such as "Tell me about . . ." sometimes elicits an abbreviated or noncommittal response—"What do you want to know?" "I just like it!"—or a quizzical look.

In these circumstances, alternate forms of grand tour questions, especially those involving activity, may enhance opportunities to elicit responses from children and enable them to explore and express their experiences. These include:

Typical grand tour questions—"What usually happens. . . .?"
Specific grand tour questions—"What happened last time the class . . .?
Guided tour questions—"Can you show me around your classroom and tell me . . .?
Task-related questions—"Can you show me how . . .?" "Draw me a picture of . . ."

This latter form provides multiple ways for children to express their thoughts and feelings, or to reveal details of their experience. Activity questions are particularly fruitful in work with children. Art enables children to draw and talk about aspects of their experience. Care needs to taken to ensure the child is engaging actual events, rather than extrapolating to an imaginary world, as creative children sometimes do. You might ask the child to draw some aspects of his or her experience by requesting "Can you draw me a picture of . . .?" Then "Tell me about the picture."

In some cases, especially where sensitive issues are explored, some people use scenarios, asking children to recount a story using imaginary or fictional characters representing types of actors in the context. Drawings or doll figures also may be used for these purposes. It also may be useful to use reversal questions such as, "If you were a teacher, what would you do if . . .?" or future-oriented questions such as, "What would happen if . . .?" The problem with these types of question, however, is the risk that children will engage in fantasies having little bearing on the reality at hand.

It is often difficult for children to talk openly and honestly with an adult, especially an authority figure such as a teacher. For this reason it is necessary to spend time and effort developing an easy and friendly relationship that allows a child to respond more empathetically to researchers. Teachers engaging in research in their class or school may need to develop a different type of relationship to enable children to speak freely. They may also provide training and practice in interviewing techniques so the children can interview each other. This is especially useful with older children, providing a safe environment for them to explore their experience. In these circumstances, group techniques (see "Using Focus Groups to Gather Data" section) that mask the identity of the participants can also be fruitful.

The time, place, and style of interviews with children are particularly important. Children are likely to feel uncomfortable if a teacher interviews them individually in a classroom. They may feel as if they are "in trouble," or wary of being asked to divulge information about their classmates. This is especially true of "problem" students who may be central to a research process. Where they are included as participants in the research process, however, the rewards are often enormous, providing children with increased ownership and understanding of events and activities occurring in their school or classroom.

As qualitative and naturalistic studies increasingly engage children, a variety of resources in the literature can assist researchers in including children in the processes of investigation (e.g., Edwards, Gandini, & Forman, 1993; Fine & Sandstrom, 1988; Graue & Walsh, 1998; Greig & Taylor, 1998; Helm, 1999; Malaguzzi, 1995; Meerdink, 1999; Selekman, 1997). It is essential that children are able to describe and interpret experiences in their own terms, rather than being asked to respond to questions derived from a teacher's or an adult's perceptions of what *should be* important for a child. Often there is a tendency

Rhonda Petty (1997) describes her methods of working with a small group of boys from her class. She met with them in their homes, at McDonald's, in parks, and on small excursions. She was amazed at the difference in their demeanor and communicativeness in these contexts. They talked animatedly and easily, a far cry from the rather silent and uneasy conversations possible in the school context. She was able to elicit a broad range of information and gain a much clearer understanding of the boys with whom she worked, and to provide a richly evocative account of the way those interactions dramatically changed the images she had formed of them.

for educational researchers to mentally list issues derived from their professional repertoire of experience—materials, lessons, learning processes, timetables, homework, reading, behavior, and so on. These issues may be of peripheral relevance to children as they focus on a more existential response to their situation. Ultimately we wish to understand children's experience and perceptions of the issue we are investigating. The process enables the children to clarify and extend their understanding of events and to be able to participate in plans to remedy the situation.

I have many times had my faith in the integrity and good sense of children confirmed in research activities. I have seen high school dropouts engaged in extended research processes culminating in the development of a new alternative high school in my city. I have seen how seriously even young elementary children engage processes of inquiry focusing on issues about which they are concerned. Children, even those labeled as "at risk" or "problems," generally respond intelligently and with passion when they are engaged as competent, intelligent persons, actively engaged as members of a team, rather than being treated as as "miscreants" or "students" subject to the often directive dictates of authority figures. The principles of participatory action research are especially rich and rewarding when applied to young people.

Using Focus Groups to Gather Data

Traditional research practices focus largely on gathering data from individuals and using that information for an abstracting process of analysis. Data gathering in action research, however, becomes more effective when individuals are able to explore their experiences interactively. Although it is important for people to have opportunities to explore issues individually in the early stages of inquiry, joint processes of collaborative inquiry considerably enhance the power of a research process. Individual interviews followed by focus group exploration provide a context for participants to share information and extend their understanding of issues.

In recent years focus groups have emerged as a useful way to engage people in processes of investigation, enabling people to share information and to "trigger" new ideas or insights. A focus group may be envisioned as a group interview, with questions providing a stimulus for capturing people's experiences and perspectives. It provides the means for including relatively large numbers of people in a research process, an important consideration in larger projects.

When we bring diverse groups of people or children together, however, we need to carefully manage the dynamics of interaction and discussion to ensure the productive operation of focus groups. Too easily they sometimes degenerate into "gab-fests" or "slinging matches" where unfocused discussions or argumentative interchanges damage the harmonious qualities characteristic of good action research. Literature providing guidance for focus group facilitation includes publications by Barbour and Kitzinger (1998), Morgan (1997a, 1997b), Morgan and Krueger (1997), Krueger (1994, 1997a, 1997b), Krueger and Casey (2000), and Greenbaum (2000).

Bringing People Together To initiate focus group explorations, the research facilitator should seek out opportunities to bring people together to discuss issues of common interest. "I've spoken with a number of people about this issue and some of them have similar views to yourself. Would you be willing to meet with them to talk about the issues you've raised?" Or, "As you know, I've been speaking with other teachers and many are concerned about. . . . Would you attend a meeting with people like Janet Jones, Bill Rochon, and Maria Garcia to discuss this issue?"

As with interviews, the time and the place must be conducive to the process. People should have adequate time to explore the issue, and should be in a place where they are comfortable and feel they can express their views and experiences freely. A rushed meeting during recess time, or in a common room where others can overhear, is likely to limit the information shared or to limit the types of interaction leading to positive working relationships between people. These issues are especially important when working with families or children. As with interviews, meetings away from school or other formal settings may be more conducive to the easy and communicative atmosphere that provides the basis for ongoing development of productive action research processes.

Initially, research facilitators may arrange focus group meetings for small groups of stakeholders, but as the processes of inquiry develop it may be fruitful to bring larger groups of participants together. Larger meetings become more productive when all individuals have opportunities to express their thoughts and experiences, so focus groups may be used to enable greater active participation of all people present. Since information gathering is often concomitant with information processing (analysis or interpretation), processes for facilitating focus groups will be discussed in greater depth in the following chapter.

The size of groups is important, with four to six people being the optimal number in each group to enable everyone to participate effectively. When dealing with large groups, then, it is usually best to form subgroups, with each subgroup recording its exploration and reporting back to the whole group.

Focus Group Processes Research facilitators should ensure that focus group sessions are carefully planned and facilitated to ensure the productive use of time. It is all too easy for poorly prepared groups to degenerate into gossip sessions, to be dominated by a forceful person, or to create antagonisms derived from intemperate debates. As with data gathering, researchers may engage single focus groups, though multiple groups may be used

Focus groups can be used in many contexts, large and small. When I worked with staff of the Brazos School to facilitate an internal evaluation, I interviewed each person individually, then wrote a short joint report revealing issues emerging from these interactions. After staff had read the report I facilitated a focus group meeting, enabling them to clarify issues emerging in the report and to identify and prioritize issues on which they wished to take action. Because it was a small school, we were able to complete this process in only a few days.

On another occasion I worked with a small team of researchers to facilitate review of a large regional organization. We spoke with staff and clients at local centers, assisting them to talk of their perceptions of the purpose of the organization, the services it was providing, and the problems they perceived. We then facilitated focus group meetings of staff and clients in each locality, enabling them to clarify the issues that had emerged. Finally, representatives from each of these localities met to explore issues emerging from these meetings and to formulate an action plan. As a result of these activities the organization was restructured, resulting in more effective services and greatly increased activity. The process took six months, but was highly effective in revitalizing an organization that was in danger of closing.

productively when meeting with diverse groups of stakeholders. The following steps provide a basic procedure for running focus groups:

1. Set ground rules.
   - Each person should have opportunities to express their perspective.
   - All perspectives should be accepted nonjudgmentally.
2. Provide clear guidance.
   - Provide and display focus questions.
   - Designate a time frame for each section/question.
3. Designate a facilitator for each group to:
   - ensure each person has an equal chance to talk.
   - keep discussions on track.
   - monitor time.
4. Record group talk in each group.
   - Designate a person to record proceedings.
   - Record the details of each person's contribution, using their own words.
   - Where appropriate, each group should summarize their discussions, identifying and recording key features of experience and significant issues or problems.
5. Elicit feedback and clarification.
   - Bring groups together, ensuring adequate time is available for feedback and discussion.
   - Have each group present the summary of their discussions.
   - Provide opportunities for individuals within each group to extend or clarify points presented.

- The facilitator should ask questions of each group designed to have them clarify and extend their contributions.
- Ensure that new information emerging from this process is recorded.
6. Analyze combined information.
   - Identify common features across groups.
   - Identify divergent issues or perspectives.
   - Rank issues in order of priority.
7. What next: Plan for action.
   - Define what is to happen next: What actions are to be taken, who will be responsible for them, where and when they will be done, what resources are required, and who will organize these actions.
   - Designate a person to monitor these actions.
   - Designate a time and place to meet again to review progress.

The rather bland description of these procedures masks the exciting and rewarding possibilities emerging from dialogue, discussion, and personal interactions common in these types of processes. There are many benefits gained through these processes. By providing participants with the space and time to engage in open dialogue on issues about which they are deeply concerned, they gain increased clarity and understanding of those issues and begin to develop the productive personal relationships so important to the effective enactment of action research.

Focus Questions   Focus groups require careful facilitation to ensure people are able to accomplish productive purposes in the time they spend together. The purpose for meeting should be clearly described by the facilitator, and discussion should be focused on specific issues related to that purpose. As with individual interviews, the major purpose of these types of sessions is to provide people with opportunities to describe and reflect on their own experiences and perspectives. A general statement by the facilitator contextualizing and framing the issue should be followed by a series of *focus questions* similar in format to those provided for individual interviews:

> **Grand tour questions.** These questions enable people to express their experience and perspectives in their own terms: "We're meeting today to think about ways we might more effectively link with families in our community. I'd like to give you time, initially, to talk about ways you currently link with families, then extend our discussions from there. Please focus initially on the first question 'How do I link currently with families?'"
> **Mini-tour questions.** As people explore these issues, further questions may emerge from issues arising in their discussion. "There's not enough time," "There are some parents who never contact me," and so on. These statements are reframed in question form and become subjects for further sharing of information: "What are the different ways we currently make time to link with parents?" "What are the ways we currently link with parents who are difficult to contact?" The sharing of information in this way not only enables people to benefit from each other's experience, but also provides possibilities for directly formulating solutions to issues as they emerge.
> **Guided tour questions.** Focus groups may engage in a guided tour, in which people tour a classroom, school, or other sites, sharing their experiences or perspectives of events related to those environments.

Task-related questions. Groups may also benefit from task-related questions, so that members are able to demonstrate how they go about achieving some purpose. For example, "Could you show us how you organize the lessons you've been talking about?" "Could you show the group how you present this type of material in your class?" Having people express their perspective *artistically* can sometimes provide very evocative understandings of their experience, and *maps and diagrams* provide highly productive ways for people to explore and express their ideas or issues. Facilitators may ask people, either individually or as a group, to draw a picture, a map, or a diagram illustrating their experience of the issue on which they are focused. These productions then become the focus for further discussions, extending people's understanding of participant experiences and perspectives.

Facilitators should ensure that each group keeps an ongoing record of their discussion. This may take the form of notes, recorded by a volunteer in the group, but sometimes may be recorded in summary form on charts. Where multiple groups are engaged in discussions, a plenary session should provide opportunities for participants to share the results of their exploration.

PARTICIPANT OBSERVATION

The principal purpose of observation is to familiarize researchers with the context in which issues and events are played out, or to provide participants with opportunities to stand back from their everyday involvement and watch purposefully as events unfold. This extends both their perceptions and understandings of the everyday features of their life-world, and provides information for the construction of reports. Careful observation enables participants to "build a picture" of the context and the activities and events within it, revealing details of the setting as well as the mundane, routine activities comprising the life-world of teachers, students, and administrators. Sometimes, however, the opportunity to observe is revelatory, providing keen insights or illuminating important but taken-for-granted features of school and classroom life.

Observation in action research is very different from the highly structured types of observation required in experimental research. Here the researcher notes the frequency of specific types of behavior, acts, or events using a highly structured observation schedule. Participant observation in action research is much more open-ended, its purpose being to provide more detailed descriptions of the people's actions and the context in which they occur—to come to a deeper level of understanding through extended immersion in that context and interaction with people and events within it.

As I facilitated the internal evaluation of BSIC (see page 184), I recorded observations of the school as field notes. This information provided the basis for a description of the school and the community context in which it was located. Readers of the report were able readily to locate themselves and their context as a precursor to reflecting on the events and activities on which the remainder of the report focused. A number of people commented favorably on this process, noting the way the description enabled them to focus on the events described as part of their own experience.

At another time, I engaged in an extended study of classrooms in a school in my state. As I watched children and teachers interact in classrooms over an extended period, a different picture of classroom life emerged for me. As a teacher I had experienced classrooms as intensively busy places, with activities and events unfolding in rapid and complex interaction. As I observed each child for an extended period, however, I saw a completely different picture emerge, one composed of long periods of silence and inactivity, the boredom and impatience of the children almost palpable. I now see classrooms in quite a different way.

As with interviews, observation needs to be focused, so that only details relevant to the issue investigated are recorded. Spradley (1979b) suggests that observations should always be accompanied or preceded by asking participants relevant questions, the answers thus guiding researcher observations. A research facilitator may ask participants for a "guided tour," with the underlying question in mind "What do I need to know about this school/classroom to understand the issue investigated?" As the tour progresses, the researcher might say "Tell me about this school [or classroom, community, etc.]." Observations will focus on any of the following issues:

- **People:** students, teachers, administrators, specialist staff, and so on
- **Places:** classrooms, play areas, offices, homes, community contexts, locations of activities and events; physical layouts
- **Acts:** single actions that people take (e.g., a child erasing some words)
- **Activities:** a set of related acts (e.g., a child writing a story)
- **Events:** a set of related activities (e.g., a written expression class)
- **Objects:** buildings, furniture, equipment, books, learning materials
- **Purposes:** what people are trying to accomplish
- **Time:** times, frequency, duration, and sequencing of events and activities
- **Feelings:** emotional orientations and responses to people, events, activities, and so on

The purpose of this process is to provide a clear record of events and activities as they actually occur, rather than relying solely on participant accounts. It provides researchers with information that enables them to construct a general picture of the context in which events occur, as well as record details of particular sets of events. The researcher should, wherever possible, check his or her observations with participants, since it is easy to misinterpret what is happening. A yawn may be indicative, for instance, of boredom, nervousness, tiredness, or cynicism.

In one study I summarized a meeting in this way: "The principal met staff to present the new school policy. The faculty appeared rather disgruntled with the new policy but made no comment about it." Here I noted information related to (a) the purpose of the meeting and (b) the feelings of the staff. When I checked with the staff to verify the authenticity of my interpretation I discovered that I had misinterpreted the situation. They were not particularly concerned about the new policy, but were unhappy with other (hidden) agendas they felt to be implicit in the principal's presentation.

Recording Observations

Field Notes Field notes enable researchers to record detailed descriptions of actual places and events as they occur naturally. As researchers meet members of stakeholding groups, they will have opportunities to gain a clearer picture of the research context by observing the settings and events in which participants carry out their daily educational activities. They should record their observations in field notes that provide ongoing records of important elements of each part of the setting. In some contexts it is not possible to record field notes immediately. In these cases, observers should record events as soon as possible after they occur.

The task may appear quite daunting, as any context contains huge amounts of information that could be recorded. As indicated earlier, researchers should record the information needed by an audience to understand the *context* and *social processes* related to the issue investigated, using the previous framework as a guide (people, places, events, etc.). The recorded information provides material that will later be used to provide descriptions of the context of the research, or of events and activities.

Written descriptions may be supplemented by hand-drawn maps or pictures that provide increased clarity. A map of a school or classroom, for instance, provides a pictoral representation that may be later used to provide increased understanding and clarity. Observers may "set up" their observations by describing and drawing the setting, then recording pertinent events and activities as they occur over a period of time, then member checking to ensure appropriate renditions of both setting and events.

Photographs Photographs provide a useful record, enabling later audiences to more clearly visualize settings and events. Photographs may be used to stimulate discussion during focus groups, or provide the basis for focusing and/or extending interviews. A grand tour question such as "Tell me what's happening in this photograph" can provide richly detailed descriptions, an especially useful process when working with children. Photographs may also be used to enhance reports presented to participants or to other research audiences.

Video Recording The increasing availability of video equipment provides an important research resource. Written descriptions are necessarily limited, focusing on specific features of the situation and providing what is really a rudimentary understanding of the events and the context. Video recording has the advantage of making the scene immediately available to viewers, providing a far greater depth of understanding of the acts, activities, events, interactions, behaviors, and the nature of the context. Extended video recordings can reveal highly informative pictures easily viewed by large audiences.

Careful consideration needs to be given to the specific settings and events to be recorded. Schouten and Watling (1997) suggest a process by which participants "*beacon out*" their fields of concern, exploring the extent of their investigations through dialogue, then focusing on salient features to be recorded. They suggest the following basic procedures:

- Leave a 10-second gap at the beginning of each tape.
- Make a trial recording to ensure equipment is working.
- Enable people time to "warm up" before recording.
- Check the material immediately after recording.
- Stick to a designated time limit.
- Allow time for people to comment after recording.

Videos, however, do not reveal "the facts" or "the truth." They still provide only partial information, since only small segments of time may be recorded, and the lens focuses only on particular features of the context or events, according to the particular interest or interpreting eye of the photographer. A useful way of using this particular tool is to record events identified by preliminary analyses of interview data. The camera then focuses on features of the scene identified as significant by participants in the process.

ARTIFACTS: DOCUMENTS, RECORDS, MATERIALS, AND EQUIPMENT

In traditional anthropological investigations, understanding a cultural context sometimes requires an intensive study of artifacts related to the daily social life of the setting. This is true to some extent in action research, though the focus on artifacts is somewhat different in nature. Much information related to educational issues investigated in schools can be found in documents and records, and useful insight may be gained by perusing books, materials, and equipment used for teaching, learning, or administration. A survey of the physical facilities—furniture, buildings, classrooms offices, and so on—may also be instructive.

Researchers, however, need to be parsimonious and focused, since huge and unwieldy piles of information—most of which has little apparent pertinence to the issue investigated—may overwhelm an investigation. In participatory action research, participant accounts provide a frame of reference to focus further observation. Preliminary analysis of interview data reveals the features and elements of experience or context that might benefit from the gathering of additional information. Comments such as "I hate the text we're using. It's so boring," or "I'm learning so much more this semester," may lead to a review of texts used in the class, or an examination of achievement records.

Ultimately, however, material is collected according to whether or not it appears pertinent to the issue investigated. Researchers do not determine which artifacts are to be reviewed prior to commencement of the study, however, since their pertinence or relevance to the research question is revealed as participant perspectives emerge. Whether school grades, classroom texts, furniture, school facilities, or other items are included becomes evident when they are mentioned in participant interview responses. Reviewing interview field notes or transcripts therefore enables researchers to identify the artifacts to be included in the study.

Documents

Researchers can obtain a great deal of significant information by reviewing documents in the research context. In classrooms, a syllabus, curriculum, or timetable may provide crucial information about the teaching/learning features of the setting. At the school or district level, policy documents may include rules and regulations providing insight into institutionally approved behaviors, activities, or procedures. Policy documents also provide information about a school, school district, or state department. These may be complemented by annual reports containing details of the structure, purposes, operations, and resources of the school, district, or state department. Memos, meeting minutes, procedure statements, school or district plans, evaluation reports, press accounts, public relations materials, information statements, and newsletters likewise extend understanding about a school's organization and operation. Researchers should keep records of documents reviewed, noting any significant information and its source. In some cases, they may be able to obtain photocopies of relevant documents to add to the body of data.

In reviewing documents and records, research participants should always keep in mind that they are not finding "the facts" or "the truth." Information is always influenced by the authors or written in accordance with particular people's motives, agendas, and perspectives. This is as true at the organizational level as it is at the level of the individual, since people or groups in positions of influence and power are able to inscribe their perspective, values, and biases into official documents and records. Documents and records, therefore, should always be viewed as just information from another source or stakeholder, having no more legitimacy or "truth value" than that of any other stakeholder.

Records

Confidential records often are not available for public scrutiny, and researchers may need special circumstances and appropriate formal approval to gain access to them. Where research is "in-house," however, review of records can often provide invaluable information. Individual records of student behavior and achievement, school records of student numbers and attendance, and district or state records may provide information central to the investigation. Comparisons with other students, classes, or schools often reveal interesting information that provides a much-needed perspective to an investigation. Perceptions that a school is poorly funded or that achievement levels are low may not be borne out by a review of the records of other schools in a district or state. As with all information, however, such information needs to be carefully evaluated, since much of it is recorded in a statistical form that requires careful interpretation. In circumstances where statistical information is used, the research team needs to include someone with the relevant expertise to interpret the information acquired. Figure 4.3 lists types of documents and records.

Student Work Samples

Student work samples provide a wonderful resource for investigation, providing highly informative, concrete visual information. They enable research participants to gain rich understandings of the types of activity in which children have engaged in classrooms, or lesson plans and syllabi used by teachers in formulating teaching/learning processes. Work samples provide useful material when constructing reports, enabling audiences direct access to the outcomes of people's activities. As with documents, however, they should be collected parsimoniously, since they tend to accumulate with astonishing speed. Work samples should be gathered once preliminary analysis of interview data provides a focus for selection.

As with participant sampling, work samples may be selected to demonstrate:

- variation in student work.
- extreme examples of student work.
- typical student work.
- student work that exhibits particular characteristics.
- exceptional cases of student work.

As with other artifacts, student work samples should be selected according to their relevance to the research issue, as becomes evident in the course of interviews with participants.

Lesson plans	Research reports
Syllabi	Demographics
Curricula	Statistics
Projects	Databases
Assignments	
Timetables	Legislation
	Rules and regulations
Grades	Policies and procedures
Achievement records	Annual reports
Work portfolios	Budgets
Attendance records	Archives
Report cards	
Case records	Constitutions
	Meeting minutes and
Books	agendas
Texts	Rosters
Book lists	Correspondence
Reading lists	Email
Bibliographies	Memos
	Reports
Diaries	
Calendars	Circulars
Phone logs	Notice boards
Schedules	Pamphlets and brochures
Appointment books	Lecture notes
Mileage records	

Figure 4.3
Documents and Records

Materials, Equipment, and Facilities

A review of material and equipment (see Figure 4.4) provides useful input to the investigation, since education is affected by a vast array of artifacts that influence events in classrooms and schools. Books, stationery, storage space, furniture, laboratory equipment, computers, art equipment, music materials and instruments, physical education equipment, play space and equipment, buildings, rooms, offices, and so on, may all have a significant effect on schooling. Students and schools may, for instance, be hampered by lack of equipment or by facilities in a poor state of repair. Research participants should carefully review these types of items, in conjunction with other data gathering processes. As with other observations, the focus and direction of reviews will depend, to a large extent, on information acquired in interviews.

Recording Information

As researchers review artifacts they should take careful note of information they consider relevant to the investigation. They should list information they have reviewed, together

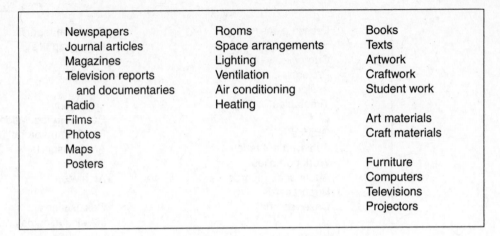

Newspapers	Rooms	Books
Journal articles	Space arrangements	Texts
Magazines	Lighting	Artwork
Television reports	Ventilation	Craftwork
and documentaries	Air conditioning	Student work
Radio	Heating	
Films		Art materials
Photos		Craft materials
Maps		
Posters		Furniture
		Computers
		Televisions
		Projectors

Figure 4.4
Materials, Equipment, and Facilities

One of the best schools for Aboriginal children I have observed was also the poorest, in material terms. Despite the dilapidated furniture, obsolete texts, and paucity of materials, the school rang with the life and vitality of the children and parents who participated in its programs in an ongoing way. It made me rethink my cherished notions about what was necessary for an adequate education for children. Sometimes in focusing on the material artifacts of schooling, we miss important truths about the emotional, intellectual, and spiritual features of people's experience. Observations need to be treated warily as a source of understanding.

On the other hand, teacher perceptions of deficiencies in teaching and learning materials in a recent school evaluation were confirmed by a review of that school's inventory. Triangulation, the comparing of different sources of data, can greatly enhance participant perspectives.

with a summary description of the nature of the material. In the process, they should record which information may be made public and which must be kept confidential. The intent of the summaries is to provide stakeholders with information about materials that might enhance their investigation. If, for instance, stakeholders have a perception that student achievement levels are declining, then access to appropriate records will enable them to check whether or not this is so. This information will enable participants to extend, clarify, or enhance existing issues and perspectives as they emerge.

SURVEYS

A survey is another means of providing input into an action research process. Unlike "quasi-experiments" that use statistical analysis to test a hypothesis, surveys are sometimes used in action research to acquire information from larger groups of participants. A survey may be used, for instance, to acquire information from parents whose children attend a school. The major advantage of surveys is that they provide a comparatively inexpensive means to acquire information from a large number of people within a limited time frame. Their disadvantage is that it is frequently difficult to obtain responses from those surveyed, and the information that can be obtained by this means is generally fixed.

Creswell (2002) describes the different ways surveys can be administered: self-administered questionnaires, telephone interviews, face-to-face interviews, computer-assisted interviews, and website and Internet surveys. He suggests there are two basic survey designs: a cross-sectional design that collects information from people at one point in time, and a longitudinal design that studies changes in a group or population over time. Surveys always obtain information about people's perspectives on an issue, rather than their actual behaviors. A study of student perspectives on "homework," for instance, may focus on student attitudes, beliefs, and opinions, or be designed to elicit information about their perceptions, feelings, priorities, concerns, and experiences of "homework." The latter is more appropriate for action research, which focuses largely on revealing the perspectives and experiences of participants.

Researchers may increase the validity of a survey by ensuring it is grounded in concepts and ideas that more closely fit the experiences and perspectives of those surveyed, by doing face-to-face interviews with a small sample of participants (see earlier "Interviews" discussion). They may then use that information to formulate questions for the survey instrument. Surveys can be conducted through face-to-face interviews or through paper-and-pen questionnaires, and each type may be administered to individuals or groups. Paper-and-pen questionnaires are useful when researchers require specific information about a limited number of items, or where sensitive issues are explored.

Questions in action research surveys may be comparatively unstructured and open-ended to maximize opportunities for respondents to answer questions in their own terms, or highly structured to acquire specific information related to issues of concern.

Conducting a Survey

- **Determine the purpose, focus, and participants.** Prior to constructing the survey instrument (questionnaire), carefully define:
  - issues to be included.
  - the type of information to be obtained.
  - the people from whom it will be acquired.
- **Formulate questions.** Ensure that questions:
  - cover all issues and all types of information identified.
  - are clear and unambiguous.
  - do not include two issues in one question (e.g., Should students be able to be in classrooms at lunchtime and after school?).
  - are framed in positive terms, rather than negative.
  - do not contain jargon likely to be unfamiliar to respondents.
  - are short and to the point.

- **Responses.** Provide appropriate response formats. Formats should provide sufficient space for responses to open-ended or semistructured questions. Questions may take the following forms:
  - **Open response:** "How many minutes should be allocated for lunch break? _____ minutes"
  - **Fixed response:** "When should children leave school after classes finish—within 5 minutes, within 15 minutes, or within 30 minutes?"
  - **Dual response:** Responses choosing between two alternatives (e.g., yes/no, agree/disagree, male/female).
  - **Rating response:** These questions end with a statement similar to: "Using the following scale, circle the most correct response 1 (strongly disagree), 2 (disagree), 3 (neutral), 4 (agree), 5 (strongly disagree)."
- **Provide framing information.** Inform potential respondents of the purpose and nature of the survey. Include information about the likely duration of the interview/session and the types of responses required (e.g., extended responses or precise responses).
- **Trial.** Test the adequacy of the questions by having preliminary interviews or questionnaire-completing sessions with a small number of people. Modify questions that prove to be inappropriate or ambiguous.
- **Administer** the questionnaire, or conduct the survey.
- **Thank** people for their participation.
- **Analyze** the data.

Where more complex, extended, and/or analytic surveys are contemplated, researchers should use appropriate sources to ensure effective and valid designs (e.g., Bell, 1993; Cook & Campbell, 1979; Creswell, 2002; Fink, 1995; Oppenheim, 1966; Youngman, 1982).

The Barrios Juntas Neighborhood Collective worked with parents and teachers to improve communication between families and the schools. They interviewed parents and teachers to explore ways of improving parent–teacher conferences. Parents were asked the following questions following their conference with teachers:

1. How do you feel about your parent–teacher conference?
2. How does it compare with other conferences?
3. What did you and the teacher talk about?
4. What would you have liked to talk more about?
5. How could teachers make your next conference better?
6. How could parents make the next conference better?

Similar questions were put to teachers. Results of both sets of information were analyzed separately using categorizing and coding techniques, suggesting a number of ways in which parent–teacher conferences could be improved. The school was able to put a number of recommendations emerging from this survey into practice in following parent–teacher conference days.

Quantitative Information: Statistical and Numerical Data

In their day-to-day classroom tasks, teachers will work with a variety of statistical information—student scores on classroom tests, state and national tests, and diagnostic tests; attendance records; intelligence and aptitude test scores; and so on. Statistical information provides data relevant to the assessment of student learning (How well has each of my students learned this material/skill?), and evaluation of teacher performance (What is the overall performance of my students?). In this era of "accountability," however, statistical information takes on even greater significance, with teachers and administrators now being held "accountable" for the performance of their students on standardized tests. Regular, centralized testing is used to evaluate the level of student performance in core content areas, and in some cases, as in the No Child Left Behind regime in the United States, punitive action is taken for poorly performing schools.

Unlike in experimental research, where statistical data is used to test hypotheses, action research uses quantitative data as another form of information to extend or clarify participant understandings of an issue or problem. Numerical and statistical data are particularly useful where there is lack of clarity about the occurrence of particular phenomena. Depending on the nature of the study, statistical information may provide descriptive information related to:

- **occurrences** of a phenomenon, for example, the number of girls in a school, the number of students in a class.
- **comparisons** of different occurrences, for example, the number of girls compared to the number of boys, or girls' scores compared with boys' scores on reading tests.
- **trends,** or **history of occurrences over time,** for example, reading scores are declining over time.
- **central tendencies**—mean score of students on an achievement test.
- **distribution of scores**—whether there is a wide spread of scores in a classroom achievement test, or whether most students have similar scores.
- **correlations,** which measure the degree of relationship between any two phenomena, for example, whether success in reading is related to gender, social class, or ethnicity.

The following section describes some of the more common types and forms of quantitative data that might be incorporated into a traditional action research study. Treatments of the sophisticated and complex statistics required to enact or evaluate more extensive studies can be found in a wide range of texts designed for these purposes (e.g., Creswell, 2002; Gay, Mills, & Airasian, 2006).

Teacher-Made Tests

Teachers construct tests to monitor the performance of students, measuring the extent to which each student has accomplished the learning objectives of a lesson. A well-constructed test will provide a clear measure of attainment for each competency or proficiency, measuring each of the different types of knowledge or skills described in the lesson objectives. A record of results provides the means to track a student's progress in each area of the curriculum, or to gain a clear picture of the overall performance of the class. This type of data is therefore useful for monitoring student performance or evaluating the effectiveness of instruction.

Textbook Unit Tests

School textbooks often provide unit tests that, like teacher-made tests, are designed to measure student learning on a particular content area or skill. Like teacher tests they measure mastery of specific learning goals and objectives.

Standardized Tests

An action research process might also require information available from the wide range of standardized tests now applied to students; these may provide measures of intelligence, aptitude, personality traits, literacy, numeracy, speech, listening, hearing, and so on. Standardized tests may provide purely *descriptive* information about levels or types of attributes or performance, but may also be *diagnostic,* indicating the source or nature of problems indicated by the test.

School Report Cards

School report cards provide a summary of the level of mastery attained by a student in each area of the curriculum. Information is sometimes conglomerated to provide a grade point average (GPA), indicating the average level of attainment of that student. The average (mean) of GPAs within a group may also indicate the level of attainment of a class or of different groups of students (girls, boys, and so on).

School Records

School records provide a wide variety of quantitative information relevant to the performance of students, their capabilities, and their behavior. They also provide information about classes, teachers, resources and facilities, staffing levels, student numbers, and so on.

Forms of the Data

Numerical Data Much of the data of student performance is recorded in numeric form, indicating the extent to which the student has attained the desired learning objectives. Scores may be expressed as raw scores (numbers), as a percentage, as a fraction or decimal (8/10 or 0.8), or in terms of a scale. Scores are often reported in letter form (A, B, C, etc.), but these often need to be converted to a numerical score if they are to be subject to analysis.

Likert Scales Likert scales are often used in questionnaires to record the level of a person's response to an issue, experience, or event. Commonly, an item in a questionnaire will present a statement and provide a range of possible responses. For example:

"I like the way the desks in this classroom are organized."

5—Strongly Agree   4—Agree   3—Undecided   2—Disagree   1—Strongly Disagree

Semantic Differential A semantic differential is similar in purpose to a Likert scale, providing the means for people to put a number or value on their experience of a particular event, activity, or object. A statement is presented and respondents are asked to assess the degree or extent of their response to a set of descriptors in terms of a set of polar opposites. For example:

"The book we read for this lesson was . . ."

Boring __ __ __ __ __ __ __ Interesting
　　　　-3 -2 -1　0　1　2　3

Irrelevant __ __ __ __ __ __ __ Relevant

Useless __ __ __ __ __ __ __ Useful

Selecting Quantitative Information

The primary purpose of any set of information in an action research study is the extent to which it sheds light on the issue being investigated. If student performance is a primary concern of the study, then relevant data from tests and records may be incorporated into the study to clarify the nature of student performance. As indicated in the following chapter, however, careful interpretation of quantitative data is essential to ensure that teachers and other stakeholders clearly understand the nature and extent of learning for the different students being tested. Once that has been accomplished, then continuing processes of investigation incorporating interviews, observation, and so on lead to greater understanding about why and where learning problems are occurring, and what can be done to improve student learning.

Quantitative information, however, is not just relevant to student learning—but it also may provide the means to clarify a whole range of issues related to the operation of the school. The information selected should be specifically relevant to the issue investigated, since unfocused data gathering may bury researchers in a large body of unrelated material.

REVIEWING THE LITERATURE

In action research "the literature" is positioned quite differently from that in traditional quantitative research, where the gaps or contradictions in the literature form the basis for the research questions. The preliminary literature review in action research reveals the types of information available in the literature that might be incorporated into a study. The literature is viewed as another source of information, together with perspectives of stakeholders, observations, and so on, that enables research participants to extend their understanding of the issue investigated. Literature reviews should be quite thorough to ensure that limited perspectives are not used as "ammunition" to force particular types of action. The voices of proponents of both phonics and whole language, for instance, should be included in any review of literature related to methods of teaching reading.

In an action research process, therefore, the literature might best be seen as another set of perspectives, providing useful information to be incorporated into the perspectives and

Figure 4.5
Literature as a Source of Information

accounts emerging in the research process. In Figure 4.5, teacher and student perspectives are obtained through interviews, analysis of which provides understanding of stakeholder experiences and perspectives on an issue. A review of literature may reveal perspectives, interpretations, or analyses emerging from other studies of that issue—providing research participants with information that can enhance, complement, or challenge the information emerging from other sources. The literature search also reveals the breadth or depth of the problem investigated, indicating whether the problem is widespread and broadly studied or generally nonproblematic in other locations, or poorly studied.

Procedures for Reviewing, Summarizing, and Critiquing the Literature

A variety of sources—academic texts and journals, professional journals and publications, and institutional or departmental publications and reports—may contain useful information that speaks to the issue investigated. The information may include accounts of successful practices, projects, or learning processes; demographic information pertinent to the location or group studied; or indications of factors likely to have an impact on the study. Sources may provide information about previous research on the issue, existing programs and services, or accounts of similar projects. Care needs to be taken in applying generalized information from these sources to the specific site of the study, however, since it is possible that the conditions in the setting or the nature of particular groups differs significantly from those of other studies. As a generalized set of outcomes, the results of other studies may not provide the basis for action in any particular local setting.

The literature is not a body of "truth." Studies may be comprised of a range of different theories and diverse ways of conceptualizing an issue, and may have different assumptions, values, and ideologies embedded in the research. These often-unrecognized assumptions and sets of ideas sometimes unconsciously impose a way of conceptualizing a situation or an issue that fails to take into account the concrete realities facing people in their specific situations. Part of the researcher's task, therefore, is to critique the literature, revealing the inherent concepts, ideas, theories, values, and ideological assumptions embedded in the texts of their writing.[1]

Researchers will need carefully prescribed procedures to identify literature relevant to the issue investigated, and to distill information specifically relevant to the study. Researchers should:

- **Identify key terms** that characterize or capture the essence of the issue investigated. These key terms are often embedded in the research question.
- **Web search.** Use key terms to enage in a web search using one of the major search engines (e.g., Google Academic).
- **Library search.** Use search facilities available through most university and college libraries.
- **Journal scan.** Scan the tables of contents of educational journals in the library stacks.
- **Locate relevant studies or book chapters.** Identify literature focused on the issue studied.
- **Summarize.** Record relevant material in note form.
- **Literature map.** Construct a literature map that places together literature that speaks to similar issues or parts of the study and indicates relationships between different parts of the literature. Draw a concept map to assist this process. (For example, group study that focuses on student performance may include issues such as motivation, interest, relevance, and so on.)

Using the Literature Review

As information from the literature enters the research cycle, participants can make decisions about its worth or relevance. It may provide information enhancing or confirming the perspectives already reported, or challenging the views and experience of stakeholder participants. The literature may also contain information suggesting actions to be taken or provide examples of actions taken in similar contexts. For formal reporting procedures, an extended review of the literature also provides evidence that participants have thoroughly investigated a variety of sources of information and have taken this information into account in their investigations.

Information emerging from the literature review, therefore, may be used:

- as part of the ongoing processes of reflection and analysis.
- as information to be included in emergent understandings.
- as material to be included in reports.

EMERGENT UNDERSTANDINGS

Researcher participants will accumulate information from a variety of sources, acquiring materials that extend their understanding or provide diverse perspectives on the issue studied.

---

[1]The emphasis on critique is another facet of qualitative research. Quantitative research assumes value-free or value-neutral research generalizable to all contexts. Qualitative research highlights the cultural and context-specific nature of knowledge, and the importance of understanding an author's perspective, since authors often infer truths about an issue on the basis of their own experience and perspective, and fail to take into account the often different experiences and perspectives of those about whom they write.

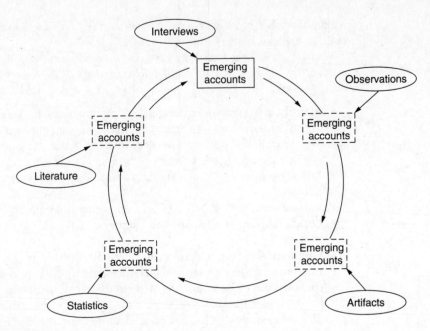

Figure 4.6
Building the Picture: Emerging Accounts

As the following chapters indicate, this information will be subject to analysis, interpretation, and, ultimately, actions to resolve the issue investigated.

As indicated in Figure 4.6, participant accounts derived from interviews provide the primary material for constructing emerging understandings, incorporating as they do information that resonates with the experiences and perceptions of research participants. These preliminary accounts, however, are modified, clarified, enriched, or enhanced by information from other sources. Information from observation, together with material derived from reviewing documents, records, and other artifacts, may extend and enrich accounts derived from participant perceptions. Insightful or useful information may also be obtained from the literature reviewed during the processes of inquiry.

The accounts and understandings emerging from these processes of data gathering and analysis are not static, however, and continue to be enriched, enhanced, and clarified as researchers enter continuing cycles of the process, adding further information from the same or other sources. The art and craft of research is in the skillful management of this diverse body of information, distilling and organizing data into a coherent and clear framework of concepts and ideas that people can use for practical purposes.

SUMMARY

Gathering Data

The major purpose of this part of the research process is to gather information from a variety of sources. *Stakeholder experiences and perspectives* are complemented by *observations* and reviews of *artifacts* and *literature.*

This process requires research facilitators and other participants to develop *trusting relationships* that enable the easy interchange of information.

The *interview* is the primary tool of data gathering, providing extended opportunities for stakeholders to reflect on their experience. Key features of the interview process include:

- *Initiation* of interviews
- *Grand tour* questions to elicit participant responses
- *Mini-tour* and *prompt* questions to extend participant responses
- Special techniques for *working with children*
- Use of *focus groups* to work collaboratively

Information is also acquired through *observing* settings and events.

A review of *artifacts* provides a rich additional source of information. Artifacts may include:

- records
- documents
- student work samples
- materials, equipment, and facilities

Numerical and statistical information from these sources, or from a project survey, can provide other useful resources.

Academic, professional, and institutional *literature* also provide useful information to extend participant understanding.

Identifying Key Issues: Data Analysis

RESEARCH DESIGN	DATA GATHERING	DATA ANALYSIS	REPORTING	ACTION
INITIATING A STUDY	CAPTURING STAKEHOLDER EXPERIENCES AND PERSPECTIVES	IDENTIFYING KEY ISSUES AND EXPERIENCES	WRITTEN REPORTS	CREATING SOLUTIONS
Setting the stage			Formal reports	Problem solving
Focusing and framing	Interviewing	Analyzing key experiences	Narrative accounts	
			Joint accounts	Creating syllabi and lesson plans
Participants	Observing	Categorizing and coding	PRESENTATIONS AND PERFORMANCES	
Literature review	Reviewing documents, records, and materials	Incorporating quantitative data	Presentations Drama	Curriculum development
Sources of information			Poetry Song	Evaluation
	Quantitative data	Enhancing analysis	Dance Art	Family and community links
Ethics			Video	
Validity	Reviewing literature	Using concepts and categories	Multimedia	School plans

Contents of the Chapter

This chapter presents detailed procedures for two approaches to data analysis.

It commences by explaining the *purpose* of data analysis in action research, then presents two distinct approaches to analysis.

The approach focuses on the analysis of *key experiences*. The main thrust of this method is to identify and *deconstruct*, or "unpack," significant experiences to reveal the key elements that comprise them.

The next section describes *categorizing and coding* procedures for analyzing data. Researchers "unitize" the data, identifying discrete pieces of information that comprise interview data, then select and sort those units into a *system of categories*.

The final sections suggest how data from a variety of sources can be incorporated into a study, providing the basis for formulating effective solutions to the problem or issue investigated.

INTRODUCTION

The major purpose of qualitative research is to identify those issues or features of a situation that "make a difference"—that are responsible for, or have a significant impact on, the issue investigated. "What are the key features of the situation that affect the issue we are studying?" "How can we choose what is significant from all the acts, activities, events, and interactions we observe or record?" The process of identifying key features and selecting from the multitude of events observed is the process of *analysis*. It is through sorting, selecting, and organizing elements of the sometimes large body of information we have gathered that we are able to understand more clearly the nature of the events we have observed.

The process of data analysis requires participants to sift through the accumulated data to identify that information most pertinent to the problem being investigated. This process of distillation provides the material for an organized set of concepts and ideas that will enable researchers to achieve greater insight or understanding of events and to formulate effective solutions to the problem on which the study is focused.

The following framework therefore signals the move from data *gathering* to data *analysis*. In terms of the simple look-think-act cycle of action research, the "think" component indicates the need for participants to *reflect* on and *analyze* the information they have gathered (Figure 5.1).

This chapter presents two approaches to data analysis. The first seeks to identify *significant experiences and events* as the basis for analysis. The ultimate intent is to identify the key elements of those experiences and thus gain a clearer understanding of how and why events unfold as they do. The second approach presents a more traditional form of qualitative analysis, *categorizing and coding*, that distills large amounts of data into an organized body of concepts and ideas. The purpose of this process is to reveal patterns and

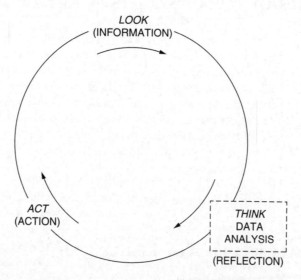

Figure 5.1
Analysis in Action Research

themes within the data that enable us to understand more clearly why and how events occur as they do.

Other information—statistical data, records, observations, and so on—clarify and add detail to the pictures—or accounts—that emerge from these processes.

Teachers rarely have time during the busy and demanding routines of everyday life in their classrooms to stand back and reflect on their work. Having the luxury to sit back and talk about and reflect on their classroom practices often provides them with opportunities to gain significant insights into their professional lives. I've frequently seen teachers' eyes light up in the course of interviews or focus group dialogues as they "see" themselves or aspects of their work in new ways. Merely having time to focus their attention in a systematic way is illuminative.

This does not always happen immediately, however. The students in the sexual harassment study (see Chapter 9), for instance, required an extended period of reflection and analysis to identify the nature and key features of their experience of harassment. The Barrios Juntos group (see Chapter 9) also needed to work through a systematic process of data analysis to reveal the key features of parent experiences of parent–teacher conferences. In each case, however, the process of data analysis enabled participants to extend their understanding of the issue investigated, providing concepts and ideas that enabled them to devise effective actions related to the problems they investigated. Data analysis, for them, was not just a technical research routine, but the means to inform their actions.

THE GOALS OF DATA ANALYSIS IN ACTION RESEARCH

The ultimate outcome of data analysis is to enable participants to clearly understand the nature of events that are the focus of the research process. The intent is to understand how people experience and respond to the events and activities that comprise the ongoing reality of the situation. We thus employ modes of analysis that enable us to capture participant perspectives and focus on the significant features that shape their actions and behaviors. The features and elements of experience that emerge from analysis provide the means to formulate actions to resolve the problems that are the focus of the study.

In order to accomplish these goals we engage the concepts and ideas people naturally use to observe, describe, and interpret their own experiences (Spradley, 1979a; Spradley & McCurdy, 1972). As Denzin (1989a) has suggested, the focus on meanings people give to events enables us to understand actions, activities, behavior, and emotions that comprise the ongoing reality of human experience (Denzin, 1997).

DATA ANALYSIS (1): KEY ISSUES AND EXPERIENCES

Key issues and experiences are those aspects of a situation that have a significant impact on the events studied. In a study of parent concerns about formation of mixed grades in their school, for instance, the "children's educational achievement levels" were identified as a central issue. Another study of poor student motivation toward reading revealed that "ways of learning reading" were of primary importance to the students. Key experiences therefore enable researchers to understand those features of the situation that have marked impact on the issue studied.

A variety of ways of conceptualizing key experiences is evident in the research literature, each revealing a particular way of understanding the underlying dynamics of a set of events. They may be called *illuminative* or *transformational moments, epiphanies,* or *criticial incidents*, but each points to features of experience that in some way "make a difference" or are significant to the people involved.

Key experiences may take a variety of forms, from the devastating event that enters a person's life but once, to an accumulation of relatively minor events that result in problematic outcomes. Key experiences can be either positive or negative, and may include the exhilaration/despair at passing or failing a particularly significant examination, the sense of wonderment (or frustration) emerging from a particularly difficult learning process, or a sense of injustice emerging from an unfair or particularly distressing comment from a teacher, colleague, or administrator.

Key experiences therefore may vary in intensity, from the life-shattering moment of complete failure or triumphant success to the relatively mundane events that are built into the fabric of people's day-to-day lives. They emerge as moments of human warmth or hurt, or moments of clarity that add new dimensions to a person's life experience, investing them with new ways of interpreting or understanding their lives. They may emerge instantaneously—the "ah-ha" experience, the "light bulb" that enables a person to say "so that's what is going on"—or gradually, through a cumulative awareness that emerges through an ongoing process of experience and reflection.

Rhonda Petty reveals how she came to understand the concept of *epiphany*, a key experience of the "light bulb" variety. She writes, "When I first read Denzin's (1989a) definition and description of epiphanies I associated them with psychotic behavior or life-threatening diseases. My interpretation was too narrow. As Denzin wrote, epiphanies are turning-point experiences, interactional moments that mark people's lives and can be tranformational. My own experience demonstrates, however, that epiphanies can stem from the unlikeliest of sources—a book, a conversation, or the click of a telephone" (Petty, 1997, p. 76). Key experiences can emerge from seemingly minor events, and may be best thought of as significant events that stand out from the hum-drum, routine events that are of little consequence, and in some way result in particular comments or responses from those involved.

Analyzing Key Experiences

Interpretive data analysis first identifies key experiences in the lives of research participants, then deconstructs or unpacks those events to reveal the features and elements that comprise them. By starting with events significant from the participants' perspectives, and building understanding in their terms, we seek not only to give voice to the participants, but to create insights that resonate with and are consistent with the world as they know and understand it. We therefore seek emic (insider) constructions that are true to their worlds and their purposes.

We do not seek only accounts of individual experience, however, but to understand the experience of different *groups*, since individuals will interpret events according to their membership in a particular group. Teachers, parents, and students, for instance, are likely to see an issue from quite different viewpoints. Figure 5.2 shows how data related to the perspectives of teachers, students, and parents are analyzed and used as the basis of a report on a school issue.

Procedures for this form of analysis require researchers to:

- *Review information* acquired from stakeholders in the data gathering phase.
- Identify *significant or key experiences* within each participant's data.
- Deconstruct or "unpack" those events to reveal the detailed *features and elements* of which key experiences are constructed.
- Use those features and elements to construct *individual accounts* describing how selected individuals experience and interpret the issue investigated.

Figure 5.2
Analyzing Key Experiences

- Use the features and elements within individual accounts to construct *joint accounts* revealing the perspectives and experiences of each stakeholding group.
- Finally, use the joint accounts to provide the material for a *collective account*, an overall version chronicling events by comparing and contrasting the perspectives of the different stakeholding groups within the setting. The collective account identifies points of commonality among perspectives and experiences, and points of discrepancy, diversity, or conflict.

In action research, points of commonality provide the basis for concerted action, while discrepant perspectives, viewpoints, or experiences signal the need to negotiate agendas and actions around unresolved issues.

Selecting key people In many studies it is not possible to focus on every person's perspective because of constraints of time or resources. As in other forms of research, it is necessary to select a sample of people who will become the focus of research activity (see Chapter 3). When we come to the process of data analysis, it is likewise sometimes beneficial to focus attention on a smaller number of people to explore their experiences in depth and to reveal with clarity which elements and features drive events in the setting. Our purpose in selecting people, therefore, is to isolate those individuals whose experiences or perspectives seem either *typical* of other people within the setting, or whose experiences or perspectives appear particularly illuminating or significant (Creswell, 2002).

Sometimes individuals may be chosen because other people in their group hold them in high esteem, or because their contribution to the life and work of the group is seen as particularly significant. Significance is a flexible term, since it may connote negative as well as positive events and behaviors. A child in a classroom whose behavior is disruptive, or a teacher who constantly complains about school organization, may have a significant effect on ongoing events in the classroom or school. Their perspectives may be as important to a research process as that of a school principal, a highly popular student, or a well-liked teacher in illuminating events.

Key people may be thought of as those likely to provide important information, or to have a significant impact on events within the school. In commencing interpretive analysis of data, research participants will select a number of persons from each stakeholding group, ensuring that they choose people who:

- represent diverse perspectives from within the group.
- are likely to have a significant impact on the group.
- have seemingly typical experiences and perspectives.
- have particularly unusual or significant experiences or perspectives.

Participatory processes assist researchers to select people whose experiences and perspectives are likely to illuminate the complex and diverse nature of people, events, and other relevant phenomena. Even in nonparticipatory processes, however, participants may be used to assist in identifying key people, as researchers ask questions such as "Who do you think might provide useful perspectives on this issue?" or "Who in your group would give me a quite different perspective?"

The first step in interpretive data analysis, therefore, is to identify those people from within each stakeholding group whose combined experiences and perspectives will provide the material from which an understanding of that group will be drawn. The following steps of analysis provide the procedures through which these accounts are drawn, the experiences of those selected being subject to further analysis.

Identifying key experiences The next move—identifying key experiences—has no magical recipe for revealing the "true" or "real" epiphanies. Rather, data analysis commences with a process of selecting those events or features of a person's experience that are especially *significant*, in relation to the issue investigated. Sometimes they are most evident when strikingly significant events emerge within the research process itself or are revealed in accounts presented in interviews. At other times, however, judgments are made on the basis of an intimate knowledge of the person, events, and the context that comes from extended engagement. Significant or epiphanic events are identified according to the expression of the participant.

The first "reading" of the data by a researcher therefore requires an empathetic, interpretive analysis responding to the internal question "What are the most significant experiences for this person (in relation to the issue investigated)?" The participant's descriptions of events provide clues, but the complex nuances of emotion and nonverbal cues displayed in interviews also provide information suggesting those events that might usefully be singled out for further analysis. Sometimes significant events or features of experience are self-evident, with participants providing animated, agitated, or emotional descriptions of events and experiences that touch their lives in dramatic and consequential ways. At other times, a more focused and subtle reading is required to identify those features of experience that have a significance impact on the lives of the persons involved. Sometimes it is evident in the extent to which the person focuses on a particular event or experience, in the person's tone of voice or language and terminology, in the person's countenance and body language, or in the emphases given to certain events.

My colleagues and I often use analysis of key experiences or illuminative moments in the course of our teaching and research work. These provide a basis for understanding those aspects of people's experience that are particularly significant and assist us to understand more clearly the issues and events that most concern the people with whom we work.

During a recent class evaluation I asked participants to identify the most significant features of their experience. They interviewed each other in pairs, then each person identified those aspects of the class that were particularly significant from their perspective. As each person shared their experience, others were able to comment on those features that were similar to their own. Participants were able to construct an emerging picture of the class using this information (Stringer et al., 2001).

In study of health workers, Bill Genat (2006) focused on an epiphanic event within the work life of one of the participants. Though other health workers were not involved in that particular event, they were able to identify similar experiences that were characteristic of their own situations. The information acquired by exploring one person's experience provided the basis for a richly textured description relevant to others.

Key events, therefore, take on a range of complexions, both in terms of their intensity and their meaningfulness to participants. Sometimes a relatively trivial event can create great emotion, while at other times what appear as momentous events create little response. Examples of epiphanies and significant events are comments such as the following:

"If he does that one more time I'll scream!"
"Is she just dumb? I've explained it to her six different ways and she just doesn't get it."
"I passed! I passed! I passed! I passed!"
"Oh, Jane. That is just wonderful. That is the best work I've seen from you in a long time. I knew you had it in you."
"It was so important that we did this work ourselves. If others had done it for us we wouldn't have learned anything!"

Sometimes the meanings of the words are self-evident, but more usually it is necessary to provide information about the ways in which the words were delivered and other associated information. It is not unusual for people to be led to tears as they speak of events with sometimes barely contained emotion. In the example just listed, the meanings are reasonably clear, but it would be necessary for people engaged in analysis to take into account the levels of excitement, frustration, anger, and/or voice tone, such as the shining eyes and excited tones of the research participant, in order to understand the significance of the words spoken. The *expression* of the words is at least as important as the words themselves.

Sometimes key experiences are revealed unexpectedly. Many times as I've interviewed people I've been struck by the emotive force of their description of particular events. I was recently surprised, however, to find my eyes "leaking" as I was being interviewed about a cross-cultural training program in which I had been involved. Though I thought I was recounting events in a fairly objective way, I had not realized the extent to which they had moved me. The interviewer informed me that it was not unusual for people to be moved to tears as they described events within this program. I coined the phrase "ethnographic tears" as a way of indicating the possibility of engaging people's deeply felt experience within an interview.

Recently I interviewed a student who revealed, in the course of a very ordinary discussion, that she had recently failed a test. As she spoke of her disappointment the tears welled up in her eyes. She described events that seemed related to her failure and the effect it had on her schoolwork. In the process she revealed much about her classroom life, her approach to school, and her relationship with her teachers and classmates. In this case, the "real" life that existed beneath the surface of her apparently benign experience provided significant insight into her experience of school.

Ultimately, however, the choice of key experiences or significant events requires direct use of member checking, since it is easy to misinterpret or wrongly choose events in other people's lives. Ideally, when the data is member checked (i.e., when the research facilitator allows the participant to read or read back the provided information), participants should be asked which events were most significant—a "grand tour" question (Spradley 1979a)

framed something like, "What, in all this, is most significant for you?" This provides opportunities for each person to identify those events most important in their lives. One step
back from this is a procedure in which the researcher identifies significant events and
checks their importance with the participant.

Although I focus on "events," sometimes significance is not found in a particular event,
but in people's actions and/or responses, or the impact of features of the environment—
physical space, dress, and so on. Significance is revealed in body language, the nonverbal
communication that gives us clues about the impact of events. A frown, a smile, a look of
pain or anger, or forceful language suggests the need to focus on what is said:

> "She's such a *bitch*—dressing like that and talking like that. I just can't stand being
> around her."
> "I won't work there much longer. The office is so small I can't even *think*, let alone do
> my work."
> "When I saw the work that kid had produced I almost cried. It was fabulous."

Thus as we explore people's description of events, we may identify a set of related elements impacting their lives. The feature of the experience, "The office is so small I can't
even think," may lead us to explore related components of a participant's experience.
Comments on the size of an office, in this instance, were related to the number and complexity of the person's work activities, and the space she felt she needed to store materials and do the work required of her. As became evident in reviewing the data, the work
itself was the significant feature of the experience, even though the size of the office was
the "straw that broke the camel's back" and became the immediate focus of an agitated
comment. Identifying epiphanies and significant experiences therefore requires a researcher to search for significant events in people's lives, but also to make connections
between related phenomena.

Key experiences do not need to be associated with momentous events. They may occur quietly and easily as people reflect on their experiences, sometimes commenting on the
"little light bulb that went on in my head" as they realize the significance of something they
have described. These might be more appropriately called illuminative moments, since they
reflect processes of understanding and clarity that sometimes emerge as people reflect on
their own experience, or hear other people's stories.

Unpacking key experiences: features and elements of experience Ultimately our purpose is to evoke an understanding of the way people experience events and phenomena in
their lives. We need, therefore, to identify the information that will enable us to construct
accounts for that purpose. The next step in this process is to "unpack" the key experiences,
establishing those elements and/or features that enable an audience to understand the nature of the experience. We need to ask, "How is this event significant for each person?" or
"What are the features of this event they would see as significant?" We are, in effect, unpacking or "interrogating" the epiphany, seeking to reveal the web and warp of the tapestry
of people's lives. In doing so we use information drawn from the data, using the concepts,
terms, and language used by the people as they described events, behaviors, responses, and
so on—we apply the verbatim principle described later in this chapter.

Figure 5.3 provides an example of this process. The participant, reflecting on her experience, described how doing research had been, for her and other parents, "an empowering

In reflecting on the community-school research process enacted by Barrios Juntos, one parent-researcher exclaimed excitedly, It w as such an empowering experience!" Her framing of events as "empowering" was obviously significant, taking into account the excitement of her voice, her shining eyes, and the intensity signaled by her body language (i.e., body leaning forward and hands gesturing). From her talk, it was possible to ascertain that the empowering features of the research process related to the fact that "We did it ourselves," "We were listened to," and "We learned so much."

Exploration of what was involved in "We did it ourselves" revealed the processes of making up the questions, doing interviews with parents, analyzing the data, and writing reports as key elements of this feature of her experience. Structurally, we could map this out in the following way:

Key Experience   [Doing research] was an empowering experience.

Major Features   We did it ourselves.
                       We were listened to.
                       We learned so much.

Key Elements (of "We did it ourselves.")
                       Making up the questions
                       Doing interviews with parents
                       Analyzing the data
                       Writing reports

Deconstruction of other features—"We were listened to," and "We learned so much"—revealed the elements of those aspects of her experience. The final structure of the analyzed information—epiphany, features, and elements—provided materials from which an account of this person's experience could be formulated.

Figure 5.3
Analyzing a Key Experience

experience." The major features of this empowering experience, revealed in interview field notes and member, checked with the participant, were that "We did it ourselves," "We were listened to," and "We learned so much." Further analysis of field notes indicates the elements of experience associated with each of these. "We did it ourselves," for instance, was associated with "making up the questions," "doing interviews with parents," "analyzing the data," and writing reports. Elements of "We were listened to" and "We learned so much" would likewise emerge from further exploration of the data.

After having identified a key experience, researchers should therefore ask, "What are the major features of this experience? What comprises its key features? And what details (elements) would need to be included in a description so that an audience could understand the significance?"

Researchers should deconstruct each key experience to reveal the different features inherent in the event. Sometimes a single event or experience is sufficiently powerful to provide the basis for a detailed analysis of a person's experience, while other accounts may require ongoing analysis of a number of related minor epiphanies, illuminative moments, or significant events.

As research participants work through this process of analysis they may use other analytic frameworks that alert them to the types of information that might usefully be extracted from the data. A framework of concepts drawn from ethnographic observation (Spradley, 1979b) indicates the types of phenomena that might be used as epiphanies, features, or elements of experience. These include **acts, activities, events, times, places, purposes,** and **emotions.**

Another useful framework—**what, who, how, where, when, why**—also may be used to assist in identifying useful or relevant detail. In all this we are not attempting to include *all* possible detail, since the possibilities are infinite. We do not need an extended description of the more mundane, taken-for-granted properties and features of everyday life, but to identify the essential features of people's experiences or perspectives. It's important that we don't let the framework drive the data analysis process, starting with "acts" and working down through the concepts. The trigger for selecting features and elements are those aspects that are seen or felt by participants to be a central part of their experience. Framework concepts merely serve as reminders of the types of phenomena that might be included.

In all this, researchers need to focus their analysis by ensuring that the information revealed is associated with the issue or question that provides the focus for the study. They should ask "How does this event illuminate or extend our understanding about the issue we are investigating? Does it provide answers to the questions that assisted us to frame our study?" In some cases, the analysis will reveal information indicating the need to extend the boundaries of the study, or to focus on issues that were not part of the original plan. The iterative or cyclical nature of the research process enables us to build understanding and extend our study accordingly.

Identifying Key Experiences Within Observations and Other Data

Sometimes key experiences occur as researchers are observing events within a research setting. Observers in any classroom or school are likely, over a period of time, to view disruptive events that disturb the relatively orderly routines of school life. A student outburst, conflict between a teacher and student, or an altercation between staff members signals a key experience that may provide a worthwhile focus for further exploration. The event itself tells part of the story, but description and analysis by participants reveals the meanings and experiences associated with the event that have the potential to greatly increase understanding about the issue investigated. Significant events therefore provide the focus for follow-up interviews to enable participants to explore and deconstruct events and probe the meanings embedded in singular events. A single event sometimes provides more insight into the underlying structures of behavior, or the ways everyday events are experienced or interpreted by the people involved.

Key experiences may also appear in representations. They may be depicted in artwork that enables students to explore or represent their experience of a particular issue, or in naturally occurring representations, such as the graffiti that often appears on school buildings or furniture, in the form of pictures or slogans—"Mr. Jones is a. . . . .," "School sucks," and so on. While all graffiti expressions are not significant, they may be associated with particular events or people that signal unresolved issues in the life of a school, thus providing a focus or a context for further exploration.

Constructing Conceptual Frameworks

Once key experiences have been deconstructed, revealing the key features and elements inherent in participant experiences, the analyzed information is organized into a carefully structured system of concepts that assists people to clearly understand the import of what has been revealed. These structured systems of concepts not only provide a summary of important information, but also supply the basis for writing reports and planning actions.

The following outlines provide examples of how deconstructed epiphanies—the analysis of significant events within two action research projects—provided the framework for written accounts of each.

Example One
"Everthing Is Different Now: Surviving Ethnographic Research" (Petty, 1997)

This account emerged from a study of a small group of African American boys from a school in an "undesirable" neighborhood. An elementary school teacher describes how she came to understand herself and her place in society differently, and how, in consequence, she was able to explore larger issues related to minority students on the basis of what she learned in a very small arena. She uses four *major features* as the basis for constructing her account, representing particularly illuminating aspects of her experience—"Doing Ethnographic Study: A Wake-Up Call," "Contextualizing Experience," and "Surviving Qualitative Research." The *key elements* of each are used as subheadings—"Setting Myself Up," and so on. Her account emerges from an analysis of one key experience she describes in the section labeled "Doing Ethnographic Study—A Wake-Up Call." The structure of concepts derived from the study include:

"**Lived Experience**": in which she presents the methodology of the study.
"**Doing Ethnographic Study—A Wake-Up Call:**" This section presents the difficulties she experienced initiating a "minority study." Key elements of her experience are described under the following headings:
  "**Setting Myself Up**" reveals her reflections on her perspective in the early stages of this study.
  "**Is This a Minority Study?—Suspicion and Resistance**" describes the negative responses of some parents when approached for permission to study their sons and the feelings of devastation she felt as a result.
  "**Aftermath**" provides an account of how she came to terms with the situation and the sense of hope she developed for these boys as she continued her work with them.
"**Contextualizing Experience**": "As I reflected on these events, emergent themes helped me understand the nature of my experience, organize my thoughts and think constructively about a situation that had once seemed hopeless." These themes (*key elements*) included:
  "**Contradictions: Expectations and Experience**" describes the discrepancy between the expectations with which she entered the boys' social worlds and the reality of the events that occurred.

"Assumptions and Stereotypes" reveals how the boys failed to live up to her assumptions or to manifest behaviors her stereotypes had predicted.

"Ignorance and Indifference" describes how she became aware that her "unconsciously purposeful ignorance showed [her] indifference" to the issues of race surrounding her study.

"Surviving Qualitative Research": Articulates the lessons she learned from the *processes* of the study.

"Naïve Realism" reveals how she originally viewed the project through her own cultural lenses and acted accordingly.

"Support for Survival" presents an account of how others supported her as she worked through these experiences and explored her responses so that the events became a learning experience.

"What Can Be Learned from My Experience": Reveals the broader lessons emerging from the research—that policies and programs fail because they fail to consider the perspectives and attitudes of those who formulate and implement them. "In the end I realize that developing a genuine connection with someone of another culture or race requires an approach that acknowledges the person as authentic rather than as someone with quaint customs or unexplainable beliefs or desires."

Example Two
"High School Students' Participation in Action Research: An Ongoing Learning Process" (Baldwin, 1997)

This project presents an interpretive account of how Shelia Baldwin taught a group of high school students to use ethnographic methods to explore cultural diversity in their school and community. The following framework emerged from deconstruction of a major epiphany—that students could be researchers. Exploration of the data revealed the *major features* (called "themes" by the author) of participant experiences—"Getting Started," "Relationships," and so on. *Key elements* of each of these features provide subheadings and descriptive details within each section—"Teacher as Facilitator," and so on. These formulated a framework that became the basis for the project report:

Introduction: Describes how the project was initiated.

Ethnographic Methods: Describes the research methods.

Emergence of Themes: Provides a description of the major themes emerging from the study.

Getting Started: Provides a detailed description of how student participants commenced work on the project.

Relationships: Describes how relationships between teacher, students, and other participants developed in the course of the study. Two major elements of the development of relationships included:

"Teacher as Facilitator" describes how Shelia acted as a guide to help the students develop the tools necessary for doing ethnographic work.

"Students as Ethnographers" provides an account of the way students assumed the ethnographic role.

"School–Community Interrelations": Tells how students came to increase their understanding of their families and communities and relations with the school, characterizing the school as a microcosm of the larger community.

"Place—The Temporal and Physical Context": This section illustrates how *time* and *place* were important elements of the study. Both time and context appeared to affect other features of the study.

"The Teacher's Reflections": Reveals how the teacher developed her facilitating role in the project and, in the process, learned to relinquish control and trust her students.

"An Ongoing Learning Process": Reviews the outcomes of the project, finishing with the words " . . . action research can revitalize the entire learning community and can aid teachers in changing or reflecting on their classroom practices."

Using People's Terms and Concepts: The Verbatim Principle

As we engage in data analysis it is particularly important to use the terms and concepts from the participants' own talk to label concepts and categories. The temptation to characterize people's experience in terms that seem to make more sense or clarify the issue from the researcher's perspective, or to translate it into language fitted to theoretical or professional discourses should be clearly resisted. Later, when the need for joint accounts incorporating diverse terms, concepts, and/or ideas emerges, we may need terminology that allows us to collectively describe similar elements or features with one term or phrase. For example, "I was angry," "She made me feel bad," "I nearly cried when he did that," and "I'm just scared of what he'll do next" may be elements of a feature described as "The Emotional Impact of . . . ." Generally, however, we should seek terms from within the speech of the participants themselves, adding additional words only to clarify meaning or extend understanding when the words themselves are insufficient for the purpose.

Maria Hines is most explicit about her experience of analyzing data in the Barrios Juntos project. With a slight frown she describes how "I never knew how difficult it was not to put my own words and meanings in. We had to really concentrate to make sure we used what people had actually said and not put in our own words. It was *hard*."

These words remind us to focus clearly on one of the central features of action research, consciously seeking to understand the perspectives of others and to use those perspectives to formulate actions. This is centrally important at the stage of data analysis, where the possibility of reinterpreting, misinterpreting, or colonizing people's words, concepts, and ideas—taking them and using them for our own purposes—is ever present.

DATA ANALYSIS (2): CATEGORIZING AND CODING

The previous sections present processes for interpretive data analysis designed to more effectively represent individual perspectives and experiences. Another process of data analysis used commonly in qualitative research is based on procedures for unitizing data and sorting units into categories, each of which is denoted by a label—a conceptual "code." The process is very useful for analyzing large bodies of qualitative data, and is especially amenable to the electronic data analysis software now available. It runs the risk, however, of losing participant perspectives in conglomerating data from a wide diversity of sources, and of revealing conceptual structures meaningful mainly to those responsible for data analysis. Using participatory processes of data analysis can minimize both of these weaknesses.

Purposes and Processes of Categorizing[1]

The purpose of analysis in action research is not to identify "the facts," or "what is actually happening," but to distill or crystallize the data in ways enabling researcher participants to interpret and make sense out of the collected materials. Initially this involves working with data and organizing them to make connections between events or ideas, and identify commonalities, regularities, or patterns. These new ways of seeing or interpreting the information gathered shed light on events, transforming people's understanding and providing the means to take therapeutic action on the problem at hand.

The process commences by reviewing interview and focus group data, dividing them into "units of meaning" (unitizing the data), then using these to construct an organized system of categories and themes. This system of categories then provides the basis for research reports and accounts, and for action agendas that guide the ongoing activities of action researchers. Continuing analysis incorporates data gathered through observation, the review of artifacts or relevant literature, and the complementing or challenging information acquired directly from research participants. (see Figure 5.4).

Reviewing Data Sets

Stakeholders in action research usually comprise groups having different roles within the context and, in consequence, experiencing events in different ways. In schools, for instance, teachers often experience and interpret events quite differently from students or administrators.

---

[1]Harry Wolcott (1994) suggests description, analysis, and interpretation as the three purposes of data analysis, the latter being generalized as theorizing not specifically relevant to the context at hand. The type of analysis presented herein makes no distinction between analysis and interpretation, as Harry depicts them. The purposes of action research require "theorizing" or "interpretation" that makes sense from the perspective of participants. Generalized theory, more relevant to theory building in the academic disciplines, has less relevance to our current purposes, though it often assists in framing the study. Shirley Bryce Heath (1983), for instance, used ethnographic methods for studying children's language use in different communities. Both data gathering and analysis were affected by understandings about the types of things associated with or affecting children's language, resulting in descriptions of the communities and the people. The "interpretive lens" filtering information was that provided by sociolinguistics.

Figure 5.4
Categorizing and Coding

Male teachers may have a different experience and perspective than female teachers, and science teachers may have quite different perspectives than teachers of English literature. Experience and perspectives of students is likewise likely to differ according to their age, family background, religion, race, ethnicity, and so on.

Often these differences in experience or perspective will become apparent in the course of the study, but one of the important features of research is that we don't assume differences, allowing them to emerge in the course of data analysis. Generally, however, we formulate data sets to acknowledge the important distinctions existing between stakeholders in a setting. This allows us to take account of the differences in perspective and experience of the types of people inhabiting the context of the study. In Figure 5.4, for instance, data from students, teachers, and administrators is analyzed separately, revealing points of commonality and difference in their perspective of school events and issues.

The purpose of reviewing the data sets is to familiarize researchers with the data, enabling them to take an overall view of the information so that links between items and elements begin to emerge. Those responsible for data analysis should therefore commence by reading through all the data.

Unitizing the Data

The next step in the process is to isolate features and elements of experience and perspective, to focus on the specific details emerging from people's talk about events and experiences. Data recorded in interviews and focus groups sessions is first printed and then divided into *units of meaning*. A unit of meaning might be a word, a phrase, or part of or a whole sentence. The sentence, "I don't really like the way I organized this class because it's too one-dimensional and I prefer to work thematically" has a number of distinct units of meaning. These include {I don't like the way I organized this class}, {the class is too one-dimensional}, and {I prefer to work thematically}. As indicated here, it is sometimes necessary to add words to a unit so it makes sense when it stands alone.

A variety of methods are used for this purpose. Some researchers isolate units of meaning by physically cutting sheets of interview data with scissors, while others use highlighters to isolate units of meaning related to emerging categories. Computer programs such as NUD*IST, Ethnograph, Nvivo, WinMAX, and Hypersearch are also used to engage in this process electronically.[2] Computer-assisted programs, however, provide only a data storage, managing, and searching tool. They cannot engage in analytic processes such as identifying units of meaning or formulating categories.

The process of unitizing the data results in a large "pile" of discrete pieces of information. From these building blocks researchers sort, select, and organize information into an organized system of categories that enables participants to "make sense" of the issues they investigate. The next phase of process of analysis, therefore, is to categorize and code units of data.

Categorizing and Coding

Spradley's (1979a) schema for *componential* analysis, similar in concept to analysis of units of meaning, provides a useful conceptualization of the process of categorization. Spradley's approach to analysis is based on the idea that people's everyday cultural knowledge is organized according to systems of meaning they give to phenomena in their lives. These systems of meaning, he proposes, are organized taxonomically, using an hierarchical structure to distinguish the different types of phenomena comprising everyday life. Category systems divide and define our cultural worlds systematically, allowing us to impose a sense of order on the multiple and complex phenomena that comprise our everyday life.

A simple set of common categories is indicated in Figure 5.5. Ingestibles—substances that can be swallowed and ingested—are comprised of food, drink, and medication. Each of these is comprised of a number of different items within the category. The category "food," for instance, is made up of fruits and vegetables. The category system is incomplete,

Figure 5.5
Category System for Ingestibles

---

[2] Reviews of these programs may be found at *http://www.sagepub.com*.

Figure 5.6
Taxonomy of School People

but provides an illustration of the way people organize phenomena in order to assist them to define and communicate objects.

Systems of meaning are inherent in every culture, and one of the early tasks in the life of a baby is to learn to understand the different types of people with whom he or she comes into contact, distinguishing "mother" from "father" from siblings and so on. The research act requires participants to uncover the systems of meaning inherent in people's way of defining their experience, and to formulate new ways of organizing that information to extend understanding of that experience.

Having identified the units of meaning inherent in the interview data, researchers will then identify those associated with each other and that might therefore be included in the same category. The example in Figure 5.6 provides a way of categorizing the different types of people in a school.

In Figure 5.6's taxonomy, two major types of people are identified from the data—staff and students. Different types of staff include "teachers," "administrators," and "support staff." Important distinctions between "teachers" are made by participants according to whether they are classified as "senior," "junior," or "part-time." As the system of categories is organized, decisions must be made about the placement of each item into a particular category or subcategory. In this example, there may be a need to decide whether a senior teacher who has administrative duties is classified as a teacher or administrator. Items are placed within particular categories or subcategories according to a system of *inclusion,* based on the *attributes* of each element. The categories "senior" and "junior" teacher, for instance, are first identified by asking *structural questions* that identify who should be placed in each category (e.g., "Can you name all the senior teachers in the school?" "Who are the junior teachers?").

We extend our understanding of the reason for placing people into particular categories by asking *attribute questions* that identify the reason for placing a person in a particular category (e.g., "What is a 'senior' teacher?"). Answers to these questions would provide the criteria employed for making a decision to define a teacher as "senior" as opposed to "junior" or "part-time." A senior teacher might be identified, according to the system of meanings used in this school, as one who:

- has been at the school for more than four years.
- is a full-time teacher.
- has some leadership responsibilities.

These *attributes* define a "senior teacher" and allow researchers to make decisions about which types of teachers are to be included in that category.

When we place phenomena into a category, one of the principal tasks is to name that category to identify the type of phenomena it contains. Apples, pears, and oranges might be identified as "fruit," for instance. This process is called "coding," so that the term used to name the category is called, by some researchers, the *code* for the category. Spradley uses the word *cover term* to refer to the code. Researchers should first determine whether an existing term occurs naturally in the language or talk of the people from whom the information has been acquired. Otherwise, they should provide a label for the category that clearly identifies the nature of the category. "Fooling around," "sitting still," "working conscientiously," and "talking loudly," for instance, might be identified by the code or cover term "student behaviors."

As information is placed in categories, we therefore become aware of the need to define more clearly the meanings intended by research participants in order to understand how the word or phrase is being used, and whether it should be included in one category or another. The codes or cover terms will eventually provide a structured set of categories that assists us to organize and make meaning of the experiences of diverse groups of people. The system of categories also provides a framework of events, activities, behaviors, and materials that assists in understanding events and formulating actions to deal with those events.

Categorizing and coding therefore requires researchers to:

- Unitize the data.
- Sort units into categories.
- Divide categories into subcategories, where appropriate.
- Code each category using a cover term expressing the type or nature of information in the category or subcategory.
- Identify the attributes defining each category or subcategory.

Other formats for coding and categorizing data may be found in Bogdan and Biklen (1992); Creswell (2002); and Arhar, Holly, and Kasten (2000). These provide detailed instructions for developing descriptions and representing findings.

Organizing a Category System

As researchers formulate categories they first place them in an organized system that identifies features and elements of experience in ways that clarify the relationship between them. Categories do not fall automatically into a structure or system, and descisions must be made about which categories are given priority, and where they are placed in relation to each other. In the school evaluation project featured in Figure 5.7, major categories identified included "Administrator Perspectives," "Teacher Perspectives," and "Student Perspectives," each containing subcategories revealing different elements of those perspectives. "Teacher Perspectives" included subcategories "Student Achievement," "Relationships with Students," "Inquiry Curriculum," and "Learning Resources." Details within those subcategories were comprised of units of meaning revealing people's experiences or perspectives of those issues. Note that there is no right way of organizing the data. It might as easily have been organized with "Student Achievement" as a major category, and administrator, student, and teacher perspectives presented as subcategories. The general process is depicted in Figure 5.7's concept map.

Figure 5.7
A Category System for a School Evaluation

In Figure 5.7, different categories of experience and perception have emerged for students, teachers, and administrators. The first cluster of units of meaning is labeled "Attention from Teachers," the next is "Improved Grades," and the final category emerges as "Freedom and Diversity." Teacher categories (i.e., labels chosen to characterize the clustered units of meaning) include "Student Achievement," "Relationships with Students," "Inquiry Curriculum," and "Learning Resources." Categories of experience and perception associated with administrators include "Demands and Resources," "Values and Behavior," and "Space." Although category labels provide no common elements across stakeholding groups, it is clear that some issues are related, and these have been identified as *themes*, each identified by a "code." The student category "Improved Grades" has been associated with teacher category "Student Achievement" and identified as a theme coded "Student Achievement." The categories "Attention from Teachers" and "Relationships with Students" have been linked as a theme having the code "Student–Teacher Relationships." Teacher and administrator categories, "Materials," "Demands and Resources," and "Space," have been linked under the code "Resources and Materials."

This system of categories provides useful information about the types of people whose perspective are presented, the issues concerning them, and the relationship between some of those issues. The way of organizing these categories into a framework assists to clarify the significant features of experience emerging in the process of investigation. At a later stage, they also provide the agenda for planning actions related to those agendas.

Researchers therefore construct a system of categories and subcategories that organizes the emerging information in ways that "make sense" to the participants. This is done by using terms or "codes" they recognize as representing or encompassing their experiences and perspectives, but providing new, interesting, and clarifying ways of organizing data.

DATA-DRIVEN DECISIONS: INCORPORATING QUANTITATIVE DATA

The research processes presented in previous chapters focus largely on discovering why and how events occur as they do. In order to understand the genesis of poor performance or problematic behavior, action research focuses on a broad range of possibilities, and seeks to understand how and why students or other stakeholders act or perform as they do.

As teachers focus on classroom problems and participants express their viewpoints and perspectives, matters of fact emerge that sometimes require the types of specific numerical and statistical information available. These can provide "hard" data that is less likely to be subject to participant impressions, biases, opinions, or fears. They provide useful information that increases participant understanding of the nature of events studied. In a previous example, for instance, parent fears for the educational attainment of their children were shown to be groundless by providing them with analyses that had emerged from a variety of studies. Teachers, likewise, may intuitively feel that student learning is improving, but they can demonstrate that improvement by examining the results of tests.

Data analysis and interpretation of results therefore provide useful information that can enhance an action research process by clearly demonstrating outcomes that can be recorded in numerical form. When matters of fact are at stake, statistical data can provide the basis for decisions about teaching and learning that are at the heart of classroom life. They can also provide information that helps schools determine the issues related to the operation of the school, providing data that, in like manner, assists participants to clarify their understanding of the situation and to make appropriate decisions in relation to the issue investigated.

The following statements provide cues to the type of quantitative information that should be part of a study:

- Children in this class/school can't read as well as they used to.
- This teaching strategy worked really well according to test results.
- Our library is poorly stocked with good reading material.
- More students have dropped out this year than in previous years.
- Absenteeism has increased since the introduction of the new rules.
- We don't spend as much time on math as we should.

Each of these statements requires validation by reviewing or collecting appropriate statistics. The level of children's reading would need to be compared with past records; an accounting of reading materials in the library must be made; student drop-out rates from the current year would need to be compared with previous years; and so on.

Note that the numbers themselves do not provide the final "proof" that the statement is true or false, since interpretation is built into each statement. What counts as "reading well" will affect the data gathered; the test results may have little to do with the particular teaching strategy used; what counts as "good" reading material is likewise open to interpretation; an increase in absenteeism may be due to causes unrelated to the new rules; and so on.

Nevertheless, quantitative data provides useful information that improves participant understanding of the nature of events studied and enhances their ability to make decisions related to actions likely to lead to an effective research outcome.

Presenting Data: Frequency Distributions and Graphs

When a test is administered, scores of each student may be presented as a *frequency distribution* that provides information about the number of students who have scored at specified levels. Thus scores on a test may be tabulated as follows:

Score (%)	Frequency
80	1
81	2
82	3
83	5
84	8
85	6
86	3
87	2
88	2
89	1
90	1

Total = 34 students

These scores may be placed in a graph that gives a visual representation of the distribution of scores. The bar graph in Figure 5.8 informs us that two students achieved a score of 81, three students scored 83, five students scored 83, and so on.

Graphs are often "smoothed out" and presented as a curved distribution. The graph in Figure 5.8 would be presented in the form of a frequency distribution as shown in Figure 5.9.

Graphs are not always symmetrical and often are skewed in one direction or the other, indicating a preponderance of high or low scores (Figure 5.10).

Figure 5.8
Frequency Distribution: Bar Graph

Figure 5.9
Frequency Distribution: Curved Graph

Figure 5.10
Positively and Negatively Skewed Graphs

A pie graph also provides the means to present numerical data, and is especially useful as a visual representation of proportions or percentages. A pie graph is a useful way of presenting information to groups of research participants. The pie graph in Figure 5.11 indicates the ethnic makeup of a school, showing the percentage of students from each group.

Measures of Central Tendency

Teachers, parents, and administrators often wish to gain an overall estimate of the quality of performance of a group of students. Technically, they may achieve this estimate in three ways—the mode, the median, and the mean. These may simply be envisaged as:

Mode—the score that occurs most frequently in a particular group. In the bar graph in Figure 5.8, the mode would be a score of 84.
Median—the middle score, above and below which 50% of scores will lay. In Figure 5.8 the median would also be at score 84.

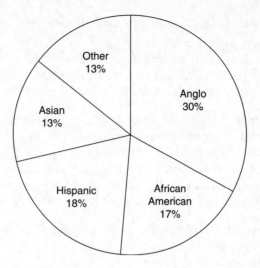

Figure 5.11
Frequency Distribution: Pie Graph

Mean—This is the arithmetic average of all scores, gained by summing all scores and dividing by the number of scores. This is the most frequently used measure of central tendency, providing, for example, an indication of the "average" score attained on a test, or the "average" level of staffing in schools in a district. For the distribution of scores shown in Figure 5.8, the mean score would be calculated in the following manner:

Score (%)		Frequency (No. of students with this score)		Sum of Each Score
80	×	1	=	80
81	×	2	=	162
82	×	3	=	246
83	×	5	=	415
84	×	8	=	672
85	×	6	=	510
86	×	3	=	258
87	×	2	=	174
88	×	2	=	176
89	×	1	=	89
90	×	1	=	90

Sum of all scores = 2,872
Divided by number of scores = 34
Mean = 85.5

Measures of Variability: The Spread of Scores

There will be variation in scores of any test given to a group of students. While the reason for these differences will not be clear, statistical information provides a clear picture of the degrees of variation that occur, providing teachers and administrators with useful indicators of levels of attainment within a class or group.

Range The *range* of scores refers to the highest and lowest scores that provide the range within which all scores lie. In the example of scores from Figure 5.8, the range of scores is 80% to 90%, which indicates that the group of students has scored very well. The range must be treated with caution, however, since one student with a very high or low score can give quite an incorrect indication of how well the group performed. If one student in our example had scored 40%, the range of 40% to 80% would have provided a quite different picture.

Percentile ranks The *percentile rank* indicates the percentage of scores that fall at or below a given score. If a student's score is 65 and corresponds to a percentile rank of 80, this means that 80% of scores in the distribution are 65 or lower. In this case the student may be unhappy with the raw score (65), feeling that she or he has done poorly, but will be much happier to know he or she has done as well or better than 80% of classmates.

Standard deviation The *standard deviation* describes the spread of scores across a group or population. It can be thought of as the average deviation of scores from the mean score of the group. A high standard deviation indicates that there is, overall, a wide spread of scores in the group. A low standard deviation indicates that student scores do not vary greatly across the group—that they cluster closely to the mean.

Normal distribution Student scores on standardized tests may be compared with a set of scores that provide an indication of how their set of scores compares with those of a large population. Graphs in standardized tests typically have a characteristic "bell curve" shape, representing, for example, the distribution of many human attributes—height, weight, and so on. Height is a good example. If we were to graph the distribution of people's height across a large population we would see very few adult people who are less than 4 feet tall, quite a number who are around 5 feet tall, many who are around 5 feet 6 inches, fewer who are around 6 feet tall, and very few who are 7 feet or over (see Figure 5.12).

| 4 Feet | 5 Feet | 6 Feet | 7 Feet |

Figure 5.12
Normal Distribution Curve

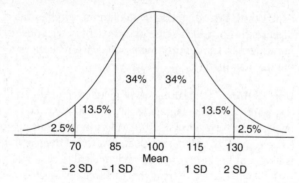

Figure 5.13
Standard Deviations Within a Normal Distribution

A normal curve indicates that scores on a standardized test are distributed in a particular way, a fixed percentage of scores being one or more standard deviation from the mean. A normal curve indicates that the characteristic variable being measured has around 34% of scores that are 1 standard deviation above and below the mean, another 14% that are between 1 and 2 standard deviations above and below the mean, and 2 ½% (approximately) that are more than 2 standard deviations above and below the mean.

The standardized scores on an intelligence test provide an example of a normal distribution, since the mean intelligence quotient (IQ) is 100, with a standard deviation (SD) being 15 points. Thus, 34% of scores lie between 85 and 100 (1 standard deviation below the mean), and 34% lie between 100 and 115 (1 standard deviation above the mean). Further, 14% of scores would be between 70 and 85 (70 being a score of 2 standard deviations below the mean), and 14% between 115 and 130 (130 being 2 standard deviations above the mean). The remaining 5% (approx.) of scores would be distributed below 70 and above 130 (see Figure 5.13).

Teachers or administrators would have an interest in these types of statistics when they wish to compare their class or their school with a state or national "average." They would calculate a distribution for their students, then compare that with state or national distributions. Care should be taken in interpreting that information, however, since scores of this nature provide very limited information and can easily be misread.

Inferential Statistics

Inferential statistics found in formal research reports use a variety of techniques—analysis of variance, multiple regression analysis, factor analysis, and so on—to tease out the effect of different factors on a phenomenon of interest (e.g., the extent to which scores on an achievement test may be attributed to or affected by age, gender, social class, race, or ethnicity). A wide range of studies and reports related to schooling and student learning has been amassed in the research literature, providing a rich body of information with the potential to inform research participants about particular aspects of issues they investigate. Classroom teachers normally will have little use for inferential statistics, since they will rarely engage in the carefully designed experimental and quasi-experimental research for which these are designed. Two common terms in the research literature—*correlation* and *significance*—provide a sense of the extent of relationship between factors influencing learning and behavior and may therefore have direct relevance to practitioner understandings of the research literature.

Correlation   The meaning of *correlation* is embedded in the word itself—co-relation—the degree to which one factor is related to another. The highest degree of relationship is designated as a correlation of 1.00, indicating that one attribute is perfectly related to another. Coefficients that approach 1.00 indicate high degrees of relationship, so that a high IQ score is likely, for instance, to be strongly related to scores of general reading ability. Scores close to 0.00 indicate that there is very little relationship between the attributes or variables measured. A score of -1.00 indicates a perfect inverse relationship, so that a rise in scores on one attribute is likely to lead to an equivalent decrease in another. The correlation coefficient is the primary basis for much research, since most educational studies seek to establish a relationship between one set of variables (e.g., teaching practices) and another (e.g., student performance and behavior).

Tests of significance   *Significance* has a particular technical meaning in statistics. A set of results is said to be "significant" if it can be attributed to the treatment or variables hypothesized—that the effects observed did not merely arise by chance. A range of measures including *t* tests, chi square, and analysis of variance (anova) provide this type of evidence. High scores on tests of significance means that there is a strong likelihood that results achieved indicate some degree of systematic relationship—that the results of the study were not merely achieved by chance. This does not mean, however, that there was a strong relationship between the variables. Sometimes an experiment can achieve results that are highly significant in statistical terms, but indicate a very trivial level relationship between the variables of interest. In such a case we might achieve, for example, a high *t* test score indicating the high likelihood that there is a systematic relationship between the variables measured, but a low correlation that indicates that the relationship is a weak one.

Numbers should always be interpreted carefully. Numerical results do not always lead to a self-evident truth—whether something worked or not. I became sensitized to that issue at a conference presentation given by a teacher who had won many local, state, and national awards for the quality of his teaching. He was in the process of completing a master's degree, seeking new instructional techniques to enhance his teaching. When asked why he should change what were obviously highly effective methods of instruction, he replied that although his students always achieved high scores on achievement tests, he had grave doubts that they really understood the material learned—that they were responding to tests and exams according to formulae they had learned in class. In this case, the teacher's deeply intuitive knowledge of his students' understanding belied the results indicating their high achievement.

ENHANCING ANALYSIS: INCORPORATING
INFORMATION FROM DIVERSE SOURCES

Thus far data analysis has been preceded by exploring information derived largely from interviews. A variety of other data also has been gathered, however, and these data have the potential to enhance or clarify information or issues emerging in the first phases of data analysis. Information acquired through *observation, artifact reviews* (test results, records, documents, materials and equipment), and *literature reviews* might be used to enhance the conclusions that participants reach and the decisions they make about actions to be taken. In the previous example, for instance, interview information related to "student achievement" might be enhanced, extended, or thrown into question by data from student records or reports. Likewise, staff perceptions about resources and materials might be given more credence or be challenged by information from the school inventory, or from comparison with district or state records about levels of resources in schools. Data from a variety of sources have the potential to provide a more effective analysis that provides the basis for more sophisticated and effective analyses.

In the Barrios Juntos school–community study, parent participants were firm in their opinion of the need for greater participation of parents within the school. A review of the literature would have confirmed this perception, since a large array of literature now signals the benefits to be obtained.

The perceptions of students and staff in the Brazos School evaluation study that student achievement had improved were verified by a review of student scores on state-mandated tests. This not only indicated increasing test scores, but showed how well the students were doing compared with similar schools in the district and state.

Diverse data sources are especially important when working with young children, who frequently have limited ability to talk of their experience in abstract terms. There are many other ways, however, in which children make meaning of their experience and communicate with others. We should carefully observe the ways children enact their work and play activities; the ways they talk to others; their drawings, songs, stories, and poems; their descriptions of events; and their responses to events and activities. These "artifacts" assist us to understand how a child makes meaning of events in his or her life, enabling us to construct accounts that clearly represent the child's perspective. If we can fathom ways of making learning activities meaningful from their perspective, then our teaching task becomes so much easier and more rewarding.

Reviewing information related to children's events and activities provides richly rewarding information assisting researchers, and the children themselves, to "make sense" of the issue at hand. It has the potential to greatly enhance the engagement of children in their learning processes and to increase the effectiveness of teaching. Analysis of these types of data requires interactive processes that first identify significant features or elements of experience, then check the ways children make meaning or interpret those features of experience. Researchers should review data related to:

- observations of children's activities, or their participation in events in classrooms, the schoolyard, or other relevant settings.

- aural or visual recordings of their activities, including verbal interactions.
- drawings and artwork.
- class written work.
- letters.
- stories, verbal and written.
- play.
- drama.

Researchers should work with children to identify significant features and elements of these types of information, constructing understandings on the basis of the way the children interpret the information reviewed.

In a study of bilingual kindergarten students, Cathrene Connery (2003) talks of the multiple ways in which children make meaning. She tells the story of a young boy who, hearing the teacher suggest to another student ways of drawing a dinghy, said "No, you're not doing it right.

You've got to go "Urrrr-Uuurrrrrr!! Aururrrrr-Aurrrrurrr!!—like that!" making pulling motions with his hands, apparently trying to invest the action and urgency into the sounds and motions of starting an outboard motor. The event was clear. What was emerging was the child's way of trying to capture that event—sight, sound, and words. We have a much clearer picture of his experience of a boat by combining elements of interview and observation.

Lisa Keck's (2000) eight- to nine-year-old students identified major features and elements of their classroom experience of art, discussing the issue verbally and drawing pictures to represent their experiences and perceptions. They used these features and elements to construct written accounts, completing a book and a mural to express their combined perspective on their experience of art in the class. As a structured research activity, it not only served to cover a number of areas of the class curriculum, but also generated considerable interest and excitement in the children.

Including information from the analysis of multiple data sources therefore provides a rich resource that can enhance a study and provide the basis for more effective action. Procedures for including the outcomes of analysis from multiple sources are presented schematically in Figure 5.14 though the cyclical nature of action research will mean that the revised analysis may be subject to further refinement in the next cycle of the study (see Figure 4.7). The end product of this process is clarity and understanding that enables participants to formulate solutions to even the most difficult problems.

USING CATEGORY SYSTEMS: FRAMEWORKS FOR REPORTS AND ACCOUNTS

Systems of categories emerging from data analysis provide frameworks of concepts that provide a clear guide to issues on which research participants need to focus in order to formulate effective solutions to the problem on which the study is centered. They also provide

Figure 5.14
Incorporating Diverse Data Sources

a structure of concepts that is a useful guide for writing reports. The Brazos School evaluation study, for instance (see Chapter 8), used the following system of categories as a framework for structuring the evaluation report:

Small Is Beautiful: Brazos School Evaluation Report[3]
Introduction
History
Student Experiences
    Attention from Teachers
    Improved Grades
    Freedom and Diversity
Teacher Perspectives
    Student Achievement
    Relationships with Students
    Inquiry Curriculum
    Learning Materials
Administration
    Demands and Resources
    Values and Behavior
    Space

Details within the report derive from the units of meaning included within each category or subcategory. Thus the evaluation report includes a heading "Teacher Perspectives" and a subheading "Student Achievement" and commences with the following text: "Teachers are also enthusiastic about the response of students to the school's model of education.

---

[3]The framework for this report has been simplified for illustrative purposes.

One teacher, comparing his experience in public schools, recounted the differences he experienced. 'You have to give students at other schools tangible rewards.' " The text continues to present details of how teachers are experiencing and interpreting student achievement, including the full range of elements drawn from the unitized data within the "Student Achievement" category. A copy of the preliminary report is presented in Chapter 8, providing an illustration of the way research materials and analysis have been incorporated.

The evaluation report provided information that informed teachers and administrators of areas of strength in the school, but also highlighted some problems they needed to address—the basis for "action" that emerged from the evaluation study.

Analyzing Data Collaboratively

Data gathering and analysis in action research is much more effective when it is accomplished as an interactive process between stakeholders. Although it is important for people to have opportunities to explore issues individually in the earliest stages of an inquiry process, continued explorations increase in power as people participate in processes of collaborative inquiry. Focus groups provide a context in which individual information can be shared and further exploration engaged. Sharing may take place initially within each group of stakeholders, though eventually diverse stakeholding groups should be brought together to share their perspectives, to identify common issues or agendas, and to explore ways of dealing with issues on which they fail to concur.

Data gathering therefore becomes an ongoing part of the look-think-act process. As information is gathered, analyzed, and actions emerge, the process often leads to the need for further exploration or the acquisition of more information, an ever increasing circle of investigation extending participants' understandings and providing the basis for strong and effective action.

Figure 5.15 represents this process. Participants share accounts emerging from individual interviews, formulate a joint account, then return to the interview phase to reflect on and extend their own accounts. There may be a number of iterations of this process during an extended study of a complex issue.

A similar process is envisaged in Figure 5.16, where initial focus group exploration provides the material to develop an initial account. This account provides a framework of

Figure 5.15
Developing Collaborative Accounts

Focus
group
exploration

Key features
of
experience

Figure 5.16
Focus Group Analysis

concepts and themes that is used for further exploration of people's experience and perspectives of the issue. Again, the process is designed to assist groups in achieving deeper understanding and greater clarity, providing the basis for actions that resolve the issue explored.

Analyzing data in focus groups enables stakeholders to come together to share information deriving from their own perspectives and experiences. This not only extends understanding between the diverse individuals and groups, but also enables them to construct a framework of ideas for ongoing collaborative action. As these procedures progress they trigger new ideas or memories in participants, leading to a productive extension of the research process. This enables participants to identify perspectives and experiences they have in common and assists in identifying areas in need of further negotiation or study.

Over the years I have been impressed by the amount of energy and goodwill emerging from well-prepared focus groups. Positive and productive outcomes are never certain, since a history of antagonisms or the presence of authoritarian figures may inhibit group discussions or interaction. I have experienced, however, a high degree of success in this type of activity. A recent half-day workshop with faculty within a college of education illustrates the types of outcomes possible. Faculty explored the use of technology in their teaching, sharing ways they currently used computers to enhance student learning and identifying future uses. The level of animation in their discussions and the extensive lists of useful information emerging from their discussions were a testament to their enthusiasm and the extent to which they appreciated opportunities to learn from each other. It also provided clear direction for the project team who had set up the workshop, indicating directions to take in resourcing faculty to extend their use of technology to enhance student learning.

The productive buzz that continued through this workshop was not the result of idle gossip or general conversation. As I walked around the room listening to group conversations to monitor the progress of their discussion, I was taken by the intensity of their focus. In professional contexts, opportunities for practitioners to get together to discuss the broader dimensions of their work are infrequent. Group discussions focused clearly on issues of interest or concern provide a wonderful context for reaffirming the broader contexts of professional work, taking people out of the sometimes humdrum organizational trivia of everyday institutional life and reminding them of the underlying nature of the work they do together.

CONCLUSION

Data analysis is the process of distilling large quantities of information, revealing the central features of the issue investigated. The process of crystallizing information into a category system provides the basis for increased understanding of the complex events and interactions comprising everyday events in classrooms, schools, and other educational settings. The process is not merely a technical routine, however, since its purpose is not to delineate a relatively small number of variables affecting the focus of study. Its major purpose is to provide the basis for richly evocative accounts and reports providing stakeholders with information and understanding upon which to make informed decisions about policies, programs, and practices for which they are responsible. It also provides the building blocks for therapeutic action within the research process, clearly delineating issues and agendas requiring attention. When engaged collaboratively it also provides a rich field of interaction that enables stakeholders to develop the productive relationships that are a central feature of a good action research process.

SUMMARY

Identifying Key Issues: Data Analysis

The *purposes* of data analysis are to:
1. reduce, distill, or crystallize large quantities of data.
2. provide clarity and enhance stakeholder understandings of issues and events.

Two processes for analyzing data are presented: analyzing key issues and experiences, and categorizing and coding:

Analyzing Key Issues and Experiences.
1. Select key people from within each stakeholder group.
2. Review the data for each selected person.
3. For each, identify significant issues or experiences.
4. Identify major features of those issues or experiences.
5. Identify the elements of experience associated with each feature.
6. Use identified features and elements to formulate a framework of concepts and ideas that represent each person's experience of the issue investigated.

7. Make connections: Identify similarities and differences between features or elements in stakeholder experiences.
8. Use frameworks to construct accounts and/or reports.

Categorizing and Coding
1. Review the interview data for each stakeholding group.
2. Unitize the data: Divide into units of meaning.
3. Formulate *categories, subcategories,* and *themes* identifying patterns, connections, commonalities, or regularities within the data.
4. Organize these into a category system.
5. Complement the analysis with information from noninterview data.
6. Use the category system to provide a framework of concepts for accounts and reports.

Enhancing Data Analysis
Incorporating analysis from diverse sources, including quantitative information, provides the basis for greater understanding and the formulation of effective solutions to the research problem.

Collaborative Data Analysis
Focus groups may be used to analyze data and share information.

Reporting: Communicating Research Processes and Outcomes

RESEARCH DESIGN	DATA GATHERING	DATA ANALYSIS	REPORTING	ACTION
INITIATING A STUDY	GATHERING INFORMATION	IDENTIFYING KEY ISSUES AND EXPERIENCES	WRITTEN REPORTS	CREATING SOLUTIONS
Setting the stage	Interviewing	Analyzing key experiences	Formal reports Narrative accounts Joint accounts	Solving problems
Focusing and framing	Observing		PRESENTATIONS AND PERFORMANCES	Creating syllabi and lesson plans
Participants	Reviewing documents, records, and materials	Categorizing and coding	Presentations	Curriculum development
Literature review		Incorporating quantitative data	Drama Poetry	Evaluation
Sources of information	Quantitative data		Song	
	Reviewing literature	Enhancing analysis	Dance Art	Family and community links
Ethics		Using concepts and categories	Video Multimedia	
Validity				School plans

Contents of the Chapter

As participants engage in research processes, they need to keep a written report of their progress. The ongoing processes and final outcomes of research also need to be communicated to stakeholding audiences.

This chapter describes:

- the *purposes* for reporting research processes and results.
- the methods of reporting, including written reports, presentations, and performances.
- procedures for developing *written reports*.
- procedures for preparing and staging *presentations*.
- procedures for preparing and producing *performances*.

ACTION RESEARCH REPORTS

The first "act" of the look-think-act cycle emerging from an action research process is a report that informs stakeholding audiences of the outcomes of analysis of the first cycle of investigation (Figure 6.1). The purpose of this process is to ensure that all acquire a body of shared knowledge to use as the basis for formulating solutions to the research problem. As will become evident in the following sections, action research reports are somewhat different in form and purpose from traditional academic research reports, being more aligned to the qualitative reporting procedures described by Creswell (2007).

This chapter presents a variety of approaches to reporting, each intended to ensure that participants and audiences of a project acquire clear understandings of both the processes and outcomes of research. According to the desired purposes, therefore, researchers may construct descriptive accounts, ethnographic accounts, or biographic accounts that can be used as progress reports, formative evaluations, or final reports. They may also formulate presentations or performances as alternative means of reporting to the diverse audiences that often comprise an effective action research study.

KEEPING PEOPLE INFORMED: REPORTING PROCEDURES IN ACTION RESEARCH

As people work through action research processes, it is essential for all participants and stakeholders to be informed of the continuing progress of the study in order for them to take part in bringing the project to fruition. As teachers, students, and other stakeholders engage in investigations, they need ways to inform other stakeholders who will be affected

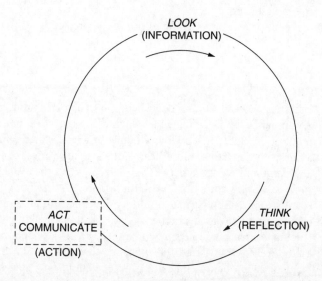

Figure 6.1
Reporting in Action Research

by their activities, or who will need to contribute to actions arising. If their work results in significant changes in the way their classroom or school operates, they may need to inform administrators and/or parents. In larger projects, such as the evaluation of a curriculum, the development of a new way of organizing the school, or the institution of a new program, the work will require ongoing communication between the various stakeholders. In all these circumstances there is a need to communicate significant features of the investigation to ensure that all parties are fully informed. Participants need, therefore, to think carefully through processes for recording and reporting their progress.

There are two aspects to reporting. One is to keep an ongoing record of the project, so that people can review their progress systematically and resolve disputes when people have different opinions about past events and planned activities. A written record is often a useful resource. The other aspect is the need to provide reports and accounts that enable participants to share their experiences and perspectives, providing the means by which larger audiences can extend their understanding or gain a better picture of "what's going on."

Purposeful reporting provides the means for all parties—teachers, students, administrators, and families—to understand the issues and events that affect the situation. As participants become increasingly aware of the influences at work, they are able to take into consideration the diverse agendas and imperatives to be taken into account, and to work toward mutually meaningful solutions to the problems they experience. Effective communication enables understanding.

Research participants may therefore report to each other for the following purposes:

- to share information, keeping people informed of the processes and outcomes of the investigation.
- to enable stakeholders and other audiences to understand the perspectives and experiences of everyone involved.
- to check the accuracy and appropriateness of the information emerging from the investigation.
- to provide an ongoing record of the project.

I recently worked in a school where the issue of communication became paramount. A number of problems had emerged that appeared to result from a breakdown in communication between school and home. Teachers, parents, and administrators became aware of the need to be more clearly informed of a variety of activities pertinent to school and classroom events. What became evident is that the usual forms of communication—such as sending notes home with the children—were not effective, so new processes of sharing information became a priority. Teachers and administrators found new ways of communicating with each other and with parents, making use of a variety of media, including written notes and memos, electronic mail, telephone trees, and verbal reports. These events emphasized the problems that arise when people are poorly informed. Many of the problems and complaints evident in early stages of the project disappeared as more effective methods of communication were developed.

Different Strokes for Different Folks: Forms of Reporting

Because action research requires all participants to understand "what is happening" to enable them to contribute to the effective resolution of the issue investigated, information must be shared with the relevant stakeholders—those who are affected by or have an effect on the issue. How information is shared is critical, since it is imperative not only that people acquire the so-called "facts," but also that they understand the dynamic ways in which significant features of the situation impact the lives of the people involved. The "objective" formal reports so common in institutions often are inadequate vehicles for these purposes, often being framed in technical language that can obscure the real intent of the study.

The type of report format therefore needs to clearly differentiate between the different research audiences and purposes, since they may be pertinent to three major audiences—academic, public, and professional/organizational:

- **Academic:** University research focuses principally on the development of a *body of knowledge,* shared with a community of scholars. The outcomes of research are reported in journals and books stored in university library collections. The knowledge is also passed on to students in order to *inform and educate future professionals.*
- **Public:** Research sometimes is used to *inform and educate the public* about *significant issues.* Research sponsored by government bodies, public interest groups, or community groups report their findings in the media, often incorporating their work into television documentaries or presenting it on stage or as street theater.
- **Professional/Organizational:** Research is increasingly used for direct *professional and organizational* purposes *to improve or strengthen programs, services, and practices.* Research outcomes can be applied directly to the development of new programs and services, or used to formulate solutions to significant problems in institutions, organizations, and community contexts.

The different audiences and purposes of action research require researchers to think clearly about the types of reporting that will enable them to communicate effectively with particular audiences. Examples of a range of different report formats are provided in Chapter 8. These do not, however, cover the full range of possibilities, as will become evident in the latter sections of this chapter. Depending on the stakeholders, the purpose, and the context, reporting may take the form of *written reports, presentations,* or *performances.*

Written reports provide an easy means to communicate information. They may take the form of short, informal reports providing limited information, or highly formalized reports providing detailed information about all facets of a project. Written reports provide the most common medium for maintaining a record of progress or recording the outcomes of a research process. They may take a number of forms, including:

- progress reports that review ongoing activities within a study.
- evaluation reports for the use of teachers and administrators.
- project reports of classroom activities for professional or parent audiences.
- case studies.

- meeting minutes that inform participants of the outcomes of planning and organizing meetings.
- memoranda that report on current activities and issues.

Chapter 8 provides examples of a number of different forms of research reports, each being written for a different purpose and a different audience.

Verbal and/or visual presentations provide richer possibilities for engaging people in processes of communication. They provide more diverse and creative means of enabling people to share focused, richly textured understandings of their research activities. Verbal or visual presentations are an especially effective means for nonprofessionals or cultural and ethnic minorities to exchange information and reveal experience. For these groups, visual, poetic, musical, or dramatic performances also provide effective ways to communicate visceral understandings of their experiences and perspectives.

Reports, presentations, and performances therefore provide diverse means for administrators, teachers, students, and parents to convey the processes and outcomes of their research. They provide multiple methods for presenting new understandings with clarity, precision, and authenticity, enabling people to contribute effectively to the ongoing development of actions and events designed to improve their situation.

WRITTEN REPORTS

Written reports are derived from the products of data analysis (see Chapter 5). Key features and elements identified in these processes provide the basis for accounts reflecting the perspectives, perceptions, and experiences of individuals and groups participating in the process. They may take the form of:

- Individual reports
- Group reports
- Progress reports
- Evaluation reports
- Final reports

As Denzin (1997) suggests, we are not seeking definitive or objective accounts, but evocative accounts that lead the reader to an empathetic understanding of the people's lived experience. Accounts or narratives thereby provide insight into people's lives, recording the impact of events on their day-to-day feelings of well-being and their capacity to interact healthily and productively with the life-world that confronts them. They reveal the rich, densely layered tapestry of human experience, and the complex emotional world lying beneath the surface of seemingly innocuous events, that breaks into view in those special moments of triumph, success, love, struggle, loss, or discord that have such a dramatic effect on people's lives.

In action research, therefore, we seek to produce descriptive accounts that convey accurate insights into and understandings of the impact of events on people's lives. Writing accounts entails more than the bland reporting of events—it requires report writers to find the means to evoke empathetic understanding of the events they describe. A government report that referred to the "inadequate sewage" in a school, for instance, failed to evoke an understanding of the stench of excreta and the parents' ongoing fear for the health of their children. Objective reports are sometimes dangerously uninformative. Extended ethnographic accounts comprised of full, richly textured narrative provide the possibility of in-depth insight into the community and/or institutional contexts in which events are played out, inscribed with the history of the situation and revealing the interactional and emotional features of people's experience. Shorter reports such as meeting minutes, team reports, progress reports, and so on, provide more condensed accounts, but should still capture the essence of people's experience.

Narrative Accounts: Biographies, Autobiographies, and Ethnographies

Action research reports therefore differ in nature from reporting procedures common in the academic research literature, their purposes and outcomes being somewhat different. The latter are based on the need to provide objective, generalizable accounts that focus on the variables or factors of interest, and often sound bland and uninteresting. Action research reports, on the other hand, require narrative accounts—stories of people's experience—that have the capacity to illuminate the often complex and deeply problematic nature of events. In contrast to academic reports that often interpret behavior from within a framework of disciplinary theory (personality, motivation, developmental stages, etc.), biographic and ethnographic accounts provide the means to understand people's lives from their own perspective. They reveal the history of their experience and significant features of their lives—key experiences or defining moments that illuminate the underlying dynamics of the situation. Thus, action research reports describe events from the viewpoint of participant stakeholders in the first instance, then compare and contrast those with other viewpoints from within the academic and professional literature.

There are multiple benefits to this process, since the mere act of "telling their own story" is therapeutic for the individuals concerned, revealing features of their lives they had inadvertently repressed or had "taken for granted" as necessary though damaging aspects of their lives. Conversely, the process may reveal hidden positive dimensions of experience, enabling them to see their worlds in a more positive light or to become aware of potentially useful aspects of the situation.

The process of writing personal accounts of experience as part of an action research project is not intended to reveal "the facts" or "the truth" of a person's life, but to enable them to look at their lives in different ways—to reinterpret events, experiences, and responses, and to come to new ways of understanding their situation. Autobiographical and ethnographic accounts provide potential useful resources, enabling individuals and groups to reevaluate their place and their interaction with others in the context, to "connect and join biographically meaningful experiences to society-at-hand and to the larger culture- and meaning-making institutions . . ." (Denzin, 1989a, p. 25).

While ethnographic accounts largely have been written by external authors, we now recognize the potential of auto-ethnographies, individuals and groups working through self-referential processes of exploration to write accounts of their own lives. Sometimes, the stories are so sensitive, reaching into the intimate details of people's lives, that people have no desire to have them made public. In these situations it is possible to disguise both the people and places by use of fictitious names or by providing generalized accounts revealing the major features of their experience, but not providing the means to identify particular people or places.

We have witnessed many situations where people have been greatly enlivened by opportunities to "tell their stories" and listen to the stories of others. In schools, workshops, program development projects, and many other arenas we have experienced
the joy that comes from this process. What we see is a *sense of worth* emerging from
people who feel, sometimes for the first time in their lives, that someone is really listening to them, that they have something worthwhile to share with others. We are no
longer surprised, but always feel gratified when people express their appreciation in
the most heartfelt terms. On more than one occasion people have burst out in the
moment, or quietly informed us later, "This changed my life!"

   Something quite wonderful happens in the process. Not only do storytellers experience the exuberance of being heard and acknowledged, but in the process they learn
something significant about themselves and their experiences. It is illuminating and
sometimes revelationary. We have often seen people—storytellers and/or audience—in
tears as their stories emerge. The teller does not need to be a practiced orator. Sometimes the straight recounting of events by simply spoken people—moms, old folk, children—has a dramatic impact on an audience, the "presence" of the people themselves
speaking volumes. When people tell stories of their lives it is no small thing.

Joint and Collective Accounts: Connecting Stakeholder Experiences

The need to present stakeholder perspectives therefore requires a somewhat different
process for constructing action research reports. Since report writers are not attempting to
provide generalized, objective accounts, but narratives that capture the experience and perspective of individuals and groups within the study, different ways of constructing a research report are required. Since it is not possible to capture accounts of all individuals in
a study, writers use joint or collective accounts to frame their reports.

   Collective accounts are based on the notion that individual stakeholder stories can reveal
singular experiences that are shared with other stakeholders. Alternatively, although they may
share the same experience, participants may be affected by the same events in different ways.
In writing reports, therefore, we need to make connections between stakeholder experiences
in order to develop an understanding of the key issues and experiences affecting events, and
the dynamic interactions between individuals and groups. Thus, when individual stakeholder
features of experience have been identified, we search for connections with others. Researchers:

- Focus on significant experiences or issues for each individual.
- Review the data for all other selected stakeholders.
- Identify features or elements of experience common to other stakeholders.
- Identify points at which other stakeholders' experiences or perspectives have been
  affected by the original key experience.
- Record those features or elements as a sublist of the original epiphany.
- Take note of the number of times an experience or element is repeated for different
  stakeholders.

By comparing information within groups and across groups researchers are able to make judgments about the extent to which events, experiences, or perspectives are commonly held by those within a group or shared with other groups. These types of comparison provide information that also is important at the "action" phase, since it enables participants to identify those common elements of experience from which productive action might be formulated. It also enables them to identify those singularly important experiences and perspectives that also may need to be taken into account in formulating solutions to the problem investigated. The terminology reveals the extent of commonality— "All teachers in this study . . .," "Many parents shared a concern about. . .," or "While some students indicated . . . others were more inclined to . . . ."

Joint accounts (Figure 6.2) therefore provide a summary of individual accounts, but focus particularly on commonalities and differences revealed through cross-analysis of major features and key elements. Common or similar features, in this case, may be thought of as "themes." Joint accounts provide ways of presenting the perspectives and experiences of stakeholding groups in a study—teachers, students, administrators, families, and so on.

Collective accounts present an overview of the major features and elements of experience and perspective from each of the major groups, so that a school report may comprise features and elements drawn from each of the stakeholding groups (see Figure 6.3). Commonalities revealed in these accounts provide the basis for collective action, while points of difference suggest issues requiring negotiation (see Guba & Lincoln, 1989).

Figure 6.2
Formulating Joint Accounts

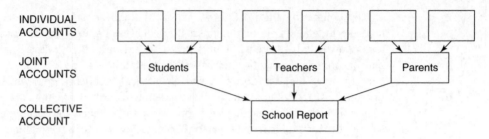

FIGURE 6.3
Individual, Joint, and Collective Accounts

In a recent research project in which I participated, analysis of data revealed that many teachers and parents expressed similar ideas about parent–teacher conferences—insufficient time, the need for more effective communication between parents and teachers, and so on.

Although each perceived the same features, they sometimes expressed it from their different sides of the coin—for instance, teachers felt that parents didn't communicate effectively with teachers, while parents felt that teachers didn't clearly communicate what was expected of parents.

These types of analysis provided the basis for changes the school made to parent–teacher conferences with the intent of making them more effective. More time was allocated for conferences, and individual teachers were able to implement group advisory sessions that provided parents with more detailed information. This included ways of enabling parents to understand how classroom learning processes were organized and how parents could assist in their children's learning.

In the process, however, a number of other issues emerged that enabled the school to take steps to improve the methods they used to communicate with families.

CONSTRUCTING REPORTS

Constructing effective and useful reports is an art form in itself, sometimes requiring years of practice to accomplish. By following some fundamental processes, however, most people can write a report containing relevant information and conveying emerging understandings. Those responsible for writing a report should:

- Describe the *audience and purpose* of the report.
- Identify *participants*.
- Identify the significant *features and elements of experience*.
- Construct a *report framework*.
- *Write the report*.
- *Review and edit* the report.
- *Member check* the report.

Describe the Audience and Purpose

Carefully define the audience and purpose of the report. Ask:

- For which particular people (or type of people) will this report be written? Teachers, students, administrators, parents, and so on? In which locations—particular classrooms, schools, or homes?
- For what purposes will the report be used? To inform people of progress on a project, assist them to understand features of people's experience, or reveal required actions?

Select Participant Perspectives

Decide which participant perspectives—individuals or stakeholding groups—are to be included. Note:

- whose experiences or agendas are central to the report.
- which people have important or significant associated experiences or agendas.

And then isolate the data for each of these individuals or groups.

Review the Data

- Read the data relevant to the identified participants to become familiar with the material.
- Note particularly effective quotations that illustrate key features of people's experience.
- Note the terminology and language used by participants to describe their experience.

Identify Significant Features and Elements of Experience

- Review the analyzed data to identify relevant material for the report.
- Make a copy of key features and elements of experience for each individual or group.

Construct Report Framework

Use the features and elements of experience to construct a framework for the report (see Figures 5.2 and 5.8). Note:

- key features as headings or subheadings.
- elements or units of meaning as the content of each heading/subheading.

Write the Report

Write the report using the framework as a guide, incorporating the terminology and language of participants in the body of the narrative. The framework guides the writing process, but is not by itself sufficient to adequately capture people's lived experience. Authors of reports and accounts need to encompass in their writing the multiple dimensions of human experience, including emotional, physical, and interactional elements of behavior and perspective, as well as the organizational and procedural components. The framework that guides data collection is useful as a checklist of what can be included in a narrative—people, acts, activities, events, purposes, emotions, places, times, and objects. In all this it is important for the words of participants to provide the terminology and language of the report. Not only should they provide the wording of headings in the report/account, but their words should make up the body of writing. Some writers string together sections of the unitized data to form the body of the account. Others use quotations prolifically to clearly illustrate the points they are making or the contexts they describe.

> The BSIC evaluation report (Chapter 8, p. xx) includes a heading "Teacher Perspectives" with a subheading "Student Achievement." The latter includes the following text: "Teachers are also enthusiastic about the response of students to the school's model of education. One teacher, comparing his experience in public schools, recounted the differences he encountered: 'You have to give students at other schools tangible rewards.' " The text continues to present details of how teachers are experiencing and interpreting "student achievement," including the full range of elements drawn from the unitized data within the "Student Achievement" category.

Review and Edit

Review the report. Check that:

- Its stated purposes have been accomplished: Does the report provide adequate and appropriate information to inform the intended audience?
- All relevant participant perspectives have been included.
- The language is appropriate for the intended audience.
- The report accurately reflects the perspectives and experiences of participants, rather than that of the author or one stakeholding group.

> Whenever I'm facilitating report writing, I continually ask authors the question, "Who is speaking here? Whose perspective is being presented?" It is surprising how often even the most careful report writer will allow his or her own perspective to intrude. When we write accounts we must take great care to ensure that we don't unwittingly present material reflecting our own perceptions and interpretations of the situation. The exceptions are those situations where we overtly include our perspective as a participating stakeholder in a research process.

Member Check

Give a draft to those about whom the report is written:

- Provide time for them to read and respond.
- Talk with them in person, if possible, or by phone if not.

- Check for accuracy, sufficiency, and appropriateness of information contained in the report.
- Modify or correct the report according to their input.

WRITING FORMAL REPORTS

Formal reports are those presented to professional audiences that have a significant stake in the research project and need to be fully informed about the purpose, procedures, and outcomes of the study. Formal reports therefore will be written for:

- administrative, professional, and funding bodies.
- academic and professional publications and research journals.
- theses and dissertations.

A formal report should include the following sections:

1. **Introduction**—describes the focus of the study.
2. **Review of the Literature**—presents an overview of current academic and professional literature related to the research problem.
3. **Methodology**—details the methodology and research procedures used.
4. **Findings or Outcomes**—presents an account of the outcomes of the study.
5. **Discussion or Conclusion**—describes actions emerging from the study and implications for further investigation.

Section 1: Introduction—Focus and Framing

This section of a report presents an overview of the study. It describes:

- the problem or issue on which the study focuses.
- the context of the study—where it is located and the people involved.
- the research question.
- the purpose of the research—generally, to seek an answer to the research question.
- the significance of the study—why the issue is important, or why the problem needed to be resolved.

Section 2: Literature Review

The purpose of a literature review is to summarize information about the research problem/question that has been gleaned from studies reported in the research and professional literature. It both describes and critiques those studies, assessing their strengths and weaknesses, and revealing the concepts, theories, and underlying assumptions on which their various claims and viewpoints are based. The review also points to gaps or inadequacies in the literature, in terms of its applicability to the current study. The review of literature may also point to the significance of the issue or problem as being worthy of study. The review and analysis of this literature sets the stage for a later process (see Section 5 discussion) in which official and academic viewpoints are compared and contrasted with research participant perspectives.

Section 3: Methodology

This section of the report presents a rationale for the approach to research used in the study (philosophical assumptions) and describes in detail the people involved (sample), the context in which it takes place (site), and the procedures used to conduct the research (research methods). It informs readers of why this approach to research is appropriate to the issue investigated and indicates steps taken to ensure the study was rigorous and ethical. In doing so it may cite sources that enhance the legitimacy of the study (e.g., Denzin & Lincoln, 2005; Lincoln & Guba, 1985; Reason & Bradbury, 2007).

Section 4: Research Outcomes/Findings

Section 4 is sometimes described as the "results" section of the report, enabling researchers to present what they have discovered in their investigation. It presents detailed accounts that describe the nature of the problem from the perspective of different stakeholders, including the events, behaviors, or responses having a significant effect on the issue investigated. These accounts not only identify the factors affecting the issue, but describe the dynamics of the situation in which they emerge.

The "what, who, how, where, when, why" framework is a useful tool for capturing these issues. This framework triggers report writers to identify: *what* the key events are; *who* is involved; *how, when,* and *where* these events unfold; *why* they occur as they do; and *how* they are experienced by different stakeholders. The intent is to provide readers with an empathetic understanding of how stakeholders experience and interpret issues and events surrounding the research problem, and the effect that has on their activities and behaviors.

The following list provides another useful conceptual framework to assist report writers:

- **Actors:** The people who are significant or relevant to the story.
- **Acts and activities:** The things people do; activities in which they engage.
- **Events:** Significant events or incidents that take place.
- **Place:** Where those activities or events take place.
- **Time:** When events occur and for how long.
- **Purpose:** What people are trying to accomplish; why they do what they do.
- **Emotion:** How participants feel about what happens; how they respond.
- **Objects:** Buildings, goods, materials, clothes, cars, books, reports, and so on.

The report will also describe solutions to the research problem formulated by participants, the way those solutions were implemented, and the effect of those solutions.

Accounts should provide sufficient material to enable intended audiences to understand the experience and perspectives of key people in the primary stakeholding groups, as well as information incorporated from other data sources. A report of an investigation of school dropouts not only would focus on the perspectives and experiences of students who left school early, but also should provide an understanding of the perspectives of peers, teachers, parents, school administrators, and others having a stake in the issue, and incorporate statistical information that indicates relevant information from school records—numbers of school dropouts in current and previous years, absenteeism, levels of educational attainment, and so on.

Section 5: Conclusion—Discussion of Findings

The final section places the results in a broader context. This is the "so what" section of a formal report or dissertation that enables writers to articulate newly emerging understandings of the issue and to compare and contrast them with perspectives that exist in the academic literature or in department/agency reports. In effect, it presents succinctly what has been discovered and explores the implications of those findings. This section does the following:

- summarizes the outcomes of the study.
- places stakeholder viewpoints in the broader social context of the issue by comparing and contrasting their perspectives with those presented within the literature.
- explores the implications of the study for practices, policies, programs, and services.
- suggests actions that may be initiated or extended, or modifications of activities and/or procedures that will improve existing practices, programs, or services.
- suggests the need for further research to enhance or extend the outcomes of the current study.

The overall purpose of this section is to show clearly how stakeholder perspectives illuminate the issue investigated and to suggest the changes in practices, programs, and services implied by the outcomes of the research. In the academic world, it may also propose ways that existing theoretical perspectives are enhanced or challenged by the new understandings emerging from the research process.

A report on an action research study of parent involvement in schools included the perspectives of parents, teachers, principals, superintendents, and personnel from the education agency. The report presented the perspective of each of these stakeholding groups, and included a wide range of possibilities for ways in which parents could participate in the schools to enhance their children's education. These reports and the recommendations that emerged from them became the basis for a series of parent–teacher workshops in a sample of schools in the district that clearly defined actions parents themselves wished to take in their particular schools. A report on the widespread success of this pilot program provided the means for the district education agency to formulate a policy that provided the impetus for similar developments across the school system (Stringer, in Reason & Bradbury, 2007).

PRESENTATIONS: EFFECTIVE COMMUNICATION

Presentations provide exciting ways to communicate research results to participants and stakeholding audiences. Constructed from multiple materials and using diverse presentational modes, they can captivate audiences, powerfully presenting participant perspectives and illuminating key features of the research. Presentations provide the possibility of clear and effective communication based on richly evocative accounts that accurately capture and represent people's experiences. They may range from simple verbal presentations to complex performances incorporating multiple forms of visual and electronic media that effectively communicate with a wide variety of audiences.

Even academic and professional conferences now provide opportunities for staging a wide variety of presentations. Though direct verbal addresses from prepared papers are still common, many presentations involve creative and innovative approaches that incorporate charts, overheads, electronic materials, roundtable interactive presentations, poster sessions, and structured dialogues. Presenters seek forms of communication that enable them to communicate information efficiently and effectively. These types of presentations are becoming increasingly common in professional and school contexts as teachers and administrators share information or report on school activities.

Such flexible formats are especially relevant in contexts where lengthy written reports may actually inhibit communication with important stakeholding audiences. Children and some adults from poorer or culturally different contexts may not have sufficient familiarity with professional or technical language to enable them to read lengthy formal reports. Further, written reports are often an inadequate vehicle for expressing the full range of participant experiences. They fail to convey the emotional, interactional features of experience, the nature of their social circumstances, or the complexities of their cultural realities. Presentations, when carefully prepared and authentically presented, provide the means for more clearly and effectively communicating the concrete reality of people's lives and the elements that need to be taken into careful account when taking action. As with written reports, presentations need to be carefully and creatively planned to suit the audience, the purposes to be achieved, and the outcomes expected.

A group of graduate students presented an evaluative account of their experience of coursework in their program. Direct verbal presentations were supplemented by role plays, poetry, and art. Their presentations were richly peppered with Aboriginal names and terminology, and humor was an integral feature of the dialogical interaction between participants. Not only were they able to provide an enjoyable and informative experience for the audience of students and academic faculty from around the university, they were also able to embody the Aboriginal cultural ethos that was central to the program of study they had engaged. Derived from a preliminary focus group exploration, their presentations clearly depicted the joys, struggles, and other major features of their learning processes. It provided a dramatic counterpoint to the rather soulless, form-filling exercises usually used for class evaluations.

Audiences and Purposes

Research participants using presentations to communicate information about their research will need to identify carefully their audience and purpose in order to achieve the effectiveness of their project. The major question to be asked is "What information should be presented, and how can we communicate most effectively with this particular audience?" In school contexts, audiences of teachers, students, parents, and administrators may require somewhat different presentations, since different agendas will be relevant to each of those audiences, each of whom may have a different part to play in actions emerging from the research process. All groups, however, will need to understand each other's perspectives, so that they are able to work in unison to achieve their desired purposes.

Presentations therefore will vary according to purposes to be achieved. Short, informal presentations assist participants to communicate the progress of activities to each other, enabling progress to be monitored effectively and ensuring that all are working in unison. These types of presentations will be very different from more carefully structured and planned presentations required at key points in the research process. If participants wish to inform a key stakeholding group—administrators, funding body representative, supporters— of the issues emerging from their inquiries to garner support for actions they wish to take, then more detailed and carefully structured presentations may be necessary.

Presentations will also be affected by desired outcomes. If participants wish to generate a clear or deeper understanding of people's experience, then participants will prepare evocative presentations designed to achieve that effect. Such presentations will be multidimensional, providing a clear picture of significant events, the context in which they occur, and their impact—rational, physical, emotional, and spiritual—on the lives of participant stakeholders. This is a more emotive presentation seeking to engender understanding of the dynamics and complexities of people's experiences and perspectives. If participants wish an audience to focus on more practical issues for planning purposes, then the presentation will take a more didactic form, focusing on key features and elements of the issue investigated. Presentations that keep people informed of activities in progress but require no action on their part will differ from those presentations requiring decisions, inputs, or actions on the part of the audience. In the latter case, the presentations themselves must be structured to make provisions for audience participation at appropriate points.

In recent years I was involved in a curriculum development project to institute a graduate program in indigenous studies. Preliminary research with prospective students and associated audiences identified the content of the program—the skills and knowledge required by the students to achieve their educational, social, and cultural purposes. These provided the basis for content of study, teaching/learning processes, and program organization, including staffing, budgeting, space, timetable, and so on.

As we worked through developmental processes, different means were employed to inform the different audiences of program details. A charted summary of the content areas was produced and used to talk with prospective students about the program. A flow chart assisted the planning team to work through organizational issues with administrative personnel. A series of reports provided relevant information to a variety of other stakeholders, including institutional committees and a community advisory group. These forms of presentation enabled stakeholding developmental partners and participants to maintain a clear picture of the program as it developed and ensured wide acceptance within the institution and the community.

A smaller research study at a local school developed small reports for teachers, administrators, and parents. These were presented verbally to the principal, to a meeting of school staff, and to a meeting of parents. The project was marked by high degrees of participation by parents, and enabled school staff to make changes to ways in which they communicated with parents. The combination of written and verbal presentations provided the means to reach a wide range of participants.

Planning Presentations

Well-planned presentations ensure that stakeholding audiences are well-informed, enabling them to maintain clarity and gain deep insights into the issues investigated. Research participants will use similar processes to report writing for planning presentations (see previous discussion), defining:

- **Audiences:** Who are the audiences to whom we wish to present?
- **Purposes:** What are our purposes in presenting to this audience?
- **Understandings:** What do we wish our audiences to know or understand?
- **Content:** What information or material will assist in achieving this purpose?
- **Format:** What presentational formats might best achieve this purpose?
- **Outcomes:** What do we wish to achieve; what outcomes are desired?

Planning presentations

- Identify the **audience** and **purpose**.
- **Identify participants** whose experiences and perspectives are pertinent to the presentation.
- **Review the data** for each of these participants.
- **Review the categories and issues** emerging from analysis of data for each participant.
- Use categories to **construct a framework** of headings.
- **Write a script,** using units of meaning and/or elements within the data.
- **Review and edit** the script, checking for accurate rendering of participant perspectives and appropriateness to audience.
- **Member check** by having participants read the script.
- **Practice** the presentation.

The basic outcome of presentation planning is an *outline* or *script* presenting the information in easily accessible form. An outline in dot-point form provides a script that guides people's presentations. The script may be complemented by additional material, including quotations from people's talk or documented information to be read verbatim to an audience. For more formal presentations, people may rehearse their presentation to ensure they are clear about the material to be presented and to keep their presentation within the allotted time.

Research participants therefore need to carefully prepare a script that has the following basic format:

- **Introduction**
    The focus of the project—the issue investigated
    The participants
    The purpose and desired outcomes of the presentation

- **Body of the Presentation**
    Previous and current activities: What has happened and what is happening
    Key issues emerging from research: What has been discovered; what is problematic
    Implications: What needs to be done (actions, next steps)

- **Conclusion**
  Review of major points covered

Presentations should be carefully scripted and directed so that each participant knows precisely where and when to speak, and the material for which they are responsible. Practice provides both clarity and confidence, maximizing the possibility of an informative and effective presentation. This is especially important for people who are not used to speaking publicly, because their inclusion—the effect of people speaking for themselves in their own voice—dramatically increases the power of a presentation.

Only in rare situations should people read from a pre-prepared written report. Though these types of presentations provide people with feelings of safety and accuracy, they usually detract from the purpose of the event. The written word is different in form and function from the spoken word, and people reading from a paper usually fail to convey the meaningfulness that is a necessary function of a presentation. We have all experienced forms of presentation, delivered in mournful monotone or excited exuberance, that rattle or drone on and on. Usually there is far too much information for the audience to absorb and little opportunity to process that information. Rarely do audiences in these situations gain appreciable understanding, and retention of information is limited. Presenting an address by reading from a pre-prepared paper is an art that few possess.

Members of a neighborhood collective planned a presentation to a national academic conference, a rather grand event that seemed somewhat imposing to them. After carefully identifying the purpose of their presentation—the major message they wished to present to a largely academic audience—they carefully reviewed the material they had accumulated, identifying and assessing those features that appeared central to research in which they had engaged. These features were ordered into a framework of ideas—headings and subheadings—and persons were allocated to take responsibility for the various sections. They rehearsed their presentation a number of times, reallocating some material to different people or places until all participants were clear on what they needed to say and when. The actual presentation at the conference was highly successful, providing the audience with a clear understanding of the power of community participation in a research process. The degree of engagement of the audience was evidenced by their rapt attention and the diversity of questions they asked. The participants were highly delighted by the success of their presentation, an event that further heightened their research skills and feelings of empowerment.

Enhancing Verbal Presentations: Audio/Visual Materials

"Talk is cheap" is a common saying that has relevance to presentations. Though parsimonious verbal presentations can sometimes be effective, it requires a skilled and practiced orator to hold an audience for an extended period. Interest and understanding is greatly extended when visual and auditory materials are incorporated into presentations, aiding in clarity and enabling significant quantities of factual information to be presented. Statistical summaries, numerical information, or lists of features and elements may be presented in chart form or as overheads. Charts have the advantage of providing a constantly available record of issues, but suffer sometimes from problems of size. Overheads and other electronic means of displaying information have great clarity, but can only be projected one sheet at a time, thus placing limits on the flexibility of a presentation.

A variety of visual aids will complement and enhance verbal information. Diagrams, maps, concept maps, symbolic representations, figures, and so on, provide effective ways for presenting information and focusing attention. Whiteboards or chalkboards also enable the active construction of illustrations and diagrams to stimulate attention and enable the structured exposition of a wide range of subject matter.

These processes can be presented in highly sophisticated form using electronic media in the form of audio or video recording, or electronic presentations derived from such software as Microsoft PowerPoint. It is important to ensure that these are used in moderation, since extended use of videos or electronic media can be detrimental to a presentation, creating a passive audience and detracting from feelings of engagement. Judicious use of electronic media, however, can provide vivid illustrations or large bodies of information, greatly enhancing people's ability or willingness to participate in ongoing dialogue. As a stimulus they are sometimes unparalleled.

At each stage, therefore, we need to ask how we can best achieve the types of understanding we desire. Presentations can be greatly enhanced by using:

- Maps
- Charts
- Artwork
- Concept maps
- Lists
- Figures
- Overheads
- Audio recording
- Video recording
- Electronic presentations

For some years colleagues and I have provided workshops on cultural sensitivity or race relations for a variety of audiences. The intent was to assist them to investigate ways of modifying their professional work practices to ensure greater effectiveness in cross-cultural contexts. These sessions have been greatly enhanced by having participants view short segments of a video film showing indigenous people presenting accounts of their experiences. One popular segment presents an old man talking of the time police and welfare officers came to take away his children. Moved to tears, he narrates the way he was prevented from taking any action as his children were driven away. Returning the next day he talks of how he put a piece of old tin over his only remaining reminder of his children, their footprints in the sand. This segment, used many times in workshops and presentations, never fails to evoke rich and sometimes intense discussions. It provides keen insight into the way past events continue to affect community life. Sometimes a picture is worth a thousand words.

For some audiences, presentations may take on an almost concert-like appearance. Creative presentations may incorporate a variety of materials and performances (see following discussion), providing a rich body of factual information and authentic understandings of people's lived realities. Presentations, constructed from materials derived from the analysis of data, use key features and elements as the basis for a script, incorporating "quotes" from the data to highlight important information. Presenters may incorporate tape-recorded information derived from participant interviews, read from reviewed materials, or incorporate, as appropriate, segments of video or audio recordings, poems, songs, or role plays. The rich variety of possibilities enables audiences of children, youth, and adult participants to fully express the ideas with which they have been working.

Interactive Presentations

Presentations are more effective when they are interactive. It is difficult to stimulate interest or involvement in a research process when the audience is passive and uninvolved. When presenters dominate presentations, other participants are likely to feel "left out," or marginalized, as if their perspectives and issues are less important. Wherever possible, presentations should provide opportunities for all participants to interact with the material presented. At regular intervals, audiences should have opportunities to participate in the unfolding presentation, commenting on issues, asking for clarification, or offering their perspectives on issues presented. As part of an "hermeneutic dialectic"—meaning-making dialogue—these processes not only enable people to extend and clarify their understanding, but also increase their feelings of inclusion and ownership in the project at hand.

Presentations may also include small-group work, enabling participants to explore issues in greater depth by engaging in dialogue, or peruse related documents or materials. Feedback from small-group discussions provides a further means to gain greater clarity and understanding, especially about points of contention or uncertainty. This points to the need for flexibility, to allow participants to take advantage of opportunities arising in the course of presentations. It is possible to turn a presentation into a workshop or focus group, so that audiences become active participants in the ongoing development of the investigation. In these circumstances time may be allocated for this purpose to allow participants to take advantage of the ideas emerging from their work together.

When I work with research groups I often have them chart the key elements of their recent activities. Each group then speaks of their chart, reporting on their progress and any issues arising. The audience is able to comment or ask questions to clarify or extend the presenters' comments. This not only informs the audience clearly, but assists the presenters to extend their thinking about the issues raised—an integral part of the process of re-searching.

PERFORMANCES: REPRESENTING EXPERIENCE ARTISTICALLY AND DRAMATICALLY

Performances extend the possibilities for providing deeper and more effective understandings of the nature of people's experiences. They present multiple possibilities for entering people's subjective worlds to provide audiences with empathetic understandings that greatly increase the power of the research process. Performances enable participants to "report" on their research through:

- Drama
- Role play
- Song
- Poetry
- Dance
- Visual artwork
- Electronic media

By engaging their work performatively, research participants use artistic means to enable audiences to take the perspective of the people whose lives are performed, to enter their experience vicariously, and therefore to understand more empathetically their life-worlds. Using artistic and dramatic media, researchers are able to capture and represent the deeply complex, dynamic, interactive, and emotional qualities of everyday life. They can engage in richly evocative presentations comprehensible to children, families, cultural minorities, the poor, and other previously excluded audiences.

Poetry, music, drama, and art provide the means for creating illuminative, transformative experiences for presenter and audience alike, stimulating awareness of the different voices and multiple discourses occurring in any given social space (Denzin, 1997; Prattis, 1985). They provide the means to interrogate people's everyday realities, by juxtaposing them within the telling, acting, or singing of stories, thus revealing the differences that occur therein and providing the possibility of therapeutic action (Denzin, 1997; Trinh, 1991). While performances fail to provide the certainty required of experimental research, or to reinforce the authority of an official voice (Atkinson, 1992), they present the possibility of producing compassionate understandings that promote effective change and progress (Rorty, 1989).

This is clearly a postmodernism response, making possible the construction of evocative accounts revealing people's concrete, human experience. Performances provide the means of complementing or enhancing reports and presentations by:

- studying the world from the perspective of research participants.
- capturing their lived experience.
- enabling participants to discover truths about themselves and others.
- recognizing multiple interpretations of events and phenomena.
- embedding experience in local cultural contexts.
- recording the deeply felt emotions—love, pride, dignity, honor, hate, envy—and the agonies, tragedies, triumphs, and peaks of human experience embedded in people's actions, activities, and behavior.
- representing people's experience symbolically, visually, or aurally in order to achieve clarity and understanding.

In recent years I have observed some stunning performances that have greatly extended my understanding of people's experience. I have seen class evaluations including poetry, song, role play, and art that provided me with deep insights into the learning experiences of my students, enabling me, as teacher, to extend my thinking about the ways my classes are organized and operate. I have seen the powerful artistic work of small children provide wonderfully illuminative representations of their classroom experience. I have sat in the audience, deeply moved by middle school children's dramatic presentation of an issue touching their school lives. In all these, I have been surprised by the depth and extent of my responses to these performative presentations, feeling deeply "touched" by what I have seen and heard, and more sensitive to the nature of the performers' experiences and how the issues they represent fit within and affect their lives.

Planning Performances: Developing a Script

Performances are built from the outcomes of data analysis, using similar techniques to those used to fashion reports and presentations. Key features and elements provide the material from which a performance is produced, with participants working creatively to develop effective means for representing their experience. These may be constructed as **poems, songs,** or **drama,** or represented as **symbolic** or **visual art.** As with written and other forms of representation, performances need to be conducted with a clear understanding of the *purpose* they wish to achieve with a specific *audience.* Participants should ask: "What do we wish this audience to know or understand? And how might we best achieve that knowledge or understanding through our performance?"

- Identify the **audience** and **purpose**.
- **Identify participants** whose experiences and perspectives are to be represented.
- **Review the data** for each of these participants.
- **Review the categories and issues** emerging from analysis of data for each participant.
- Use categories to **construct a framework** of key features of experiences and perspectives.
- **Write a script,** using units of meaning and/or elements within the data.
- **Review and edit** the script, checking for accurate rendering of participant perspectives and appropriateness to audience.
- **Member check** by having participants read the script.
- **Rehearse** the performance.

Producing Performances

As with any script, there will be decisions to be made about who will perform which roles, how the setting will be designed, what clothing or costumes will be worn, and who will direct the staging of the performance (i.e. take responsibility for overall enactment of the performance).

Rehearsals are an important feature of performances, enabling participants to review the quality and appropriateness of their production and providing opportunities to clarify or modify the script. People will also become familiar with their roles, sometimes memorizing the parts they need to play, though readings may be used effectively where people have minimal time for preparation or rehearsal.

Sometimes action research requires research participants to formulate on-the-spot performances, so that role plays requiring minimal preparation provide an effective means for people to communicate their messages. For this mode of performance, participants should formulate an outline of a script from the material emerging from their analysis, ad-libbing the words as they enact the scene they wish to represent. Role plays are especially powerful when participants act out their own parts, speaking in their own words and revealing, in the process, clear understanding of their own experiences and perspectives.

Video and Electronic Media

Although live performances provide effective ways to communicate the outcomes of research, video and other electronic media offer powerful and flexible tools for reaching more extended audiences. Not only do video productions provide possibilities for more sophisticated performances, but they enable the inclusion of people whose personal makeup inhibits them from participating in live performances. The technology now available enables video productions to be presented on larger screens, to be shown on computer screens, or to be incorporated into more complex online productions.

Dirk Schouten and Rob Watling (1997) provide a useful model for integrating video into education, training, and community development projects. Their process includes:

- making a recording scheme.
- recording the material.
- making an inventory of the material.
- deciding what functions the material will serve in the text.
- making a rough structure for the text.
- making an edit scheme on the basis of the rough structure.
- editing the text.

Although producing a quality video requires high levels of expertise and careful production, current technology enables even amateurs to produce short and effective products. By recording events in schools, research participants can provide engaging and potentially productive productions that extend the potential of their work. This type of recording enables people to provide sometimes dramatic renderings of their experiences, and to engage in forms of research from which they were previously excluded.

Videotaping also provides research participants with a variety of means for storing and presenting their material. Possibilities today include storing productions in videotape form, on CD/DVDs, or within computers, and these can be viewed or transmitted through a variety of media, including video and DVD players, streaming video, and community television. These formats provide the possibility of reaching a wide variety of audiences and using video productions for many effective educational purposes.

Examples of Performances

Case One: Art in the Classroom

An elementary teacher was concerned that the district was cutting funds for art, restricting her possibilities for both teaching art and engaging in art-like activities for student learning processes. She worked with her elementary students, engaging in an extensive exploration of how art was part of their classroom experience. Through extensive dialogue, writing, and drawing, they mapped out the different ways they experienced art and the ways art was incorporated into their learning. By sorting through the information and materials accumulated in this experience, individual students were able to identify important features of their experience of art, and to represent them artistically and in writing. These products were incorporated into a book produced by the class that the teacher intended to have presented to the district superintendent. The class also produced a large mural, to which everyone contributed, using similar materials to represent the class perspective on the issue.

Case Two: Sexual Harassment in School

Following a classroom discussion a teacher met with five of her female middle school students to explore the issue of sexual harassment in their school environment. She facilitated a process of inquiry in which they first spoke of their experiences and perspectives on harassment, then identified key features of that experience. This was extremely helpful in keeping their focus clear and their thoughts manageable. They decided to incorporate boys into their exploration, and extended their understanding of how males are affected by sexually oriented harassment. They wrote a performance piece—"Speaking Out"—based on what they had learned, then made a tryptich—a three-paneled piece—on which the audience could write down their ideas about harassment after the performance. This was performed at the school and later at the university. Three of the students also wrote an article—"Students Against Harassment"—for publication in the monthly school newsletter. By the end of the school year the number of reported incidents of sexual harassment had dropped from four or five each week to one or two every two weeks.

Case Three: A Classroom Opera

Pam Rossi (1997) wrote her doctoral dissertation as a libretto (a script for an opera) based on her work with 31 children in a bilingual grade 1 classroom. The opera, composed by the children and their teachers, describes how the children, in the course of a two-way bilingual program, came to view Spanish, English, and Chinese as among many choices available when creating meaning. By the end of the creation of the opera all the students had achieved some degree of bilingualism. The libretto is comprised of a plot synopsis, a cast of characters, an overture, and a traditional act/scene structure. Pam notes (2000):

The children were participants in a creating, producing, and performing community of inquirers whose interests and ideas informed and contributed to the process and product, making and sharing meaning in a variety of modes. . . . [O]pera is an awakening to multiple literacies through the facilitation of adults who were mutually engaged in a challenging project, shared their expertise and offered the opportunity for guided practice and ongoing critique in different sign systems. [It] is a vehicle for creating synergistic culture with assessment embedded in the process of doing and undergoing, acting and reflecting.

Case Four: Transformative Evaluation

A university professor asked students in his graduate class to reflect on their experience of the class. They interviewed each other in pairs, then identified the key features of their individual experiences collaboratively. Each person used material from his or her own interview to formulate a performance representing the meanings the class had for them. Through poetry, art, song, drama, dialogue, symbolic presentation, and the use of a fractal, each provided a wonderfully descriptive and powerful representation of their experience of learning. The instructor was able to gain deep insights into the types of learning that were important for them, the extent of their feelings of competence, and the features of the class that enhanced their learning. Dialogue following these performances greatly enhanced class members' understanding of their own learning processes, providing ideas they were able to use in their own teaching. It was a dramatic and forceful indication of the way performances might be used to enhance the power and utility of an evaluation process.

Case Five: Quilt-Making: Understanding Teaching History

Ann Claunch (2000), an elementary school teacher, wished to understand how children learned history. Frustrated by textbooks and a curriculum presenting isolated facts along a timeline dissociated from the larger picture of social events, she moved from presenting history inductively, small to large, to a more deductive approach using narratives rather than textbooks in her teaching of history. She used a conceptual plan of a year-long curriculum as a road map to broaden her thinking. Through reflection, dialogue, and review of literature she recorded key features of what she learned as she reformulated her teaching, creating visual representations of her ideas and experience. "Representing my thoughts with images forced me to sort my thinking into concise statements and the artistic representation of understanding paralleled what I had asked elementary students to do in my research." These images were fashioned into a quilt design, providing a unique and informative display of her project.

SUMMARY

Representation: Communicating Research Outcomes

This chapter presents three main formats for presenting the outcomes of research: *written reports, presentations,* and *performances.*

These provide evocative accounts enabling empathetic understanding of participant experience. They should:

- clearly and accurately represent participant *experiences* and *perspectives.*
- be constructed to suit specific *audiences* and *purposes.*

Written reports may take the form of *accounts* and *narratives, biographies,* or *ethnographies* written as individual, joint, or collective accounts. They may take the form of *informal summary reports* for project participants, *formal reports* for professional and administrative audiences, or *academic reports* for research journals.

Presentations may integrate *a variety of media,* including verbal reports, charts, flow charts, maps, concept maps, art, figures, overheads, audiotapes, and video and electronic presentations.

Performances may include *drama, art, poetry, music,* or other formats. These may be stored, displayed, and presented in a variety of visual, aural, and electronic forms.

Procedures for constructing *written reports,* or *scripts,* for presentations and performances include:

- identifying *audience* and *purpose.*
- selecting participant *perspectives.*
- reviewing the *data.*
- selecting *key features* and *elements* of experience from the analyzed data.
- constructing a *framework/outline* using these features.
- *writing* the report/script.
- *reviewing* and *editing* the report/script.
- *member checking* for accuracy and appropriateness.

Taking Action: Passion, Purposes, and Pathways

RESEARCH DESIGN	DATA GATHERING	DATA ANALYSIS	REPORTING	ACTION
INITIATING A STUDY	GATHERING INFORMATION	IDENTIFYING KEY ISSUES AND EXPERIENCES	WRITTEN REPORTS	CREATING SOLUTIONS
Setting the stage	Interviewing	Analyzing key experiences	Formal reports Narrative accounts Joint accounts	Solving Problems
Focusing and framing	Observing		PRESENTATIONS AND PERFORMANCES	Creating syllabi and lesson plans
Participants	Reviewing documents, records, and materials	Categorizing and coding		Curriculum development
Literature review		Incorporating quantitative data	Presentations Drama Poetry	Evaluation
Sources of information	Quantitative data	Enhancing analysis	Song Dance Art	Family and community links
Ethics	Reviewing literature	Using concepts and categories	Video Multimedia	
Validity				School plans

Contents of the Chapter

This chapter describes ways to use action research as the basis for systematic professional practice in classrooms and schools. It describes how to:

- solve specific problems in classrooms.
- formulate and implement planned activities within school settings.

The chapter then describes how action research can be incorporated into processes of *curriculum development*, *syllabus construction*, *lesson planning*, *learning projects*, and *student assessment*.
Two approaches to curriculum planning are presented:

- Traditional curriculum planning
- Transformative curriculum leadership

The chapter also describes how action research may be used for purposes of evaluation and assessment. Three models are presented:

- Responsive evaluation
- Action evaluation: open inquiry
- Action evaluation: audit review

Action research is also presented as a method for developing *professional development* programs, as a means for developing purposeful *links with families* and the community, and as a *strategic planning* process for schools.

INTRODUCTION

The second "action" phase of inquiry applies the knowledge and understandings emerging from research inquiry to immediate practical purposes—resolution of the problem or issue on which research has focused. The next step, therefore, is an important transition, moving from essentially reflective and communicative processes to practical actions that enable researchers to achieve the purposes of their inquiry. It is here where "the rubber meets the road," where people take specific actions to modify teaching practices, develop new classroom procedures, or engage in new learning processes. Action research is used at the school, community, or district level to enhance the effectiveness of such activities as curriculum planning, program evaluation, strategic planning, and policymaking.

The look-think-act cycle signifies the need for research participants to "look" at the new understandings emerging from data analysis; "think" about the implications of that information; and plan appropriate instructional, curriculum, or evaluative "actions" (Figure 7.1).

Action research can be used to discover solutions to discrete problems that emerge in any school or classroom. This does not, however, encompass the full potential of action research as a tool of inquiry. Many of the educator's regular tasks—curriculum development, syllabus construction, evaluation, and so on—may be greatly strengthened by the application of systematic processes of inquiry. Curriculum development, for instance, is not merely a process of constructing the scope of sequence of a fixed set of topics. It is the development and application of an educational philosophy that formulates a set of educational objectives and seeks to systematically and creatively construct teaching/learning processes for accomplishing required outcomes. Curriculae are not arbitrary collections of bodies of information, but complex constructions that often require careful gathering and analysis of a large body of information. Curriculum development can be seen as an ongoing process of action research. Similarly, planning and development of classroom teaching/learning

Figure 7.1
Taking Action

processes, or the evaluation of a program of learning, may be fruitfully engaged as a process of systematic inquiry.

The central feature of such developments is that a "culture of inquiry" emerges in the classroom or school, so that students, teachers, and other stakeholders increase their research skills and capabilities so that they become able to apply them automatically to everyday educational problems. As a "culture of inquiry," action research therefore becomes an integral part of the teaching/learning, curriculum, assessment, and planning processes of classroom and school.

ENGAGING PEOPLE'S PASSIONS

Education is a wonderfully multifaceted activity, requiring carefully structured and skillfully implemented programs of learning to provide for the complex needs of students. Schools are not just credential factories, but institutions whose purpose is to engage the highly sensitive task of extending human learning so that students become well-rounded, healthy individuals, living as productive, moral, and knowledgeable citizens in safe and democratic communities. Well-structured school programs are the manifestation of carefully constructed educational philosophies encompassing the physical, social, cultural, moral, and spiritual dimensions of human life.

Although programs of learning can easily become so highly routinized and ritualized that people lose sight of the underlying purposes of education, there is enormous scope for people to creatively engage educational practices that provide innovative, exciting, and effective approaches to learning. It is possible to attain any set of educational objectives in a variety of ways—to take a seemingly dull set of learning content areas or procedures and invest them with highly productive life and energy.

These kinds of outcome are increased dramatically when teachers, students, and/or families participate in the development of educational plans and activities. The success of a research and learning project rests as much on the development of high levels of commitment and ownership as on the skilful enactment of techniques of inquiry (see "Index of Engagement," Chapter 3). When people are truly invested in activities enabling them to take action on an issue about which they are concerned, they often do so with *passion*, taking on feelings of ownership that enhance their capacity and willingness to invest themselves in the project at hand.

When taking action, we thus need to continue engaging the working principles of action research presented in Chapter 2:

- **Relationships:** Maintaining positive working relationships with all stakeholders.
- **Communication:** Informing stakeholders of ongoing activities.
- **Participation:** Providing opportunities for stakeholders to engage in worthwhile activities.
- **Inclusion:** Including all stakeholders and all relevant issues.

A key feature of this process is the need to ensure that the primary stakeholders—those principally affected by the issue—are centrally involved in the process. If student apathy is an issue, then apathetic students need to be involved centrally in the process. Where teachers and/or administrators are concerned about the lack of involvement of parents, then it is

As a teacher, I am aware that the best classes I have taught are imbued with this sense of passion. In recent years I have taught many courses by formulating and enacting the class syllabus in conjunction with class members, consulting with them about the aims of the class (i.e., what they wished to acquire through participation), the course content, learning processes, and evaluation procedures. I review class learning processes regularly, seeking to ensure that the content of the class is meaningful and applicable to their everyday professional and/or private lives. With few exceptions this process has produced highly successful classes, with participants evincing high levels of commitment and demonstrating high levels of skill and understanding. In a number of cases the relationships nurtured through these participatory processes have endured, with class participants continuing to meet, sometimes over a period of years, to share and explore features of what has become a life-long process of learning (Stringer and colleagues, 1997).

necessary to find ways to include uninvolved parents in the research process. The relationships that emerge provide the basis for extended and ongoing actions having the potential to transform people's attitudes and to energize the whole context in which they live and work. As we move from analysis to action, therefore, plans made for the ongoing work of school and classroom will be greatly enhanced by the inclusion of stakeholders in the process. From little things, big things grow.

SOLVING PROBLEMS: ACTION PLANNING IN CLASSROOMS AND SCHOOLS

Sometimes solutions to the research problem emerge spontaneously, with people seeing clearly what steps they need to take to work toward resolution of the issue they have studied. Often, however, careful planning is required to ensure successful resolution of the problem investigated. Researchers need to analyze the results of the first phases of the research process to identify the particular features of the situation affecting the problem, and to formulate effective strategies for its resolution.

The resolution of problems related to student learning is particularly significant in this era of high-stakes testing. The imperative to increase test scores, especially in the basic skills areas, signals the need for systematic action to accomplish this goal. One of the fallacies generated in this ethos is that the application of a specific teaching/learning routine will provide the means for raising test scores, a pathway unlikely to make significant differences in student performance outcomes. Where groups of students are performing poorly, the causes are usually deeply rooted in the complex interactions between classroom, school, family, and community life. To seriously address the issue of poor classroom performance requires more than a superficial search for a "silver bullet" instructional technique. Systematic processes of investigation that include the students and their families are likely, over time, to produce more viable and effective learning outcomes.

Carefully devised plans therefore provide the means for teachers and other stakeholders to accomplish effective solutions to the problems that confront them in their classrooms.

The following section delineates a simple planning process that will provide clear guidance for this purpose.

Setting Priorities: Establishing an Action Agenda

Having engaged in data collection and analysis, research participants need to step back a few paces to scrutinize the information they have acquired. They will review information contained in reports, presentations, or performances and identify key issues to be addressed. From these they will construct a set of agendas upon which they will take action.

Research participants will:

- Review the research *focus, question,* and *objectives.*
- Review the framework of *issues, key features,* and *elements* emerging from data analysis.
- From these, select *agendas* requiring action.
- *Prioritize* the issues, distinguishing those to be subject to immediate action from those that may be handled in the medium or long term.

As part of the BSIC evaluation, the school staff reviewed the report based on the framework of concepts and issues emerging from investigation:

Student Experiences
Attention from Teachers
Improved Grades
Freedom and Diversity
Teacher Perspectives
Student Achievement
Relationships with Students
Inquiry Curriculum
Learning Materials
Administration
Demands and Resources
Values and Behavior
Space

After discussing all of the issues contained in the report, they decided that their priorities for action would focus on curriculum development, learning materials, professional development staff orientations, and organizational planning. This action agenda defined areas in which staff would work to improve the effectiveness of the school.

Creating Pathways: Constructing an Action Plan

Carefully formulated plans enable research participants to envision the concrete steps needed to accomplish a desired outcome. Participants devise action plans for each issue identified as a priority in the action agenda. Each plan will:

- Review the *problem, research question,* and *research objectives.*
- Review the analyzed data to identify significant *issues* and *features.*

- From those issues and features, select items requiring attention.
- List items in order of priority to formulate an *action agenda*.
- Distinguish those items requiring immediate action from those requiring medium- or long-term attention.
- For each agenda, devise an action plan that includes:
  - a statement of overall purpose (*why*).
  - a set of *objectives* to be attained (*what*).
  - a sequence of *tasks* and *steps* for each objective.
  - the *people* responsible for each task and activity (*who*).
  - the *place* where the tasks will be done (*where*).
  - the *time* when tasks should commence and be completed (*when*).
- Make arrangements to monitor and support people as they enact their tasks.

Some of my colleagues were involved in a project focusing on "increased juvenile crime." Participants restated the issue as a goal: "To decrease juvenile crime." Reviewing the analysis from previous phases of research revealed objectives related to this goal. In a context where both parents were often engaged in the workforce, factors related to increased juvenile crime had included "lack of youth leisure activities," "poor school attendance," and "lack of after-school programs." These were restated as three objectives: To develop youth leisure activities, to improve youth school attendance, and to organize afterschool programs. Teams of relevant stakeholders developed a plan for each issue and brought them to a combined planning session for the discussion, modification, and endorsement of all stakeholders. In this case, each planning group included a member from each of the primary stakeholding groups. The issue of "poor school attendance," for instance, had a team that included teachers, young people, school administrators, and parents.

A simple six-question framework—why, what, how, who, when, and where—provides a useful basis for systematic planning. Using the example just provided as the basis, it would look like this:

- **Why:** State the overall purpose of these activities—for example, to reduce juvenile crime. This *purpose* or *goal* statement describes the ultimate end point of the project.
- **What:** State what actions are to be taken in the form of a set of *objectives*—for example, to organize an afterschool program for teenagers or to develop a youth center.
- **How:** Define a sequence of *tasks* and *steps* for each objective.
- **Who:** List the *people* responsible for each task and activity.
- **Where:** State the *place* where the tasks will be done—at a school, a community center, a youth club, people's homes, and so on.
- **When:** State the *time* when work on each task should commence and when it should be completed.

PURPOSE (Why): What are we trying to achieve?							
OBJECTIVE What	TASKS How	PERSON(S) Who	START When	FINISH	LOCATION Where	RESOURCES	FUNDS

1. Establish a
youth center
	a. Obtain
	   permission
	b. Repair
	   and renovate
	c. Plan
	   organization
		Ms. Jones
		Lions Club
		Students
		Volunteers
			6.3.02	12.6.02	Disused
					church
						Paint
						Timber
						Tools
							$1,500
							School disctict
							Town council
							Goverment grant

2. Establish
after-school
program
	a. Establish an
	   art program
	b. Establish a
	   sports program
	c. Establish
	   tutoring
	   program
		Mr. Whipple
		Jenny
		Bruce
		Jose
		Venus
			1.5.02	4.4.02	Youth center	Art materials
						Sports equipment
							$350
							School district
							Fees

Figure 7.2
Planning Chart

A planning chart may be used to clearly articulate all facets of the work (see Figure 7.2). The chart clearly defines all dimensions of the project and allows people to see their places in the broader scheme of things. It also identifies the resources required to complete the tasks and identifies the source of funds. It provides a concrete vision of the active community of which participants are a part, and enables them to check on their progress as they work through the various stages of the project together.

Reviewing the Plan

Once details have been entered on the chart, participants can review the plan to check and clarify each person's responsibilities, the sequence of activities, and materials and resources required for each task:

- Have all needed materials and/or equipment been identified? Who will obtain them? Where from? When?
- Are funds needed? Where will they come from? Who will organize them? When?
- Do people have adequate time to accomplish their tasks?
- Should other people be involved? For what tasks? Who will ask them? How will they become part of the process? Who will describe the project to them? How can they become part of our community?

Each of these elements is included in the review of the plan, with objectives, tasks, and activities carefully defined and assigned. Larger or more complex issues may require the monitoring of an extensive array of activities, but smaller projects usually need only limited time and resources for planning.

A recent study by a classroom teacher investigated why children were not completing assigned reading for homework. The teacher assumed the children didn't like reading, which accounted for noncompletion of homework, a perception reinforced by the fanciful excuses students provided for their noncompliance. A systematic investigation, however, revealed significant degrees of interest in reading, but only in certain circumstances and for certain types of reading. Having completed her data gathering and analysis, she reviewed the basis for her study:

- **Research problem:** Students are failing to complete reading assignments.
- **Research question:** Why are students failing to complete reading assignments?
- **Research objective:** To find ways of improving student engagement in reading.

She then reviewed her data analysis, identifying the most significant ideas and issues emerging from her observations of student behavior and student accounts of their experience. These included:

- Disinterest in silent reading activities
- High levels of interest in group reading activities
- High levels of interest in oral reading activities

As a result of this investigation the teacher was able to define an action agenda and to incorporate a new plan for reading into her class syllabus. She placed more emphasis on oral reading and group reading activities in class, and placed less reliance on individual silent reading, in class or at home.

Sometimes planning procedures become stalled because people focus on emerging difficulties. Statements such as "What about. . .," "Yes, but we can't do this because . . .," "The principal won't allow . . .," "Parents can't . . .," "Students aren't capable of . . .," "We haven't the time to . . .," "The funds aren't available to . . .," and so on can stall the process. If these statements are left unanswered, people will soon become de-energized and an air of futility will arise.

Each of these concerns needs to be formally acknowledged, clearly recorded, and then incorporated into the planning process. It is essential that these issues be seen as problems to be solved rather than reasons not to take action. Most such statements are easily resolved, but sometimes they need careful and creative thinking to enable effective action to continue. Each needs to be reformulated from a *problem* to a statement of an *objective or task*, which is entered into the action plan. The problem "Funds aren't available," for instance, might be formulated as an objective "To seek funds from . . . ," or "To search for sources of funding for . . . from . . .." This objective would be extrapolated through *tasks and activities*, a *person* responsible for the tasks, and a *timeline* for beginning and completing the tasks.

Some of the example statements just noted point to the need to include other stakeholders in the process. If the principal and students, for instance, are included in the process, then their perspectives and agendas can be accommodated immediately. If not, then work needs to be done to ensure their perspectives and agendas are included in the plan, so that "What the principal will/can allow" becomes part of the creative formulation of the plan of action.

Supervision: Supporting and Monitoring Progress

It is important that someone supervises the implementation of the plan. A designated person will confirm that people are able to carry out their tasks in the time allocated, and assist them to work through minor problems. The person supervising will communicate with participants regularly, using informal conversations in staff rooms or other common meeting places, or by phone messages or email. In monitoring progress the supervising person should also see himself or herself as offering personal support, especially for people working in difficult situations or carrying out difficult or complex tasks. Often, in these situations, supervisors merely need to be a "listening ear," providing a means for participants to debrief, vent where necessary, or review the work they are doing.

Progress should also be monitored at meetings of participants. Meetings should be regular enough to ensure people remain committed to the project and to each other. Meetings should provide opportunities for people to report on their activities, to review the overall plan, to make any modifications or changes in objectives and tasks, and to celebrate successes.

CLASSROOM TEACHING AND LEARNING

Action research may be applied to a wide range of teaching/learning processes, including the construction of a class syllabus, lesson planning, and student assessment. Essentially it enables teachers to engage inquiry learning as a tool for instruction, providing rich possibilities for engaging students in learning processes that greatly enliven and enrich their classroom lives. The look-think-act process applied to lesson planning enables teachers to systematically acquire and analyze information that will enable them to construct highly effective programs of learning. It provides opportunities to inquire systematically into the meanings embedded in state or district curriculum standards, extending understanding of the broader purposes and possibilities for student learning.

Engaging students in the development of class syllabi may appear time-consuming, but the deeper understandings of the purposes, the curriculum, and the increased levels of ownership students acquire are likely to lead to more meaningful and effective learning. Where students can "make sense" of the purposes and processes of the curriculum—their own learning—they are apt to engage with interest and energy.

Constructing Programs of Learning: Creating a Syllabus

As an action research process, syllabus construction commences with a review and analysis of a mandated curriculum. Research questions investigate features of the curriculum and lead to the development of a program of learning:

- **Purpose:** What do (we) students need to accomplish? What is the goal or purpose to be achieved?
- **Objectives:** What would (we) students need to do to achieve this goal/purpose?

GOAL/PURPOSE: Statement of broad goal or purpose to be achieved.				
OBJECTIVES	LEARNING PROCESSES	CONTENT	LEARNING OUTCOMES	LEARNING RESOURCES

Figure 7.3
Syllabus Framework

- **Content:** What knowledge and/or skills would (we) students need to learn in order to accomplish this goal/purpose?
- **Learning Processes:** How would (we) students learn these sets of skills and knowledge?
- **Learning Outcomes:** How would (we) students demonstrate the skills or knowledge acquired? How can (we) students apply these skills and knowledge to demonstrate accomplishment of stated goals/purposes?
- **Resources:** What resources or materials are needed?
- **Organization:** How can answers to these questions be organized into a coherent program of learning?

These questions provide the basis for exploration, description, clarification, and construction of sections of the syllabus that may be recorded within a syllabus framework, as shown in Figure 7.3.

The first time I tried a truly participatory approach to construction of a syllabus was in a research class I taught at Texas A&M University in the spring semester of 1993. In the first class session I asked students, "What would you like to learn? And how would you like to learn it? I'd like you to help me formulate a syllabus for the course." My intent was to model a community-based approach to course-planning processes. I wished to demonstrate how we could determine objectives for the class appropriate to their academic and professional needs, that the content and strategies suited those objectives, and that these could be encompassed within course requirements that their schedules could accommodate.

The silence that followed was underlined by the emotions reflected in the eyes of the class members, the worry lines that furrowed their brows and wrinkled their eyes. Some kept very still. Others stirred restlessly, moving cautiously in their seats and quietly shuffling their feet under the desks.

Eventually someone provided a suggestion. "I would like to learn how to do observations in the real world."

"Real-world observations," I wrote on the board.

"How to do ethnographic studies," a thick Texan drawl suggested.

"Applying research across the community," came another response.

"As the list emerged, a spark of interest was ignited that I continued to fan with affirmative comments. As we reviewed the completed list, I commented on the variety of interests and agendas and indicated that these items would provide the basis for the syllabus. I then asked for suggestions about how the syllabus could be organized, what types of learning activities might be relevant, what projects might be appropriate to provide them with opportunities to practice what was learned, how they might evaluate those projects, and so on.

As we explored these issues some people became excited as the range of possibilities emerged—presentations, debates, practice sessions, "fish bowls," group projects, discussions, ethnographic studies, journals, and so on. For many, however, the levels of discomfort became increasingly evident and some started to ask, at first obliquely, then more pointedly, when they were to get a class syllabus, when they would know the class requirements, and the dates on which assignments and projects would be due.

By the end of class the energy levels, both positive and negative, were high, some students talking excitedly about the possibilities that were emerging while others huddled in small groups exchanging obviously worried comments. Though I had provided a syllabus labeled "preliminary," the content and requirements of the class were described in only the very broadest of terms. By the end of the class more detail of content had been negotiated, but "course requirements" had not been specified. The participants' body language spoke to me more clearly than their voices. "What are we going to do?" their worried frowns asked. "I don't know where I'm going, or when I will have to do my assigned work. How can I prepare a study schedule? How will I fit my class work in with my work requirements?" Some were unperturbed and their voices expressed excitement and interest, while others, although intrigued by the process and interested in the content of the course that had emerged, exhibited responses that ranged through consternation, concern, annoyance, doubt, disquiet, and anxiety.

By the next class I had prepared a more detailed "supplementary" syllabus, written on chart paper and taped to the board, and asked for comments and suggestions, explaining that I had crafted it, as far as possible, to fit the inputs they had provided the previous week. I sought their approval of the syllabus I had planned, and asked whether they had additions or amendments to suggest. There was some discussion and debate about the projects I had assigned and we were able to make a number of modifications and amendments, including the times when work would be due, so that by the end of the first hour the syllabus had been ratified by all members of the class. Once again, the range of emotions present in the class was evident in the participants' responses, as excitement and energy competed with relief as the predominant emotions.

From the energy that emerged from the interest, excitement, doubt, and disquiet of those students, I was able to fashion an ongoing process of inquiry and discovery that I marked as one of the most exciting I have taught in my teaching career. Such was the feeling of community generated by this process that members continued to meet on a regular basis, staging an annual retreat where they share ideas and reflect on their professional experiences.

The experience has changed my approach to teaching dramatically. I rarely engage students, even small children, without asking them to assist me in constructing their learning process. Teaching, for me, has become a continuing process of inquiry and discovery that continues to enhance my educational life.

Lesson Plans

In general terms, the syllabus framework presented in Figure 7.3 provides the basis for planning lessons. Students may work with the teacher, within groups, or individually to construct a plan for a learning program. By working through iterations of the look-think-act process they may identify:

- **Goals/Purposes**—the broad purpose to be achieved in the lesson.
- **Objectives**—the objectives through which this broader purpose might be achieved.
- **Learning processes**—the specific learning activities in which they will engage to accomplish each of these objectives.
- **Content**—the particular topics, concepts, or issues that comprise the content of the lesson.
- **Resources**—books and materials required in the process.
- **Outcomes**—how they will demonstrate they have accomplished learning objectives.

All of these may be associated with state or district curriculum guidelines and standards.

Lessons may also be formulated using problem-based inquiry learning processes. Lessons emerge by focusing on an issue, problem, theme, or topic, then use action research processes—look-think-act—to develop a solution to the problem and/or extend children's existing stock of knowledge. The teacher should facilitate the process by asking students:

- what they already know about the topic, issue, or problem.
- what they would like or need to know.
- how they can learn about identified issues or topics.
- what resources they will need.
- how they can demonstrate their competence or a proposed solution.

Exploration of any topic often elicits considerable information from children, to which the teacher contributes by assisting them to build order and coherence into the emerging body of knowledge. Information may be written on the whiteboard as it emerges, then organized appropriately (a quick form of data analysis) and complemented by reinforcing activities that assist the children to acquire a deeper understanding of the topic. The teacher may provide additional information from her or his own stock of knowledge to round out the lesson.

Although inquiry learning may not be suitable for all lessons, it provides the basis for rich and active alternatives to standard information-transmission approaches to instruction. It is surprising how much information may be acquired from a classroom of even young children who are apt to become enthusiastic and engaged as they construct a body of knowledge that they themselves generate.

Outcomes-Based Learning Projects

Outcomes-based learning projects can derive from many sources, including prescribed curriculae; special events occurring in neighborhood, town, or country; or a topic of interest arising in the children's experience. The purpose of a learning project is to provide opportunities for children to explore an issue or topic and to present the outcomes of that learning in multiple ways. Standards and outcomes from literacy, mathematics, social studies, and science curricula may be incorporated in the one project, providing students with integrated and effective learning experiences. Learning projects may incorporate many sources of information (data gathering), including library research, community visits, interviewing and observing, materials and artifacts, and so on. By selecting and organizing relevant information (data analysis), children may formulate a coherent body of knowledge related to the desired outcomes. This body of knowledge may be presented in multiple forms—for example, written reports, presentations, and performances (see Chapter 6). All have the potential to enrich students' educational experiences and to generate high levels of motivation and competence.

Proponents of the Reggio Emilia approach to learning provide many useful examples of the ways research can productively be incorporated into children's learning (Edwards, Gandini, & Forman, 1998). They suggest that including students, parents, and other adults from the neighborhood or community, even in the planning stages, can enhance learning projects. This, they suggest, not only provides rich resources for child learning, but also enables adults to extend their understanding about schools and education.

The Foxfire approach to learning also provides rich possibilities at the high school level (Wiggington, 1985). Students collect folklore in their communities by interviewing people in the community about what they do or know, sometimes also observing them at work on a chore or craft, and in some instances taking photographs. Students therefore gather an extensive body of local knowledge or historical information that is then incorporated into a magazine. This "cultural journalism" is accomplished through action research routines, providing rich possibilities for engaging multiple learning experiences and accomplishing high levels of learning across the curriculum. An action research process applied to inquiry learning requires students to:

- Identify a focus, topic of interest, or problem.
- Gather relevant information through interviewing, observing, and collecting artifacts, photographs, or recordings, or engaging in library research.
- Analyze the data to identify key elements of information.
- Organize those elements into a structured framework of ideas.
- Present the outcomes of their research in multiple formats—reports, art, music, dance, demonstration, drama, and so on.

I once worked with a year 3 class in Bryan, Texas, on the topic of "Australia," which was part of their social studies syllabus. I was amazed at the depth and extent of information these eight- to nine-year-old children were able to provide. They spoke, of course, about the common animals—kangaroos, koalas, and so on—that are part of the international Australian image, but then went on to give me extensive details of the life of the wombat, the platypus, and other less well known animals. The stock of knowledge in that class was extensive, ranging from information about the climate in various parts of Australia, the direction of rotation of cyclones (called hurricanes in the United States), the cities in Australia, through quite detailed information about other features of Australian life. Their questions were insightful, enabling me to complement the information they had provided. I was able to use pictures and other materials I had prepared as they became relevant. All of the children in the class were interested, excited, and engaged throughout the lesson. Participatory, constructivist processes, I have discovered, are powerful tools for learning.

Assessment of Student Learning

Assessment is an integral part of lesson and curriculum planning and is the means by which we know what students have learned. As a process of action inquiry, assessment therefore can be built into the construction of a syllabus or curriculum that links the statement of objectives, learning processes, and content with outcome assessment. Student learning processes are greatly enhanced when they participate in deciding how they may demonstrate their competence in a body of knowledge or the performance of skills. Student learning may be demonstrated (and reported) in a variety of ways. Numerically graded written tests provide the most commonly used procedure, but presentations, performances, portfolios, and projects also provide the means for students to demonstrate competence. These methods are especially useful ways of enabling students to demonstrate complex learning objectives not easily embedded in written tests.

As Astin et al. (1996) indicate:

- Assessment is not an end in itself but a vehicle for educational improvement that enacts a vision of the kinds of learning we most value for students.
- Learning is a complex process that entails not only what students know, but what they can do with what they know.
- Assessment works best when the programs it seeks to improve have clear, explicitly stated purposes and goals. It entails comparing educational performance with educational purposes and expectations.
- Assessment requires attention to outcomes but also and equally to the experiences that lead to those outcomes. Where students "end up" matters greatly.
- Assessment works best when it is ongoing, not episodic. Though isolated, "one-shot" assessment can be better than none, improvement is best fostered when assessment entails a linked series of activities undertaken over time.

An action research inquiry process provides the means to engage students in more comprehensive and exploratory processes of assessment, enabling them to systematically *evaluate* the nature and extent of their learning. This type of assessment provides opportunities for them to make meaningful connections between classroom activities and learning objectives, and their own learning processes.

Assessment as a cyclical process of inquiry involves:

- reviewing learning objectives and standards.
- describing or demonstrating the types and/or levels of skills and knowledge acquired by learners.
- judging the adequacy of learning in relation to the objectives and standards.
- formulating next steps in learning or remediating weaknesses in learning.

Teachers work with students to develop an evaluation framework to provide a clear process and set of criteria for judging the adequacy or level of learning. Although this may suggest mountains of "grading" for teachers, the reverse is actually the case, since it is possible to incorporate self-assessment, peer assessment, online grading, and a variety of other assessment tools and procedures into the process. The teacher, in other words, is not the only person who may assess student learning, though he or she bears overall responsibility for checking the veracity and authenticity of the results obtained.

Traditional classroom assessment procedures often provide a numerical estimate of the *degree* or *extent* of student learning. This information is also sometimes used to *rank* students to show how well they have performed compared with their peers. Assessment procedures also may be used *diagnostically* to indicate points of weaknesses in student learning.

CURRICULUM DEVELOPMENT

Action research provides a process for developing a rich, engaging curriculum relevant to the lives and purposes of students, engaging their interests and abilities, and serving the broad human needs of community, society, and the planet. Creative construction of curricula or syllabi provides the means whereby the needs, perspectives, and/or interests of diverse stakeholders can be incorporated into vital, creative, effective programs of learning.

Participatory curriculum development is not a new idea, emerging in the early twentieth century through the ideas of John Dewey (1930, 1916/1966). As Lois Christensen reminds us (1997, p. 65), John Dewey thought that "Learning should be approached in an integrated and participatory fashion to enable learners to construct and continually reconstruct meaning from authentic experiences." In exploring the processes of curriculum planning, Peter Oliva (2001) notes, "To varying degrees, the democratic process is accepted more and more in school systems across the [US]. Nowhere is its presence more clearly felt than in the participatory procedures that seek to involve the major constituencies of the school in curriculum development. . . . Administrators and their staffs, teachers, students and the citizens of the community."

Participatory action research provides an authentic context in which teachers, learners, and other stakeholders develop a shared culture of learning through the collaborative development of common meanings and purposes. Where educational professionals engage in curriculum development without engaging other constituencies or stakeholders, they run a grave risk of incorporating agendas derived from organizational pressures or their own social and cultural perspectives into the curriculum. In doing so they are likely to construct curricula deeply imbued with values and ideals that have little meaning or are contrary to the social and cultural context of parents and students. In such circumstances teachers are likely to face cohorts of disinterested and sometimes antagonistic students, and will search to find ways of coaxing or making them engage the content of the curriculum. While the speedy formulation of a curriculum may seem pragmatic and efficient, the outcome of such a process is likely to be a lack of ownership of and engagement in the curriculum by significant segments of a school population.

As a young teacher I taught a state-prescribed curriculum to children in an Aboriginal community. Having only recently emerged from the desert into contact with the modern world, people in the community still lived a lifestyle of the hunter-gatherer. Living in closely bonded and carefully interrelated family groups, they enacted an economic life based on sharing, and a rich spiritual tradition manifested through song, dance, and ritual. From this context the children came to school to confront a curriculum derived from the ethos of a materialistic, capitalistic, European, suburban society.

I now look back in shame at the inadequate and possibly destructive learning processes in which I engaged those children. Teaching that "Captain Cook, the English navigator, discovered Australia," and the delights of a "nutritious, balanced meal comprising the five major food groups," the curriculum failed to even attempt to incorporate the difficult but necessary task of assisting them to deal with the changes that were necessarily part of their experience as their community came to grips with the "modern" and "civilized" world.

I fear that similar processes still operate, not only in these contexts, but also in many similar contexts where the social and cultural experience of communities and students diverges significantly from those who operate the school systems. This is certainly true of many U.S. schools in which I have worked, where many African American and Hispanic students confront a curriculum with little relevance to the ongoing realities of their social and cultural lives.

Two approaches to curriculum development are presented next. The first—curriculum planning—summarizes a traditional approach to curriculum construction based on a model developed by Tyler (1949) and modified by Oliva (2001). The second approach—transformative curriculum leadership (Henderson, Hawthorne, & Stollenwerk (2000)—presents a more collaborative, constructivist approach to curriculum development.

Curriculum Planning

The complex task of curriculum planning may be engaged as an action research process, with participants investigating inputs from diverse sources (data gathering), distilling and selecting desired content and outcomes from that large body of information (data analysis), and formulating these key features and elements into a coherent curriculum framework (action).

A well-developed curriculum provides the blueprint for learning that incorporates a wide array of purposes or goals, including those derived from descriptions of human, national, social, and individual needs, and inputs from diverse sources—the academic disciplines, the human and behavioral sciences, and the community. A curriculum plan provides the means to envisage how these diverse agendas might be incorporated into programs of classroom learning at all levels of a school system.

Oliva (2001) presents a widely used model, based on a curriculum framework initially developed by Ralph Tyler (1949), that incorporates the following elements:

- **Needs analysis:** Statement of *personal needs* of the learner and *social needs* of the community/state/nation.
- **Goals and objectives:** Broad *goals* derived from those needs, together with *specific objectives* to be attained by learners, filtered through a screen of philosophical assumptions.
- **Learning processes:** What *learning activities* will enable learners to accomplish the objectives?
- **Content:** What *subject matter* will be associated with those learning activities?
- **Assessment/outcomes:** How will learners *demonstrate* they have accomplished the learning objectives?
- **Evaluation:** To what extent does the program of learning enable learners to *accomplish purposes/goals*? Do they fulfill the *personal needs* of learners and *social goals* of the community?

Action research engages relevant stakeholders in formulating each of these stages of production. Stakeholders describe and analyze student needs—personal needs, future employment needs, social needs, and so on—that will provide for the development of a healthy, harmonious citizenry. A statement of needs provides the basis for a set of broad goals and more specific objectives describing how these goals are to be attained. Learning processes and curriculum content comprised of specific skills and knowledge are then incorporated into a well-organized program of learning.

Transformative Curriculum Leadership

Henderson, Hawthorne, and Stollenwerk (2000) provide an interesting alternative to the standard curriculum processes just described. Their framework contains many of the elements of the standard model, but is much less mechanistic, taking into account the human dynamics that are an integral part of the curriculum. Their process is directly linked to action research as a process of inquiry incorporating multiple stakeholders. Speaking of the evaluation component of the curriculum, they suggest:

> Transformative evaluation assesses both the quality of school life and the quality of student learning to give students information about their own learning and ability to create meanings. This complex process must allow for multiple personal expressions. Thus, while standardized tests are part of transformative assessment, they do not dominate it. More important is a spirit of inquiry and critical analysis that takes the form of action research.

Thus teacher researchers provide "curriculum leadership," guiding others to construct a curriculum rather than constructing it themselves. Henderson et al. describe five fundamental principles for enacting a transformative curriculum leadership (the 5 C's), requiring participants to be:

- Creative
- Caring

- Critical
- Collaborative
- Committed

Working within these guiding principles, a transformative curriculum process moves through four phases: deliberating, building a vision, assessing student learning, and planning a classroom curriculum. Each of these may be thought of as a cycle of the action research process.

Deliberating about a school-based curriculum Stakeholders, including teachers, administrators, students, and others, have an active voice in reviewing, critiquing, and revising standards. They build a curriculum design platform containing the goals, criteria, assumptions, and principles by:

- describing and analyzing the current curriculum, as currently expressed in plans, policies, and materials and as experienced by students in classrooms.
- sharing personal stories of meaningful and exciting curriculum experiences, and reflecting on beliefs and values related to living in a democratic society.
- analyzing projections about national and regional economic, ethical, cultural, political, technical, and interpersonal futures.
- examining state and national standards, outstanding curriculum plans developed by others, and alternative forms of student assessment.

Building a vision of the curriculum Using the curriculum design platform as a guide, stakeholders construct an overall vision or structure for a curriculum. They:

- Identify problems, issues, and themes to focus student engagement.
- Describe the content: big ideas, perceptions, values, skills, and ways of knowing.
- Identify key forms of student inquiry.
- Provide supportive materials and equipment.

Again the process is participatory, drawing together teachers, students, and community members to visualize imaginative, exciting, and appropriate learning events in which students are actively engaged and highly interested.

Assessing student learning Assessment procedures are designed to determine what students have learned and gain insight about how students can use what they know. Students become active agents in their own learning and assessment processes. In this phase participants identify:

- what students have learned.
- how students can use their learning.
- how they are becoming active agents in their own learning.
- information about the quality of student learning.
- information about the quality of school life.

Assessment may be accomplished through:

- Standardized tests that are used for assessment processes, but that don't dominate assessment

- Performance assessments that test a student's ability to apply knowledge and skills
- Portfolio assessments that use a variety of materials to demonstrate the nature and extent of learning

Planning the curriculum in the classroom In this phase, teachers apply the curriculum in their classroom—in conjunction with students and community members, where appropriate—by creating:

- Specific objectives
- Learning activities
- Materials
- Learning contexts
- Assessment procedures

At all stages of curriculum development, therefore, stakeholders engage in participatory processes of inquiry through which they build shared understandings and commitments to the curriculum.

EVALUATION: ASSESSING THE VALUE AND QUALITY OF EDUCATIONAL PROGRAMS AND SERVICES

This section presents three models of evaluation concomitant with participatory action research—*responsive evaluation* (Guba & Lincoln, 1989), and two orientations to action evaluation: *open inquiry evaluation* and *audit review evaluation* (Wadsworth, 1997). Readers engaged in the evaluation of large and complex projects would do well to consult these sources in detail.

The forms of evaluation presented here are *formative* (Scriven, 1981a), insofar as they focus on the ongoing processes of teaching and learning, rather than describing or measuring learning outcomes, which is a *summative* (Scriven, 1981b) process of evaluation. Formative evaluation, in other words, speaks to a broader set of criteria, attempting to understand the more complex processes through which learning takes place and the types and qualities of learning that are occurring, rather than solely measuring or describing student performance on a specific set of learning outcomes.

Responsive Evaluation

Responsive evaluation is clearly aligned with the underlying principles of participatory action research revealed in this book. It has an action orientation that defines a course to be followed, and requires evaluators to interact with people in ways respecting their dignity, integrity, and privacy.

> Responsive evaluation . . . . signal[s] the idea that all stakeholders put at risk by an evaluation have the right to place their claims, concerns, and issues on the table for consideration (response), irrespective of the value system to which they adhere. It was created as the antithesis of preordinate evaluation, which assumes that the evaluator and client together possess sufficient information and legitimation to design and implement an evaluation completely, without the need to consult other parties. (Guba & Lincoln, 1989)

These features make it an especially pertinent tool in action research, since the processes of evaluation are not only responsive to participant stakeholders' views and perspectives, but also become the basis for assessing action to be taken. The principal audiences of an evaluation are stakeholders, who Guba and Lincoln (1989) define as:

- those put at risk by the evaluation.
- agents who contribute to the development of the evaluand (the "instrument of evaluation).
- putative beneficiaries who are expected to profit from the evaluation.
- secondary beneficiaries (e.g., parents of students).
- victims—those injured or deprived by the implementation of the evaluand.

Guba and Lincoln speak of the need to provide stakeholders with insights about the roles they might play and questions they might ask, as well as their right to become full partners in the evaluation.

The flow of responsive evaluation Since action research processes incorporate participatory processes, much of the following activity has already been accomplished by participants. Sometimes, however, an external evaluator is a required part of funding. Where an evaluation is set up separately, however, evaluation facilitators will move through the following steps:

- **Contracting:** Initiating contract with client/sponsor.
- **Organizing:** Selecting/training a team of evaluators and making logistical arrangements.
- **Identifying stakeholders:** Identifying agents, beneficiaries, and victims, and formalizing "conditions" agreements.
- **Developing within-group joint constructions:** Establishing hermeneutic circles (focus groups) and shaping emerging joint constructions.
- **Enlarging joint stakeholder constructions:** Incorporating new information from documents, interviews, and evaluator constructions.
- **Sorting out resolved claims, concerns, and issues:** Identifying and resolving claims, concerns, and issues.
- **Prioritizing unresolved items:** Submitting items to prioritization.
- **Collecting information/adding sophistication:** Collecting further information and utilizing further hermeneutic circles to add sophistication to stakeholder constructions.
- **Preparing an agenda for negotiation:** Defining and elucidating unresolved items and testing the agenda.
- **Carrying out the negotiation:** Selecting a "representative" circle from all stakeholding groups, shaping the joint construction and determining action.
- **Reporting:** Providing reports on the previous activities to stakeholding groups.

Guba and Lincoln's responsive evaluation process is very similar to processes involved in action research, though the terminology they use is somewhat different. Hermeneutic circles, for instance, are comprised of groups of stakeholders, and are designed to enable participants to "make meaning" together, in similar fashion to those described for focus groups in previous chapters. Nevertheless, they provide a sophisticated process for enabling stakeholders to work together to assess the ongoing progress, accomplishments, and deficiencies of their work. Responsive evaluation provides the basis for evaluating school programs and services, and may be incorporated into the evaluation phase of a strategic planning process.

Action Evaluation: Everyday Evaluation on the Run

Yoland Wadsworth (1997) presents two approaches to action evaluation—open inquiry evaluation and audit review evaluation. Like action research, action evaluation works through reiterative processes of inquiry that enable participants to collaboratively explore their work, gaining greater insight into their activities and identifying ways to solve problems or enhance the outcomes they seek. Participants build or extend their common understandings of the worth of their activities, and test the value of what they are achieving:

- **Reflection:** Observing own actions in the world and reflecting on what is being experienced.
- **Design:** "Naming the problem" and systematically answering questions that arise:
  - Who or what is to be researched?
  - Who are to be the researchers?
  - Who is it for? Whose lives will be improved (the critical reference group for whom services are provided)?
  - Who provides services, funds, and so on for the critical reference group (primary stakeholding group)?
- **Fieldwork:** All relevant parties reach an effective understanding of what different people think, value, and what things mean to them.
- **Analysis and conclusions:** Identifying themes, trends, or understandings to develop conclusions, explanations, and theories.
- **Feedback:** Checking with the researched or evaluated and the critical reference group that we "got it right" and that findings are understandable, plausible, or convincing.
- **Planning:** Realistic, practical, and achievable "recommendations" for changed and improved practices are prioritized, planned, and put into practice.

Open inquiry evaluation An open inquiry approach to evaluation, through its focus on identifying and solving problems, increases the chances of improving educational programs and services. It enables innovative, creative, and dynamic ideas and perspectives to emerge and provides participants with a sense of enthusiasm.

Open inquiry evaluation examines existing practices in the following ways:

- **Starting with general questions** How are we doing? What are we doing? What's working? What's not? How do we know?
- **Asking problem-posing and problem-solving questions** How could we improve things?
- **Asking what the community needs.**
- **Repeatedly asking "opening up" questions** Why are we doing this?
- **Starting with immediate problems.**
- **Revealing existing assumptions and intentions.**
- **Developing new and improved evaluative criteria.**

For some people in some contexts, open inquiry is not sufficiently systematic and comprehensive, and risks overlooking important matters. The uncertainty involved in the emerging construction of evaluation criteria and foci brings the consequent possibility of lack of clarity, disagreement, and conflict. Generally, however, the essentially anthropologic, interpretive approach to inquiry makes it particularly relevant to participatory processes of inquiry.

Audit review evaluation Audit review evaluation uses a more focused approach, though people sometimes see it as complementary to open inquiry. The sense of this approach is signaled by the word "audit"—meaning *to check*. The audit starts with different questions and has different end points. The audit review focuses on:

- **Objectives:** It starts with questions based on an existing set of objectives—Have we done what we set out to do? What are the signs we have done this?
- **Gaps and irrelevancies:** It asks questions about gaps and irrelevancies—What are we not doing? What are we doing that we shouldn't?
- **Needs:** Assumes community needs are known.
- **Distills information:** The questions are "narrowing down," checking activities on the basis of preexisting understandings.
- **Reveals problems:** Systematically problematizes all existing activities—that is, checks to see if they are problematic.
- **Reviews practices:** Examines practices in light of existing objectives.

An audit review has the advantage of checking all matters previously planned for, reassuring participants that much has been done and matters not yet attended to will be attended to. The comprehensive nature of this approach is especially advantageous if the prior research base was strong, enabling participants to affirm previous agreements and strengthening a collective sense of direction. The fixed nature of the exploration also can feel very comfortable, providing a sense of stability and unity.

The audit review, however, does not always discriminate between still-valuable activities and those that have become outdated. It does not identify what needs to change or how changes might be accomplished. The attention to detail enabling a comprehensive review of activity may also be tedious and wastefully time-consuming.

An audit review provides, however, a useful approach to evaluation especially loved by those responsible for administering or funding educational activities. The sense of a fixed universe and clearly defined objectives provides an illusion of expertise and "best practice" often at odds with the complex realities of educational environments. In the end, however, it can provide more concrete evidence of the extent to which a set of objectives has been achieved, though this evidence lack insight into whether those objectives are appropriate or relevant.

PROFESSIONAL DEVELOPMENT

Action research provides the means for formulating relevant and effective professional development programs. The need to improve teacher professional development has been clearly acknowledged in recent explorations (Darling-Hammond & McLaughlin, 1995;

Feiman-Nemser, 2000; Hawley & Valli, 1999; Little, 1993; McDiarmard, 1994; National Commission on Teaching and America's Future, 1996). The National Board for Professional Teaching Standards (1994) has established a set of assumptions it considers as necessary conditions for sound professional development. These acknowledge that:

- Teachers are committed to students and their learning.
- Teachers know the subjects they teach and how to teach those subjects.
- Teachers are responsible for managing and monitoring student learning.
- Teachers think systematically about their practice and learn from experience.
- Teachers are members of learning communities.

Stein, Smith, and Silver (1999) suggest that meeting the ambitious school reform goals and standards put into place in the United States over the last decade will require a great deal of learning on the part of practicing teachers and those responsible for professional development. They advocate a new paradigm of professional development that supplies teachers with assistance and resources to develop a community of practice. They suggest a professional development design process enabling teachers to engage in thoughtful, conscious decision making to create, implement, reflect on, and modify their teaching practices. Effective professional development processes have the following characteristics:

- **On-site development:** Development within professional work environments.
- **Resources:** Organizational resources—time, space, expertise, and so on.
- **Learning community:** A practice-based learning community of practitioners.
- **Networks:** Links to appropriate people and organizational resources in the community.
- **Planning:** Areas of professional development linked to organizational plans.

Systematic processes of action research enhance the design and implementation of an effective program of professional development. The research framework presented in this book provides a resource enabling teachers and other professionals to:

- Identify professional development needs.
- Identify issues related to those needs—pedagogical, curricula, administrative, and so on.
- Set goals/objectives for professional development.
- Plan strategies of professional development.
- Implement and evaluate professional development strategies.

Systematic process of inquiry will enable teachers to plan sustained and substantive learning opportunities, built into their ongoing teaching work, tapping their collective wisdom and gaining access to other sources of expertise. Through processes of reflection and dialogue inherent in action research they may work with colleagues and other stakeholders to determine:

- Their current strengths
- Problematic issues in their work
- What is to be learned by whom?
- How will these things be learned?
- Who will facilitate and support the learning process?

Figure 7.4
Strategic Professional Development

- Who will provide expertise?
- How will time and resources be allocated?
- How will new learning be supported, reinforced, and extended?
- How will new learning be assessed and reviewed?
- What financial resource will be allocated?

Where mandated administrative requirements are part of this process, they may be incorporated into a holistic program of professional development. Professional development programs will be further enhanced if they are aligned with educational planning processes in the school or district, and integrated into their ongoing organization. As Figure 7.4 indicates, the strategic directions of the school or school system have implications for the organization of schools and classroom teaching/learning processes. Professional development processes need to incorporate new knowledge and skills to be acquired by school staff in order to enact required changes.

LINKING SCHOOL, FAMILIES, AND THE COMMUNITY

The task of realizing the potential of children's home and community is not always easy or straightforward. It requires systematic processes of inquiry over time to reveal the strengths of the families and to integrate them into the curriculum and the ordinary day-to-day life of classrooms (see Chapter 8 "Listening to Families," and Stringer, 2007). By starting with small projects that link home, community, and classroom, teachers are able to build relationships with parents and their students that gradually reveal the ways home and community life can be incorporated as an integral part of the curriculum As McCaleb (1997) says:

> Through participatory research, parents can be invited to engage in dialogue, either by the teacher or by their own children, the students. When family words and experiences are turned into the printed word, the thoughts of the participants are validated. . . . Parents begin to realize that their words and experiences merit a valuable place in the education of their children. . . . Through their participation, parents and community members get a concrete view of how they can contribute to their children's education. (p. 58)

The learning, however, is multidirectional, as teachers also gain deep insights into the cultural, community, and family lives of their students (Petty, 1997), and students begin to learn from each other of the rich diversity of their own communities (Baldwin, 1997). Over time, action research projects engaging families and the community provide a wonderfully engaging context for education, affirming the multiple forms of cultural life existing in the community and providing the basis for engaging the academic life of students.

Action research is particularly effective in situations where students come from culturally diverse families and communities. As teachers, we work from within the experiences and perspectives we derive from our own upbringing and social experiences, and cannot fully comprehend the quite different worlds from which our students come. We may sometimes need to modify both the content and processes of instruction to ensure that our students' learning is accomplished in ways acknowledging, respecting, and celebrating the social and cultural strengths of home and community life. McCaleb (1997) suggests that "The school's failure to acknowledge and value the family's learning and knowledge has a detrimental effect not only on the children's image of their parents but also on the students' appreciation of themselves as members of their home culture."

McCaleb's experience led her to appreciate the following benefits of engaging in research with families (1997, p. vii):

- Co-authorship produces increased communication, dialogue, and sharing within the family and community.
- Student family voices are heard.
- Personal histories are validated.
- Self-identity and self-esteem are strengthened.
- Parents discover the validity of their own experiences.
- Through the negotiation of meaning, adults and students achieve new levels of understanding and self-knowledge.
- Children's respect for their parents and parental respect for children grows.
- The teacher comes to know the family and community better.
- The building blocks for creating a culturally relevant curriculum are laid.
- Teaching becomes easier.

Research processes presented in previous chapters provide the basis for engaging inquiry with parents, families, and other community members. Initially, informal interactions enable school staff to establish effective communication and to develop working relationships with parents. Home visits or meetings in community centers or cafes provide a better context for talking with parents than school, since many of the parents teachers most need to engage have had poor school experiences. Meeting on the parent's "turf" enables them to speak more comfortably. Small, informal lunch or coffee meetings also provide a more natural context, enabling teachers to set up other meetings with individuals or small groups as issues worthy of further exploration emerge.

As parents become interested in exploring solutions to problems, teachers can engage them in processes of inquiry and exploration to seek solutions to small problems that concern them. From these beginnings other agendas will emerge, so that, over time, parents, students, and teachers may engage in more extended investigations about increasingly significant issues.

Sometimes, however, moments of crisis may generate the conditions where groups of parents or students are willing to invest time and energy in working toward a solution to the problems confronting a school or class. A community research project with students (Baldwin, 1997; and "Students and Teachers as Co-Researchers," Chapter 8) emerged from racial problems that had erupted in a school. Student researchers initially focused on issues within the school, but discovered the need to extend their investigations into the community, leading to significant understandings about the relationship between racial dynamics in the school and community.

Engaging families, students, and community members in research entails:

- communicating personally with individuals (notes sent home with children are usually insufficient).
- identifying issues of concern to parents and students.
- engaging other stakeholders related to the issues.
- planning a research process.
- implementing research activities.
- planning actions to solve the problem.
- evaluating outcomes.

The multiple possibilities for reporting on the outcomes of action research presented in Chapter 6 are particularly pertinent to research with families and the community. Many adults in poorer or ethnically diverse communities feel inhibited by formal written reports, but the use of creative and dramatic presentations provides the means for individuals and groups to communicate comfortably and effectively. Journals, magazines, books, or other printed materials constructed within the school or community enable family and community members to present their perspectives, experiences, and knowledge. Informal presentations in classrooms, schools, or to community groups likewise provide the means to communicate research processes and outcomes. In some instances students or family and community members have been able to use concert performances to communicate research outcomes, using poetry, music, art, and drama to both entertain and inform their audiences.

The "Listening to Families" project (see Chapter 8) describes a community-based research process. Representatives of the Barrios Juntos Neighborhood Collective met with the principal of Reginald Chavez Elementary School at a local community center to discuss ways in which relationships between parents and families might be improved. After preliminary discussions, the group focused its attention on ways of improving parent–teacher conferences, and at following meetings decided to survey parents and teachers on the issue.

A framework of questions, initially framed by a university professor as "Listening to families" and "Listening to teachers," was reformulated by Barrios Juntas members using language more appropriate for the community. A group of parent volunteers enlisted by Barrios Juntos attended a preliminary preparation session during which they practiced interviewing techniques in conjunction with the school principal.

During parent–teacher conference week, a table of food was set up in the school library and parents leaving conferences with teachers were invited to snack as they were interviewed by members of the interviewing team. A total of 120 out of 200 parents with children at the school attended the parent–teacher conference, and 88 attending parents were interviewed.

The research team met in the school at a later date to analyze the results of the survey. Responses were written on charts, tabulated, and categorized. The resulting outcomes were incorporated into a one-page summary and presented to parents at a school function. Teachers were interviewed separately and their perspectives used as the basis for a teacher report on the issue. This research has been used by the school to improve the way parent–teacher conferences are organized, but potentially provided participants with insight into the more general processes of interaction between school and families.

The indirect outcomes of the process were as important as the direct outcomes. Parent participants indicated they felt empowered by opportunities to work collaboratively and listen to the views of other parents. They also gained greater understanding of the perspective of the principal and the teachers. Community participants were able to include their own cultural elements into the process—the place of food, and the language of survey questions.

STRATEGIC PLANNING: BUILDING THE BIG PICTURE

Although action research is often associated with small-scale, local studies, it is a viable tool that may be applied to the management of large organizations. Action research therefore may be used at the level of school, school system, or state educational system as a means for accomplishing large-scale developments. The collaborative strategic planning processes described next are implicit in such popular processes as Total Quality Management (Huffman, 1997; Tennant, 2001), but are relevant to more generalized processes of planning and administration (Block, 1990; Coghlan & Brannick, 2004). Action research processes enable school administrators to systematically gather and analyze the large array of information required to produce strategic plans for the operation of the systems for which they have responsibility.

Schools and school systems describe the "big picture" of their educational intents within policy documents incorporating *vision* and *mission* statements that are the manifestations of an *educational philosophy*. They include broad statements of *purpose* and *values* that define an educational philosophy. Such statements may cover fundamental issues related to democratic social and community life, as well as underlying moral and ethical principles. The following statements provide examples of common types of issues incorporated into school policies:

Purpose

- All students have an inherent right to an education that will enable them to reach their highest possible potential.
- The responsibility of education in a democracy is to make it possible for all citizens to understand themselves and the world about them, so that they can live effectively in the world of expanding experiences and constant change. (Omaha School District, quoted in Oliva, 2001)

Value

- All students are treated with dignity and respect.
- Learning is unique to each individual.
- Parents are partners in the education of students. (Orange County Public Schools, quoted in Oliva, 2001)

A coherent policy provides strong degrees of association between broad policy statements and particular educational programs enacted all levels of the system. Broad vision statements, which are essentially philosophical in nature, are specifically linked to particular programs, services, and educational activities. Carefully articulated links at each level of planning provide guidance for practitioners to move from *vision,* to *mission,* to *operational* and *action plans* detailing how these programs and services are to be instituted.

A school district may construct a vision for education through a type of statement such as the following:

- The provision of a quality education for all children, regardless of race, ethnicity, class, gender, or sexual orientation, that provides for their intellectual, emotional, and physical well-being at all levels of the school system.

Mission statements describe how this vision is to be achieved. For example:

- Provide preschool, elementary, middle, and high school education programs in all districts of the system.
- Design and implement appropriate curricula at all levels.
- Provide special services (curriculum, special education, physical plant, etc.) in support of those schools.
- Supervise and monitor teaching, administration, and special services.
- Provide funds and resources required to implement programs and services.

Each school in the district would articulate an operational plan that describes a set of specific objectives related to each of these mission statements. For example:

- Provide a fully developed program of education in all classes of the school.
- Organize and coordinate the ongoing operation of those programs.
- Provide supervision and support for those programs through the school administration.
- Provide resources—equipment and materials—and special services in support of school programs.

Figure 7.5
Strategic Planning Process

- Evaluate the effectiveness of school programs.
- Link the school effectively to families and the community.

Action plans at the classroom level establish syllabi and lesson plans enacting the educational philosophy established in the *vision*. Classroom plans derive, therefore, from curricula emerging from operational plans, and incorporate philosophical guidelines delineated in the school/district vision. The beauty of action research is that it provides the means for the integrated development of programs and services at all levels of the system. Opportunities for school and classroom stakeholders to review and re-envision their work in this way provides the impetus for thinking "outside the box," maintaining their focus on the real purposes of their endeavors and enhancing their educational life.

The strategic planning process depicted in Figure 7.5 is a nominal version of an actual planning process. It shows the levels of planning that need to occur and signals the interconnection between the different sections. The figure illustrates how classroom learning is linked to larger social and educational issues and agendas. Action research provides the means for educators to systematically acquire and analyze the complex array of information required to formulate educationally effective classrooms and schools.

SUMMARY

Taking Action

This chapter outlines the ways action research can be applied to common school educational processes. It presents frameworks for:

Solving Problems: Action Planning in Classroom and Schools
Setting priorities: Establishing an action agenda
Creating pathways: Constructing an action plan
Reviewing the plan
Supporting and monitoring progress

Classroom Teaching and Learning Practices
Constructing programs of learning: Creating a syllabus
Lesson plans
Learning projects
Assessment of student learning

Curriculum Development
Curriculum planning
Transformative curriculum leadership

Evaluation: Assessing the Value and Quality of Educational Programs and Services
Responsive evaluation
Action evaluation: Open inquiry and audit review

Professional Development

Linking School, Families, and the Community

Strategic Planning: Building the Big Picture

Case Studies: Action Research Reports, Presentations, and Performances

INTRODUCTION

Examples of action research projects in schools and other educational contexts are proliferating rapidly. The extent of interest in this form of investigation is demonstrated by the expanding audiences at action research sessions at conferences and the numerous new reports in educational and professional journals. It is becoming a recognized tool of classroom teachers and a regular part of preservice preparation and inservice professional development.

The following case studies therefore represent but a few of the creative and productive ways teachers, students, and parents have applied action research in their school and community contexts. They are real-life studies, providing some indication of the diversity of forms participatory investigations may take and, particularly, applications of frameworks similar to those described in this book. They differ in style and quality and do not necessarily represent "best practice" in report writing. They do represent, however, the diverse means the authors used to communicate information to different audiences, according to the purposes they wished to achieve. The following case studies are presented:

1. A Study of Sexual Harassment in the Lives of Middle School Students

This paper is written by a middle school teacher who reports on a research project carried out by a group of middle school students. It describes details of the research process, as well as the "actions" in which students engaged. It details the methods they used to explore the issue—gathering information by dialoguing about their experiences of harassment, including other "stakeholders" in the process, and distilling the data to reveal key features of their experience. It also describes actions taken by students, including the writing of an article for their school newspaper and a poem that became the basis for a play. The paper also demonstrates how to produce an empathetic text that speaks clearly and movingly about participant experiences.

FRAMING

Students in my eighth-grade language arts classes were excited about working on a research project concerning a school issue. In a class discussion, they had no hesitation in identifying sexual harassment as the number one issue facing them on a daily basis. My first-period class felt that sexual harassment is so pervasive that most of the 850 students in the school had experienced sexual harassment in the hallways, in class, locker rooms, the cafeteria, and on the buses. "Nowhere is safe at school," said Moira, one of the eighth-grade girls who became a participant in the study.

Students shared that sometimes sexual comments created such anxiety that it was hard to focus on class work. Some students had stayed home from school to avoid being a target. They felt that physical abuse of peers was much less of a problem than verbal, sexual harassment. In fact, sexual harassment was a way of life, "You get used to it, 'cos there is nothing you can do about it," said Katie, and many students nodded in agreement.

"Like, it happens when teachers are around," reported Moira. She noted that when teachers heard name calling in the hallways, such as "faggot," nothing was done about it. Moira went to her desk in science class to find her name written across two desks. It said, "Moira gives me a boner." When Moira asked for the names of the students who sat in those desks, the teacher said he didn't know. The following day the graffiti had been removed, but when she again asked for the names of the students from the seating chart, the teacher replied, "What do you want me to do? Write a research paper about it?" In fact, there have been many research papers written about sexual harassment, and it appears that some of them need to be presented to the faculty at my school.

In *Hostile Hallways*, a survey carried out by the American Association of University Women released in 1993, the overall national picture is revealed. Of the 91% of the students who reported some experience of harassment in school, 68% said they had been harassed at least once in the hall; 55% reported the classroom as the site of harassment; 43% reported occurrences outside school but on schools grounds; 39% reported harassment in the gym, playing field, or pool area; 34% indicated the cafeteria as the location; and 23% named the parking lot as the site of the harassment. Students said locker rooms (19%) and restrooms (10%) were also locations for sexual harassment. Overall, 83% of the girls and 60% of the boys reported experiencing unwanted sexual attention in school. When this study was shared with the class, there was relief that our school wasn't the only one with the problem of sexual harassment. There was also anger and confusion as to why sexual harassment is such a prevalent issue among teens. We started a research group.

METHOD

Five girls volunteered to meet after school every Tuesday afternoon to explore how they had experienced sexual harassment. We began in October of 1999 and continued meeting through May of 2000. Their level of concern and commitment is shown in the fact that they never missed a single meeting. The first step was to write letters to parents explaining the project and asking permission for their daughters' participation. Letters were also written to the principal, assistant principal, counselor, and our on-site police officer explaining the nature of the study.

The girls were interviewed individually using the Ethnographic Interview Questions (1979). I took notes during the interviews and collected articles that the girls brought in from their own research in magazines and from the Internet. The group was extremely involved and self-motivated. At times, our meetings were very intense, a natural response to such a sensitive issue. And I wrestled with my own ignorance of what a school day is like for an eighth-grade girl. The pressure to look pretty, to not appear smart, and to defend oneself against verbal attacks takes a huge amount of energy. Going into the project, I had no idea about the extent of the issue. One of the girls suggested I interview the counselor and the police officer, as many students sought out their help after they had been sexually harassed. I made appointments and followed through with interviews. One girl's mother volunteered to be interviewed.

The group also decided to ask other students in our language arts classes to anonymously write down their thoughts about sexual harassment. We saved these writings, and later incorporated them into a performance piece.

After the individual interviews were completed, we began by discussing the official stance on harassment: "Arnet Independent Schools (AIS) are committed to providing all members of the school community with a safe, supportive, and harassment-free environment. Members of the school community are expected to treat each other with mutual respect. Harassment is a form of disrespectful behavior that is intended to intimidate, creates a hostile environment, unreasonably interferes with an academic or working environment, adversely affects and academic and employment opportunities, or seriously alarms or terrorizes another person. The conduct to be harassing must be such that it would cause a reasonable person to suffer emotional distress, or deprive victims of access to educational opportunities or benefits provided by the district."

This policy was sent to all AIS schools as a direct result of *Davis v. Monroe County Board of Education*, in which a student had sued the school district for failing to protect the student from sexual harassment. The district was found in error and had to pay damages to the student for emotional distress. The students in the study wanted to know why the school had not told them of the policy to protect them. It made me think about the importance of sharing information, especially when harassment drains so much energy from learning. They have the right to be protected from harassment.

ANALYSIS

Moira had said that she was only just now recovering from a traumatic seventh-grade year. During most passing periods she was harassed on a daily basis. Boys taunted her with comments about her appearance, "You have a nice butt," "You are so hot," and "I heard you sucked everyone at Bellamy." During science class, a boy next to her masturbated. Moira tried to avoid going to science class by asking the teacher if he had any errands. At no time did she tell the teacher what was going on because she believed nothing would be done about it. She also said she didn't want to be known for getting someone in trouble.

At the same time, Moira was being harassed in the bathroom by girls who were calling her slut and whore, and making comments such as "You want to do it with Jeff." Moira said that the girls hate her because she is popular and pretty.

"Students tell me that teachers have a crush on me. Teachers like me for a lot of reasons, but being pretty adds . . . . A guy has never called me a slut to my face but girls have. I don't take what girls say seriously . . . . I discovered I had power over men," Moria stated.

I read my notes back to Moira at the end of the interview. It was a moment of insight for her because of the word *power*. "Oh, wow, I really said that didn't I? I like that they appreciate me. But, I don't think it's good about the power stuff."

Toward the end of seventh-grade, a male student in science class leaned over the desk and told Moira "I'm going to your house tonight to rape you." This galvanized Moira into action because she was really afraid. She went immediately to Officer Meredith, the school police officer, who talked to the boy in his office. Soon after that the young man was expelled for bringing a toy gun to school, so she didn't see him again. Moira added that she wasn't really scared because "I didn't think he would do it." And again she didn't want the boy to know "it was me who narced on him." Moira did report that she felt better after she had sought out help, and that a grown-up had listened to her. For her, anxiety stemmed from inertia.

Katie and Leslie, two of the other participants, shared their anger at not being harassed. They both perceived themselves as unattractive, fat, and "way too smart." They also believed that "only cute, popular girls get harassed." Both girls heard others being verbally harassed on a daily basis, but felt powerless to do anything about it, or too scared of reprisals. "I keep my head down so no one will talk to me," said Katie, "but I don't think it is right that everybody is calling each other names." Leslie said, "It's just a joke; they don't really mean to hurt anybody." But this was counteracted by Moira, who vehemently responded, "Yeah, they say mean things, then 'oh, I'm just joking' when they really mean it."

Rose, the fourth student in the study, left six weeks into the study. She joined the group because she wanted to represent the students who had not been harassed. Rose's reason for leaving was that she was overwhelmed by the others. She felt "no one is listening to me," and yet she rarely said anything in the group meetings. There had been an ongoing competition with Katie about grades and sharing a best friend. The group talked it over with her and tried to problem solve, but in the end, she decided to leave. She didn't feel her voice was being heard. This had a huge impact on what the group decided to do with the presentation of our research. We decided to write a performance piece in which everyone's voice would be included.

Adult Input

Our school counselor said he dealt with sexual harassment on a daily basis. Students came to talk to him about awkward situations, but often the students didn't know if it was harassment or not, they just felt bad. He talked about the lack of awareness of what harassment is, but that in coming to him with feelings of confusion, he could help clarify why they felt very uncomfortable when called *faggot* or *lesbo*. Most of the verbal harassment he dealt with was between girls: sexual name calling and rumor spreading about who did what with whom. Most of the inappropriate physical harassment was from boy to girl. This included unwanted full-body hugging, as well as pinching and grabbing of girls in the halls. Girls were more likely to report incidents of harassment than boys. The counselor said he rarely had boys in his office who wanted help with being called gay. In his experience girls report harassment more often that boys, even though the counselor observed sexual harassment as being gender equal.

When parents were called about their child harassing another child, the parent often was at a loss as to know what all the fuss was about. Two girls had gotten into a fight because one had made remarks about the size of the other girl's chest. The girl didn't think it was cruel. When her mom was brought to school, she supported her daughter by saying, "It's no big deal." It is clear we need to do more for our students and parents to increase awareness of what sexual harassment is.

The parent who volunteered to be interviewed had requested a transfer for her daughter from the neighborhood school to Bellamy. This meant her daughter had to travel an extra 45 minutes on public transportation. She felt strongly that her daughter had been seriously harassed at her home school by gang members, and teachers. "White teachers discriminated; they gave more freedom to white kids. The administration would not do anything about it. Here they listen." She felt her daughter would feel safer and more challenged academically at our school.

DISTILLATION OF DATA

At the beginning of each Tuesday meeting, we reviewed the key elements from the last meeting. This was extremely helpful in keeping our focus clear and our thoughts manageable. Then we shared any insights or research we had completed during the course of the week. This gave everyone a chance to be heard. Rose brought in an article about the restrictions placed on girls in Afghanistan. In this country girls are denied an education and are physically mutilated if they show ankles or wrists.

Leslie was vehement that we invite boys to join us. This proved difficult. None of the eighth-grade boys showed up even when they said they would, until Leslie hit on an idea. She thought we would have more success if we asked high school boys. This proved to be the key. Two 10th graders showed up and told us of their experiences in high school. They said it was much worse for boys because, "everything was gay, and about how you looked and which group you fit in." They wanted to start a group like ours at their school, so students would think about what they were doing to each other. "It's not right to treat people bad, and what if they are gay? They must feel worse. There's too much stress on sex in high school."

At the end of the year, we took all of our key elements and distilled them down into these issues:

1. Harassment is not just a boy/girl problem.
2. Harassment happens between girls.
3. Harassment is not just a middle school problem, it's worldwide.
4. Harassment causes long-term damage.
5. Harassment can be dealt with.
6. Each person is responsible for his or her own behavior.
7. We can do something about harassment.

We decided to write a performance piece based on what we had learned from our own experience of sexual harassment, incorporating the writings of other students and interviews of other adults. We decided to integrate suggestions of how to contact help, as well as suggestions of what to say to protect oneself when harassed. The group felt that sometimes students were so frozen by humiliation that they could not respond verbally. They felt this lowered self-esteem and confidence. We decided that we needed an art piece to accompany our performance, "Speaking Out." After looking through many art books, we came across the work of Keith Haring. He had a huge canvas of the Statue of Liberty on the floor of a museum in New York. Students who came to visit were able to write on the canvas about what liberty meant to them. This was what inspired us to make a triptych, a three-paneled piece, where students could speak out about harassment by writing down their ideas after the performance.

COMMUNICATION

1. *Drama: "Speaking Out"*

Framing

Voice 1:	After being harassed, I get a knot in the pit of my stomach That lasts all day.
All Voices:	I can't think!
Voice 2:	Middle school is about how I look How many boys like me?
Voice 3:	Yeah, and if the girls like my butt
Voice 4:	Who are you going out with?
Voice 1:	Am I a slut?
Voice 3:	Am I a player?
Voice 1:	Names ringing in my ears So what did the teacher say?

All:	I can't think!
Voice 3:	I want to hurt someone Please don't let it be me.

Method

Voice 4:	You started with questions
Voice 5:	"Tell me about school."
Voice 4:	Do you have a few weeks? I can tell you about fourth grade When I felt the power Of my body. That's when I smiled in a different way To get boys near me. The rush of being popular The joy of being manipulating I liked their eyes on me Now it's more than eyes And I can't give up that power.
Voice 1:	So, you want to start a meeting Like I have to talk to those girls Who look down their nose at me Because I'm a pretty slut Yes, I know I'm beautiful But don't hold that against me.
Voice 2:	Yes, she's pretty and popular If I were that pretty I would be popular too, But I'm not, so I don't get Harassed. Why doesn't Someone pinch my butt?
Voice 5:	OK, we'll meet on Tuesday's after school
Voice 2:	Anything to figure out why I feel so bad all the time.

Analysis

Voice 5:	We talk and cry and then laugh Now what are we gonna do?
Voice 1:	Enough talking already!
Voice 2:	Well, who can we tell?
All:	We start to speak in surer Voices.
Voice 4:	"Don't you ever speak to me that way!"
Voice 1:	"You're harassing me. Quit it"
All:	Speaking out and feeling Power of a different kind Strong, united, together.

| Voice 2: | For a moment that frightening Isolation is gone. |
| All: | We can think. |

Communication

Voice 1:	Writing begins with Clear words and offerings Of what to do if what happened To me happens to you.
Voice 3:	We explore the safety of the Written word together.
Voice 4:	But images pound us Memories of powerlessness Recur and recur.
Voice 2:	Words fail and we begin To imagine a canvas Full of color, bright and Potent, to catch eyes and thoughts Perhaps to change those ugly slut Words into kinder conversations.
Voice 3:	Looking at other artists Work inspires and energizes us Now we talk of Images and shape and form and Composition of creating An interactive piece where Others can add their wisdom.
Voice 5:	Adrenalin of hope replaces Tears and powerlessness.

Action

Voice 1:	Now Tuesday afternoons are full No time for questions About past inertia It's voice and art and speaking out.
Voice 3:	Guests who drop in from High school, helping out with Loud discussions and talk Of beginning another group In my school.
All:	At times, we catch each others Eyes and remember There is a different way.

2. *Newsletter Article:* We also agreed that we needed to write an article about our group for the school newsletter in an effort to let students know they could join. The newsletter would reach parents about the issue of harassment. We checked beforehand with the administration and they agreed to publish the article.

STUDENTS AGAINST HARASSMENT: ARTICLE FOR THE MONTHLY BELLAMY NEWSLETTER

By Katie Dupont, Moira Rodriguez, and Leslie Junette

Since October of 1999, a group of eighth-grade students has worked collaboratively toward making positive changes in the issue of harassment at Bellamy Middle School. Recently, they were joined by a concerned group of Francisco High School students. Together, the groups have worked on ways to identify different types of harassment and how to stop it.

The Merriam-Webster *dictionary states that harassment "is to annoy persistently." The official policy of Arnet Independent Schools states that "harassment is a form of disrespectful behavior which will not be tolerated. Harassment consists of knowingly pursuing a type of behavior that is intended to intimidate, creates a hostile academic working environment . . . or seriously alarms or terrorizes another person." It is also stated that harassment could cause substantial emotional distress. From a survey taken by eighth graders, distress caused by harassment is seriously interfering with the educational process at Bellamy Middle School.*

"I have personally been harassed and I know how it feels. The pit of your stomach turns, and the rest of the day, I feel horrible," says an eighth-grade boy at Bellamy. Several girls report harassment from girls, as well as harassment from boys, making learning in the classroom nearly impossible.

Based on the student survey and interviews with parents, students, teachers, and a counselor, as well high school students from Francisco, the Students Against Harassment concluded that harassment could be dealt with positively.

First, any unwanted actions or comments from an aggressor should be addressed immediately. Phrases like, "Don't ever talk to me that way again," and "Stop! That is harassment and I don't have to take it," are examples of proper responses because they state your demands to be treated with respect. Your voice must be clear and firm.

One way adults can help is to gain more knowledge on the topic of harassment and how to prevent it. Teachers need to teach students that harassment is unacceptable. Second, victims should report any incidents to the proper authorities. Officer Meredith at JMS reports, "When harassment is dealt

*with quickly, students realize that there are boundaries
which cannot be crossed." Officer Meredith conferences
with students and parents to clarify appropriate
boundaries. Individuals who are being harassed must
take action as soon as possible.*

So remember:

1. *DO NOT IGNORE HARASSMENT.*
2. *TELL THE HARASSER, "STOP! THAT IS
   HARASSMENT!"*
3. *IF THE HARASSMENT DOES NOT STOP,
   TELL OFFICER MEREDITH. IT'S
   CONFIDENTIAL.*

*The Students Against Harassment group has
written a performance piece to be presented at
Manzanita Center at UNM on May 10. This is the
beginning of extending public awareness of the issue
of teenage harassment. The group will also perform
on Friday, May 12, at 6:30 in the gym at BMS Student
Forum.*

*Please contact Katie Dupont, Moira Rodriguez, or
Leslie Junette if you are interested in joining Students
Against Harassment. Working together, students can
reach the goal of ZERO tolerance of harassment at
Bellamy Middle School.*

The article was submitted well ahead of the
deadline. It was never published in the newsletter.
When we asked about the omission, we were told it
was too long to be included, even though we had prior
approval. It will be resubmitted next year.

ACTION

Katie arrived for the performance at UNM. She addressed the group with confidence, describing the
creation of Students Against Harassment and what
the experience had meant to her. She stood alone,
as the other participants could not attend due to hec-
tic end-of-school activities. For a 14-year-old, Katie
appeared very comfortable speaking to a group of
adults. University class members filled in the remaining voices and performed "Speaking Out" while
standing in a "theater in the round" formation. This
was our first official "engagement," and it moved people enough for them to write on our triptych, "Speak
up against what is wrong," "Walk in Beauty," and
"Right the Wrongs." Katie reported back to the group
the next day that she saw how "it got to people." She
didn't think it odd that grown-ups were performing it

because they had been teenagers themselves once
and probably remembered what it was like to be
harassed.

When we performed "Speaking Out" during Student Forum there was a standing ovation. Students
filled the triptych with comments such as: "Yeah, you
said right"; "it happened to me too"; "have courage and
speak up"; "never again"; "we can stop harassment";
"no more silence." Some students chose to write the
names of family members who had experienced harassment. Three panels were covered with statements of strength and affirmation. It is a permanent,
artistic reminder that we can find courage together to
right the misuse of power.

Sexual harassment is an issue of power. In
Confronting Sexual Harassment (1997), Judith
Brandenburg states that sexual harassment is: "a
manifestation of deeply held beliefs, attitudes, feelings and cultural norms. In its most prevalent forms, it
is predicated on sociocultural views and sex-role
stereotypes that males are active dominant, and enti-
tled to power, while females are passive, nurturing,
submissive, and powerless."

These attitudes and beliefs shape the socialization of children and the development of gender identity. The meanings we attach to gender are the basic
underpinnings of what society expects from a girl
instead of a boy. In our study we found that boys use
physical contact and verbal comments about body
parts to harass girls. But girls use rumor and specula-
tion about sexual activity to isolate one another. Boys
who are assumed to be sexually active are "hot," while
girls who are assumed to be sexually active are
"sluts."

Throughout childhood, sex-role stereotypes are
reinforced by the media and society. Television, sports
heroes, and books tell us males should be active, independent, and aggressive. In spite of some increased
sensitivity in the media over the last decade, girls and
women still appear less frequently than men, and they
are shown largely in stereotyped roles. In ads and music videos, women are objects, a collection of body
parts. Women are valued for how they look: thin and
pretty and sexual. Moira talked about feeling the power
of being pretty and planning how to get boys to notice
her because she liked being beautiful. At age 13, she
would not go out of the house without makeup. "I don't
know how I could live, if I wasn't pretty." By fourth-grade
she had formulated the belief that her worth lay in her
outward appearance. In middle school, she found that

boys responded to her looks, vying to sit next to her in class, but girls saw her as a tremendous threat. She was labeled a "slut" because she was popular with the boys. Thus girls learn to compete against each other for the label of "prettiest." It then becomes easy to attack self-esteem with epithets of *ugly* and *fat*. Similarly, teenage boys are inundated with media images of male virility and sexual prowess with girls. How easy it is to threaten this image with insults of "queer" and "faggot."

As educators, we can talk and talk about equality and respect. When students themselves speak out about their experiences and when students are courageous enough to offer alternative ways of being, the balance of power will be impacted. In October 1999, Officer Meredith reported dealing with four to five incidents of sexual harassment every week. At the end of the school year he said the numbers had dropped to one every two weeks. When students know harassment will not be tolerated, behaviors change. Change can happen.

BIBLIOGRAPHY

American Association of University Women (AAUW). (1993). *Hostile hallways*. The AAUW survey on sexual harassment in American schools. Washington, DC: Author.

Berman Brandenburg, J. (1997). *Confronting sexual harassment: What schools and colleges can do*. New York: Teachers College Press.

Denzin, N. (1997). *Interpretive ethnography: Ethnographic practices for the 21st century*. Thousand Oaks, CA: Sage Publications.

Eaton, S. (1995). Sexual harassment at an early age: New for schools. In E. Miller (Ed.), *Ready to learn: How schools can help kids be healthier and safer*. Cambridge, MA: Harvard Education Letter, Reprint Series 2.

Hassenpplug, A. (2000). Courts and peer sexual harassment: School district liability for damages. *Brigham Young University Education & Law Journal*.

Morewitz, S. J. (1996). *Sexual harassment and social change in society*. San Francisco, Austin & Winfield.

Shakeshaft, C., &. Barber, E. (1995, January). Peer harassment in schools. *Journal for a Just and Caring Education*, *1*(1), pp. 30–40.

Stein, N. (1999). *Classrooms and courtrooms: Facing sexual harassment in K–12 schools*. New York: Teachers College Press.

Stein, N., & Sjöstrom, L. (1994). *Flirting or hurting? A teacher's guide on student-to-student sexual harassment in schools*. West Haven, CT: NEA and Wellesley College Center for Research on Women.

Tangri, S. S., & Hayes, S. M. (1997). Theories of sexual harassment. In W. O'Donohue (Ed.), *Sexual harassment: Theory, research and treatment*, Needham Heights, MA: Allyn & Bacon.

2. SMALL IS BEAUTIFUL: INTERNAL EVALUATION REPORT

Brazos School for Inquiry and Creativity

By Dr Ernie Stringer

This document was written for the Brazos School for Inquiry and Creativity, a small charter school in Bryan, Texas, as part of an internal evaluation process mandated by the State of Texas. It resulted from a five-day review process in which school staff, students, and administrators were interviewed and the school observed by the evaluation facilitator. An interim report was presented to teachers on day five of the process, enabling them to discuss the findings and identify actions they could take to improve the quality of the school's operation. These actions are included as an appendix to the report. Information included in the report was obtained from interviews, observations, and a review of school documents and records. It was produced as an internal document for the information of school staff and administration. Statistics related to student achievement levels, "at risk" classifications, and so on, were included in another report produced by an external evaluation team.

INTRODUCTION

The Brazos School for Inquiry and Creativity sits on the outskirts of downtown Bryan, surrounded by older and slightly worn houses, redolent of a past and more prosperous era. Housed in six rather cramped classrooms, nestled at the rear of a large Catholic church from which it leases the building, the school seems rather cramped for space, considering the nearly 100 children, and numerous teachers, administrators, and adjunct faculty working within. It is an impression reinforced by teachers, administrators, and students at the school, who almost with one accord spoke of the inadequacy of the buildings and the desire to move to larger quarters.

The physical surrounds, however, belie the energy and movement that envelops visitors as they walk through the busy main corridor, passing classes scattered with children that would, in other venues, be classified as "noisy." In some rooms the children sit listening to a teacher working through material written on a blackboard. In others, children laze across desks, lounge in beanbags, or talk animatedly with each other within easy reach of one of the adult figures, teachers, or adjunct faculty who appear in surprisingly large numbers for such a small school. In yet other rooms, usually housing older students, individuals or small groups work in concentrated fashion through their work, oblivious to the surrounding buzz and the ever-attentive teachers who move between them. "Chaos theory best describes us," says one teacher, referring to the patterns apparent in seemingly random sets of events, eventually emerging for the visitor, as he becomes more understanding of the nature and the purposefulness of the multitude of events happening simultaneously in this small, but busy school.

Order emerges from the chaos through the ministrations of two administrators, busily coping with a multitude of tasks and issues as children, teachers, parents, and the telephone intrude on the one small administrative space. It takes shape in the excited talk of teachers as they describe the way they attempt to turn an educational theory into the ongoing practice of a school. It reaches greater clarity in the sometimes hesitant but always clearly articulated perceptions of the students as they mull through their experience attending a school quite different from those they've previously attended.

With around 95 students, two part-time principals, five full-time core teachers, and 30 part-time adjunct faculty, known within the school as *Aggies*, the school operates on two campuses. K–2 is housed in a kindergarten facility a mile or so away, while 3–12 classes operate in the main campus, with facilities complemented by those of a nearby Boys and Girls Club used for Physical Education Classes, and a local swimming pool.

The brainchild of Dr. Robert Slater, whose passion for the children is acknowledged by teachers and administrators at the school, Brazos School for Inquiry and Creativity enacts a theory of education focused on a balanced curriculum to implement democracy. Its educational philosophy/principles, carefully elucidated on a website and espoused by teachers and administrators, focuses on the need to balance both the aesthetic and logical/rational capacities of students. It is an experiment in democratic schooling that appears to have enormous potential to provide a productive and relevant education for the children who attend.

HISTORY

The school, now seven weeks into the second year of operation, is still in its early days. Both administrators and staff recognize that they are still in the process of formulating, working through, clarifying, and improving many aspects of its operation. A recent meeting of teachers and administrators clarified details of a discipline plan, for instance, and the school is in the process of investigating the extent to which it has been able to achieve academic excellence within the framework of the democratic freedoms central to the school's philosophy. It is, in other words, still a school in process.

But the comparative constructive, productive, though jumbled order that characterizes its operation was achieved only through the determination and hard work of the people who initially gave it life. Those staff who remain from the first year of its operation tell of the difficulties and disorder arising from the growing pains of the school—the lack of order, the inability of some students to realize the implications of responsibility that went with the freedom they enjoyed, and the lack of facilities taken for granted in a fully operational school. As one administrator said, "I wasn't prepared for Inquiry and Creativity. It seemed like chaos to me. The children were eating and drinking, listening to music. They didn't have books. They had a lot of freedom, but they were used to a structured environment and couldn't use their time wisely or productively."

Coming from traditional models of schooling it was hard for teachers and administrators to adjust to the demands and practices of the Inquiry/Creativity model, though a period of orientation allowed them to come to grips with the model. Dr. Slater talked with them at length, gave them papers to read explaining the theory of the school, enabling them to better understand the task before them. As one said, "As time went on I began to see the vision and I bought into it."

Some students, likewise, found it hard to adjust to the atmosphere of the school and some left of their own

volition or were asked to leave as their behavior—responses to traditional school environments—threatened to disrupt the school too severely. Most, however, adjusted to the demands of this different school environment and settled into more productive routines. "Kids went through a metamorphosis .... But it took a lot of repetitiveness for them to understand what we're about. Some still don't [get it]. . . . We had a ton of discipline problems . . . but this year we've seen very little of children we saw repeatedly last year."

The school, therefore, though only in its second year of operation, has gone through a period of development characterized by adjustments and changes, leading to a more settled and productive atmosphere. It has discovered, to some extent, what it can and cannot do, which students are capable of sustaining themselves in the atmosphere of "freedom with responsibility," and the minimal rules required to ensure an educationally functional environment. It is a school, therefore, still in process, with administrators, staff, and students working through issues and problems as they appear, gradually building the structures and processes that enable them to enact the Inquiry/Creativity model.

At this early stage, however, it is apparent that much has been accomplished, and though it is still in the early days, both students and staff tend to look back with feelings of accomplishment, seeing the early reward in student academic achievement for their efforts. As the following report reveals, there is much to be celebrated, but also much work still to do. Though the pains of birth have passed, there is still much growth to achieve.

STUDENT EXPERIENCES

A visitor to the Brazos School for Inquiry and Creativity cannot help but be impressed with the responses of students, expressing as they do almost unanimous approval of their experience of this new institution. Almost all indicated that they much preferred this to their previous school and were intent on continuing at the school. The one standout indicated that he'd like to have experienced a middle school after elementary school instead of coming directly to the Brazos school. His, however, was a divergent opinion; all other children providing responses ranging from quiet approval to excited or wholehearted enjoyment of their experience. One girl, obviously almost ecstatic at her progress, indicated in heartfelt tones "The school is a blessing."

The reasons for this extended vote of confidence by the students relate to their comments during interviews. They felt that:

- They received more attention from teachers.
- The teachers were nicer.
- They were learning more.
- Their grades were improving.
- They had increased freedom.
- They appreciated the diversity of activities.
- They liked the small size of the school.

Students were almost unanimous in voicing their approval of the school. With very few dissenting voices they asserted that they preferred the BSIC to the school they last attended, and spoke positively of their experiences here.

More Attention from Teachers: The Teachers Are Nicer

It was clear that the students appreciated the close attention made possible by the small teacher/student ratio in this school. They commented on the nature of their relationship with their teachers and the fact that teachers knew them personally, knew their needs, and were available to help them with their work. One said, "They give you more attention, do things with you," while another indicated, "Teachers know you, work with you, know what you need. They're approachable, you can ask them things." Others compared this with the situation in their old schools, where much of the teachers' time was spent focusing on disruptive students. "At my old school, teachers spent their time giving attention to students acting up. They didn't give their time to students who wanted to learn." Another commented, "I really like my relationship with the teachers. They're, like, your friends!" The informality and friendliness of relationships between students and staff is notable to a visitor and acknowledged by all. It clearly is a significant factor in maintaining the ethos of "inquiry and creativity" that is at the heart of the school. As one faculty member indicated, "We're like a family. If something happens to someone, we all know it."

Learning More: Grades Improving

Many of the children came to BSIC as underachievers, either well behind in their schoolwork or at the point of failing or dropping out of school. Some would be classified as "at risk" from an educational viewpoint. The low student/teacher ratio, however, and the individualized learning processes ensure that children who are failing to achieve do not escape attention. In these circumstances it is unsurprising that students felt that they were learning more at school and that their grades were improving.

Although this varies from student to student, even students who did not evince much interest in their schoolwork clearly indicated increases in achievement. While observation of classrooms suggests that some still have difficulty in remaining focused, the constant attention of teachers ensures that all achieve at least a minimal amount of productive engagement with their work, something apparently able to be avoided in mainstream classrooms. For some children, attendance at the school has been a transformational experience. One student, a low achiever at her previous school, spoke enthusiastically of her progress: "I was well below my grade level, but since I've been here, I've been making great progress, working my way back up. . . . I feel as if I can really learn here!"

Like other children in the school, she works by herself doing exercises based on the TEKS. "Aggie" tutors assist her to set up assignments and projects based on the TEKS materials and she works through them, asking assistance from teachers and tutors as she requires. Individualized work is required of some students, especially at higher levels, or where they are well behind the requirements for other students at their grade levels. The flexibility of the curriculum and instruction allows each student to formulate a program of work that fits his or her grade or ability level. Tests indicated that one 15-year-old student was achieving at only grade 5–6 levels, and thus the student was allowed to start working at that level. As one administrator said, "She realized there was a gap and wanted to go to that level so she wouldn't miss any information. . . . She's really excited because she's learning." Her progress has been quite dramatic and she appears truly engaged in her learning, leaving work for tutors to review when she leaves school and communicating with teachers via email.

Although this case dramatically illustrates the potential of the flexibly organized teaching/learning processes at BSIC, it is not unique. Almost all students indicated increased learning, a fact borne out by the high TAAS scores achieved by children in this school. Figures indicate that BSIC TAAS scores are two standard deviations above the state mean, a fact made more laudable by the at-risk status of much of the student population.

Freedom and Diversity

Most children commented positively on the greater freedom they experienced at this school. It manifested itself in the choices available to them in the schoolwork, in their freedom of movement in the school, and in the activities available to them. Almost all students commented positively on this aspect of the school, one noting particularly that "We can work at our own level, at our own rate [pace]." Another noted the impact of this on his learning— "When I came here I was behind. Now I'm achieving at my grade level." He indicated that the students in the school liked working at their own rate.

The freedom that comes to the children through the enactment of the Inquiry/Creativity model is matched by the flexibility of instructional arrangements. As noted, a number of children indicated that they appreciated the opportunity to formulate their own learning levels and activities, but they also commented on the diversity of activities available in their school program. They enjoyed physical education activities, including swimming, exercises, weights, and games, activities not available at their previous schools. They were particularly enthusiastic about the field trips, from which they learned much. It is this type of activity that helps the school stand out from the education received at public schools in the region, providing diverse and active learning experiences that engage the children and provide a positive focus of attention on their schooling.

The difficulty of maintaining a model that provides freedom while expecting responsibility, however, is still evident in some of the children. With years of experience in traditional classrooms, some still maintain the attitude toward their schoolwork and behavior redolent of an authoritarian approach to schooling from which they were alienated and which they resisted through their behavior. One boy indicated, "We can get away with a lot more," referring not to misbehavior, but to the ability to make choices about work to be done, leaving the classroom, and so

on. He still interpreted these freedoms as "getting away with things."

As one might expect, in the circumstances, some children still require persistent attention to keep them focused, and appear not particularly interested in their work. This seems a greater problem for older male students whose educational experience appears to have alienated them from the productive possibilities available to them. The larger picture of the school, however, is that most students evince an interest in their work and are actively engaged in the activities and projects emanating from the TEKS formats. Even a cursory walk through the school provides evidence of energy and engagement that pervades the school and shows through some of the seeming babble that occasionally erupts when the schedule changes from one period to the next.

Small Is Beautiful

Almost all children remarked favorably on the small size of the school. When asked about their experience of the school, they noted that "Its smallness is good," "I like the small size," or "It's tight, cool." They obviously like the attention that they get, not available in the more anonymous, larger schools they previously experienced. Their comments on the attention they get from their teachers, the fact that teachers are aware of their presence and their needs and gaps in their work, all reflect the outcomes of the small size and the low student/teacher ratio. It is clearly, from the students' perspective, one of the benefits of attending the BSIC.

It does, however, have its downside. One student mentioned that she was "A social person," and would like to have more students with whom to interact. It also creates difficulties for students at higher levels of high school, who have few fellow students with whom to share their work. One noted that it took some adjustment, but that she was now able to enjoy being self-motivated and organized, though she would like to have a teacher or mentor at year 11–12 level who was more focused on college preparation.

ADMINISTRATION

Administration is a demanding occupation for the two part-time principals of the Brazos School for

Inquiry and Creativity, with all of the administrative and organizational requirements of a larger school being necessary, but fewer facilities and human resources available to complete the work. The smaller number of students does not necessarily lead to less work, though the ability to ignore the large number of rules, regulations, and requirements of large school systems is a bonus, a fact noted also by teachers. Administrators are responsible for the general organization of the school, must monitor the development of class curricula, facilitate the development of a variety of school plans, order and distribute textbooks, engage in extensive disciplinary activity, formulate and complete a variety of forms, maintain school documentation, organize report cards, and assist in the construction of the complex scheduling required by the flexible instructional arrangements in the school. Because the school is so new, much of this activity is developmental, being engaged in an ongoing way as a need arises. It is demanding activity requiring after-hours work by both part-time principals and the head of the school board.

One of the ongoing difficulties is to provide organization and structure in ways that are consonant with the values and principles of the school. As one principal says, "We try to deal with things on an individual basis, focusing on values rather than on a fixed set of rules." Only when a problem becomes schoolwide (for example, tardiness and absenteeism becoming widespread) are rules defined. In many instances, however, individual children are given counseling to enable them to understand the purposes of the school and the need for them to be responsible for their own work and behavior.

This focus on individual counseling of students has paid off, behavioral and disciplinary problems having decreased dramatically over the past year, though some older students continue to have problems taking the Inquiry/Creativity model on board. As one administrator noted, "Older male students, especially, tend to come with too much baggage. They're products of the existing system." It is clear that systematic talking through of issues and focus on individual responsibility for behavior is having an impact. Students understand and conform to the routines laid down for resolution of problems and disputes. A sense of order and responsiveness prevails among the students, despite the sometimes high levels of activity and movement.

Administratively, therefore, the school has much to celebrate. As levels of conflict and associated disciplinary problems have decreased, the students appear much happier, a facet of their experience most evident in interviews. Many children who were "at risk," being on the point of being suspended from their previous school, are becoming more settled as they become used to the way the school functions. Attendance has improved—the school attained a rate of 98% for the first six weeks of the school year—and children are increasingly engaged in productive work. As one administrator noted, "We're now starting to see the Inquiry/Creativity model coming in." It is not easy, however, and she continues to find it hard not to fall back into a traditional mode of operation, to remind themselves of why they are here. Although it is relatively clear how the model works at a classroom level, it is more difficult to imagine how to run a school accordingly. Nevertheless, the school evinces a comfortable, laid-back, harmonious ethos in tune with the spirit of the Inquiry/Creativity model that gives it life.

Although administrators focus on the needs of the children and the instructional processes to implement this innovative educational model, it is apparent that they work under difficulties. Even a short period of observation reveals the lack of space, furniture, and facilities to establish an efficient administrative system. As the school develops, it will need to acquire the resources necessary to provide space for the multitude of interactions occurring at all times—facilities for information storage and retrieval, an efficient system of records, and space for preparation of documents and the many other tasks and functions required to administer a school effectively. The administrative staff does a surprisingly effective job in the circumstances, but as the school grows, these issues will become more pressing.

TEACHER PERSPECTIVES

The dedication and vision of the teachers at the Brazos School for Inquiry and Creativity is admirable. All have a focus that speaks clearly to the principles enunciated by the Inquiry/Creativity model, which forms the central theory at the core of the school's operation. As Dr. Slater notes, "Without that theory, there would be no school," a statement pertinent to the perspectives of all teachers in the school. Though some of the teachers initially found the transition from traditional schools somewhat difficult, all are in accord with the fundamental principles of the model, and enjoy the equality they experience as staff members. One teacher indicated, "I found it difficult at first, but after about three months I liked it a lot. I find there's more will, more desire to learn than in the public schools. I like that the kids can work at their own level; they're excited, interested."

Teachers also enjoyed the flexibility and freedom allowed by the small size of the school. They enjoyed the ability to take field trips to ground the children's learning in real-life events and phenomena and to be able to take advantage of the children's interests. They spoke enthusiastically of past field trips and those planned for the future. Further, the less rigid structure enabled them to get the kids involved in activities related to careers in which they expressed interest and to get them in contact, through visits and visitors, with their own cultures.

Student Achievement

Teachers are also enthusiastic about the response of students to the school's model of education. One teacher, comparing the experience of public schooling, recounted the differences from his previous experience. "You have to give students at other schools tangible rewards. I'd buy things like games and disposable cameras. Here, the rewards are more intangible for these kids. They know they're advancing faster than they would at other schools. [That motivates them]."

Relationship with Students

The staff also appreciates the low student/teacher ratios, at some times of the day being reduced to one to two or one to three when Aggie tutors are in attendance. They comment on the attention it is possible to give to individual students, and the relationships that develop in the process. "You get to know your students. You become part of their environment; you become a friend, a part of their community. They have a lot more confidence asking you questions, showing you work. As a teacher, that's rewarding."

An Inquiry/Creativity Curriculum

The staff members also approve of the more balanced curriculum, with its emphasis on an aesthetic as well as an academic curriculum. Teachers are also aware, however, of the challenges before them, of the need to improve the quality of the curriculum as well as academic achievement. As one noted, "We have to build character and self-responsibility in kids and enduring knowledge, not just passing the TAAS test like the public schools. . . . I'd like the kids to be able to say that moving to the Brazos school changed their lives. I'd like it to enable them to go to their maximum capacity, to make them critical thinkers, not just pass the test or go to the next grade level." Another indicated, "The real power is to have the children review their portfolio. I'd like them to be able to critique their own work, to be able to review their achievement and progress, and assess the quality of their work, in terms of goals and purposes they've set themselves." Currently kids don't understand why they're learning what they're learning, except insofar as it is part of the TEKS.

This raises an important issue that points to an underlying tension in the implementation of the Inquiry/Creativity model: how to build a curriculum that enables students to formulate learning activities and focuses within a state-stipulated curriculum framework. A number of teachers and administrators spoke of the difficulty in coming to grips with this issue. One indicated that she would like to see more innovation, with the students more involved in the process of developing learning projects and less lecturing by the teachers. She'd like to hear the kids talking more about what they're doing in classrooms, getting to the point where they could work independently for a whole day. On reflection she realized that the kids were achieving much more than they had been able to earlier in the school's history, but she was still concerned to see better implementation of the Inquiry/Creativity model.

Most teachers who indicated a desire to more clearly enact responsibility in the child for learning the model they advocated also echoed this perspective. As one indicated, "The potential is there, but we're not achieving it yet. If we can get the kids' natural curiosity and apply it to the work in hand, it'll be a wonderful thing. Rather than setting up [material from a state curriculum] and teaching to it, I'd like to start with what the kids are interested in and start with that." She also saw the need to learn techniques to deal with the multiple interests and levels that would be involved in such an approach to teaching. Currently she was not sure how to handle a situation where other students were passive as she worked things through with one student of the class. "I need to think of a way to deal with this." Though the current structure revolving around the Texas Essential Knowledge and Skills has served the school well at this stage in its history, a more creative, innovative approach to curriculum processes may be required to enact the school's preferred model.

Planning and Professional Development

It is evident in speaking with teachers that all have the desire to upgrade their skills and knowledge. They are searching for ways to more effectively implement the Inquiry/Creativity model, incorporating more diverse types of activity, working in an interdisciplinary way, formulating a more integrated thematic curriculum, and/or constructing learning programs more clearly centered on student needs and interests. As one said, "We need to look more clearly at what we're doing academically; whether we're really an Inquiry/Creativity school; whether the kids are asking good questions and producing a creative product."

This points to the need for the school to make provision for staff professional development—to provide regular times, on a weekly basis and/or each semester, for teachers to work together and/or in concert with people with relevant curriculum expertise and experience—to extend their skills and build a repertoire of appropriate techniques, activities, and approaches to learning. They may also need time and assistance to formulate a more systematic, structured curriculum process reflecting the principles of the Inquiry/Creativity model. Individual teachers have some ideas and access to limited resources, but it is likely they will need an extended and systematic planning process to collaboratively plan and develop a more clearly structured and integrated curriculum.

Equipment and Materials

These issues are made more problematic by the lack of equipment and materials, a fact clearly evident to the eye of an experienced visitor. A dearth of storage space, a lack of general teaching equipment and materials, a paucity of books, including texts, books, other resource materials, and so on, all spoke to the realities of a school in its early days of operation. One teacher noted that he had heard it took five to seven years for a school to become fully operational. It is evident that to fully implement the chosen model the school will need to increase teaching/learning resources, especially in light of the highly individualized instruction required. An increase in the number of computers will alleviate this problem to some extent, as students will be able to access knowledge and information available on the Web. It will not solve the problem, however, and as the school moves towards a more clearly articulated Inquiry/Creativity curriculum, required resources should be identified. It may also need to institute a process for regular planning and ordering of teaching/learning equipment and materials.

Achievements

Despite the obstacles they face—the limited resources and the rather crowded conditions—there is a real air of achievement among the teachers at Brazos School for Inquiry and Creativity. They enjoy their relationships with students, the feeling of having achieved something significant in the progress evident in student accomplishments and engagement, and in the mere fact of having *survived*. "The school has a lot to say about how at-risk kids can learn. Most of these kids weren't making it in the public schools. A lot of people said it couldn't be done. We've done it!" Staff are also clear in their desire to maintain themselves in this type of school. As one indicated, "I couldn't go back to a public school. I couldn't overlook the structure, the kids that didn't make it, the general acceptance of that." Despite the problems they face, most staff members indicate that they "love working in this school," and are intent on maintaining the momentum toward achieving the vision that has given new meaning to their professional lives.

CONCLUSION

Dr. Slater's vision of an innovative school, an integral part of preparation for participation in a democratic society, is manifest in the operation of the Brazos School for Inquiry and Creativity. His drive and passion for this model can be seen daily in the dedicated and enthusiastic work of the staff of the school and in the quiet and productive achievements of the students. The school is far from a finished product, but has already achieved significant gains in providing an effective education for the students who attend. A steadier and more orderly educational environment has supplanted the hard work and seemingly chaotic events of the first months of the school. Those responsible should take heart in the clear achievements already evident in the lives of their students, noting carefully the results they have achieved, not only academically, but also emotionally and socially. While there is still much work to be done, the principles of the model are clearly in the minds of all who work in the school, and stand as a beacon guiding future developments. These principles will become increasingly manifest as staff and students continue to develop the structures and strategies that give form and coherence to their educational lives. The successes experienced should be applauded and celebrated and the strengths built upon. Brazos School for Inquiry and Creativity is a testament to the idea that **"small is beautiful!"**

APPENDIX

ACTION AGENDAS

Administrators and teachers reviewed the BSIC report and discussed issues within it. The following major agendas derive from this discussion:

Curriculum Development

There is little doubt that children within the school have increased their learning dramatically. At the moment, however, learning is still based on a linear movement through the TEKS, and school faculty are still grappling with ways of enacting an inquiry-based model of instruction. They are concerned about standards students have for themselves and the possibility that student learning is somewhat superficial. They seek a curriculum that is more oriented to the interests and experiences of the children and toward enduring knowledge and life skills. Action agendas include:

- The systematic development of an integrated school curriculum more clearly reflecting the Inquiry/Creativity model
- A block of time (four to five days) put aside for school staff to formulate an initial curriculum structure and a process for its ongoing development
- Although school staff are well equipped for this process, it would be enhanced by inputs from people with relevant curriculum expertise

Resources

As a new school, the BSIC is relatively poorly resourced for the rich array of materials and equipment required by the model of education it espouses. There is need for the school to:

- Systematically review current equipment and material needs related to teaching and student learning
- Acquire resources as indicated by the curriculum development process

Professional Development

Teachers and administrators indicate a desire to extend their understanding of practical ways of implementing an Inquiry/Creativity curriculum. They may upgrade their skills through:

- Regular, structured opportunities to exchange ideas and information
- Review of individual staff professional development needs
- A program of workshops or short courses to extend skills

Staff Orientation

Over time the school will experience continuing changes in staff, particularly the student tutors who provide an important resource. To ensure that people working at the school engage their work appropriately, the school will require:

- A process for orienting and training staff in appropriate teaching/learning and behavior management processes

Organizational Planning

In the early days of school development, staff were called on to engage in a variety of activities as needs emerged unexpectedly. With the increasing stability of the school's operation, staff expressed the need to:

- Engage a long-term planning process to ensure a continuity of staff and a continuing engagement with the Inquiry/Creativity vision
- Clearly define the roles and responsibilities of staff so that school needs were met systematically

3. LISTENING TO FAMILIES: IMPROVING COMMUNICATION BETWEEN THE SCHOOL AND THE COMMUNITY

A Collaborative Project of: Barrios Juntos Neighborhood Collective University of New Mexico Dominguez Elementary School

This report describes a collaborative project instigated by women in a neighborhood collective and developed by them with the assistance of the school principal, a university professor, and graduate students. It presents details of the research process, including the process of data collection and analysis, together with a report on results of the survey. It also indicates the way the school used the information emerging from the study.

I. PROJECT BACKGROUND

The focus of the research project on parent–teacher conferences can only be understood if we present the people behind the project. The project was formulated and implemented by participants from the Barrios Juntos neighborhood collective, Dominguez Elementary School, the University of New Mexico (UNM), and volunteers from the community at large.

Barrios Juntos

The project was initiated by Barrios Juntos, a group of concerned community people dedicated to addressing the many problems that exist in the localities in which the live. They believe that because of their deep commitment to their community areas, and their intimate relationship with the residents of these neighborhoods, they have a firsthand knowledge of the problems that exist. Their combined experience and successes as community activists in addressing these problems, even without financial sponsorship, places them in the best position to identify, address, and help correct many problems that exist in their identified areas. In their planning and strategy-development sessions, they have attempted to identify all of the major problems in their community, while selecting specific problem areas where their work will begin.

II. PROJECT INTENTION

Barrios Juntos planned to improve children's educational experiences by changing the role of parents and improving opportunities for parents to participate in their children's education. The first step was to bring together a core representation, which included neighborhood parents, children, residents, and educators including principals, teachers, and key school administrators to discuss these issues and to decide what could be done to improve parent inclusion.

III. PROJECT PROCESS

Surveying Parents

Preparations for conducting the survey began with the identification of neighborhood volunteers who were brought together for an initial evening and subsequent training at the Dominguez site. Volunteers included parents and grandparents, neighborhood association leaders, and former teachers and UNM graduate students and service corps members. Information covered in the training session included background on the subject, the thinking behind the survey questions, and considerations of different ways to gather survey data. During parent–teacher conference time, volunteers were carefully stationed around the school to intercept postconference traffic and then either survey on the spot or, more typically, find a quiet place such as the library to sit and talk. To make parents feel more at ease with this process, Barrios Juntos provided food and drink for all those who answered survey questions. Of the 200 families affiliated with Dominguez, 120 of these attended parent–teacher conferences, with project volunteers surveying 88. Many of those not surveyed attended conferences organized before the start of the school day.

Analyzing Results

Six survey questions were identified prior to the parent–teacher conferences. A list of these questions is documented in Appendix II. After the conferences, Professor Shaw from UNM suggested that follow-up work with parent answers focus on three questions: 1A, 3A, and 3B, with answers to other questions often proving repetitious. The Barrios Juntos/UNM group went through collected surveys, recording parent responses to each question on large sheets of paper for all to see and discuss. Where responses were repeated, a checkmark was added to the first response, with additional information added alongside in a different color.

Documenting Findings

After responses to a question had been listed, they were then all grouped by theme into four headings. The questions were reviewed by the Barrios Juntos/UNM group, with Professor Shaw leading the discussion. Responses were grouped and then woven into a written report by the UNM group, who sought to maintain documented voices as much as possible. The report was later brought back to the entire Barrios Juntos/UNM group for review and revision.

IV. PROJECT RESULTS

Question 1A: How Did You Feel About Your Parent–Teacher Conference?

Introduction

The following results were derived from an analysis of parent responses to this question. It drew responses that were grouped under four headings: communication, how parents feel about the conference, the school and the teachers, and what parents learn from the conference.

Communication

It was interesting to see that many of the parents stress the importance of "ongoing communication" with the teachers. "Open communication" and "constant contact" are identified as key to not only the success of the conference but also the overall progress of the child. The information flow, which includes to and from the child, is "useful for the teacher as well as the parent," and one parent stated that this affects "how openly I can discuss anything with the teacher" and "how well the teacher knows the children."

Almost a third of the parents were pleased with the way teachers "explain everything clearly," "answer questions," and "explain the child's progress and what's coming up." One parent put it concisely, stating that "the information is useful for the teacher and the parent, and ultimately for the child."

How parents feel about the conference

Most parents felt that the parent–teacher conferences "went well." They said the conferences are "thorough, yet quick," and a "very positive" experience. Some expressed that they "feel comfortable," "enjoy the conference," and that the "teacher is great." They feel they are "treated with respect," they have a "good relationship" with the teacher, and have "confidence in what the teacher is doing." On the whole parents expressed that the "conferences are important" and "useful" for their child's progress. A couple of parents said they feel "free to express any concerns" they have.

A few parents have some concerns about the conferences. One parent mentioned how she was "not happy with [the child's] grades." Another was distressed because "there was someone else in the room" during her conference. This turned out to be another parent waiting for his/her conference. Although the teacher apologized, the parent found this "distracting." A couple of the parents said that the teachers are "not around to meet during the school year." One of the parents wished that "conferences were longer."

The school and the teachers

Almost half the parents made general comments about the school and the teachers. The overwhelming opinion of teachers is positive, with parents stating that "the teachers are great" and that they are "happy" with them. One parent explained how the teacher "knows [the child's] strengths and weaknesses" and "is doing extra to help" both the parent and the child. The only concerns the parents have are that some "teachers don't speak Spanish," are "not around to meet during the school year," and "don't give enough help on how to help [the children] out of school time."

With regard to the school, some of the parents said they believe "this is a good school" with a "good atmosphere in the classroom." A few parents are concerned about their child being placed in special programs such as Title 1.

What parents learned from the conference

Parents leave with "more information" about their child than when they came in. For example, some parents found out that their children are "having problems of low grades" and others learned that their children are "having no problems." Some discovered that their children are "doing well," "progress was good," and the children's "reading and learning is better."

Summary

The majority of the feedback from parents was positive. However, there were some concerns that revolved around the length of conferences and the availability of teachers during the year for more frequent communication and progress reports.

Question 3A: How Can Teachers Improve Parent–Teacher Conferences?

Introduction

This question drew suggestions later grouped under four headings: scheduling, communication, life in school, and the total child. At the time, many parents had positive comments they wished to record. They noted that their conference had been "good," a number said the conference had been "great," while yet more said that the conference was "perfect." Parents who were specific about aspects of the conference that they appreciated made the following comments: " . . . everyone was ready to start the conference" and "the teacher used a form that explains the child's performance." Teachers were also praised for being "accommodating" and "answering questions."

Scheduling

One parent noted that "one of her child's teachers did not give her a conference date," while another asked for "more advanced notice, at least a week." Yet another commented "bringing problems up at a conference is too late. I want to take care of things right away," and one went so far as to ask for "weekly reports; nine weeks is too long without talking." A few parents recommended that conferences be held later in the day "at a time convenient for parents." However, by far the largest concern among parents is that there be "more time available" for conferences.

Communication

While one parent made a point of talking about "good communication in giving positive feedback," another talked of the need to "establish good communication," and yet another—speaking out of frustration—said simply that the teacher should "tell the truth." Some parents asked for "a translator/interpreter," and one asked specifically for "help with interacting with my daughter in English so she would feel better communicating with her [English-speaking] teacher." One respondent stated that "the parent shouldn't have to ask all the questions," while another requested that the teacher have "questions ready for the parent to ask." One parent hoped that the teacher would have "more to say about my child," and "be consistent in the way they go though the forms." It was also suggested that

parents be encouraged to "bring the child" to the conference. Some feedback focused on teachers making parents more comfortable. One said, "They ignored me," focusing instead on her husband. She therefore requested that the teacher make "eye contact with the person asking the question." A suggestion to make parents feel more at ease was to "have snacks" in the classroom.

Life in school

Some parents would like teachers to take time to go beyond talking about their child's progress in the last nine weeks and explain other issues relating to life in school. One parent asked that the teacher "talk about ways they deal with discipline," while others hoped that teachers would "explain math" and "talk in depth about the grading system." Yet another needed to "know more about the gifted program so I can make a decision." Other suggestions focused on helping parents better understand what is going on in the classroom, including asking for "a walk through the classroom to get an idea of what a child experiences" and for a "child's progress to be posted in the classroom."

The total child

When surveyed, one parent had only a single problem at the conference: "I disagree with putting my child on violation." This and other parent concerns that teachers "take an interest in the child" and "be aware of other needs of the child" might begin to be met through one parent's suggestion that the teacher make "home visits." Another parent went further, suggesting that her teacher "take ideas from families on how to work with children." As part of attending to the total child, one parent asked that the teachers "research and understand more about problems such as dyslexia," while another asked that school and home communicate over "hearing and eye tests."

Summary

While many parents have positive comments to share regarding their conference experience, they also have some concerns and a number of suggestions for teachers to consider. Scheduling and communication issues dominate critical conference feedback, but parents also express interest in broadening the parent–teacher interaction to cover a range of issues affecting the lives of children both in and out of school.

Question 3B: How Could Parents Make the Next Conference Better?

Introduction
This question drew suggestions later grouped under four headings: communication, parental involvement/showing concern, preparation, and showing up.

Communication
A parent noted "parent and teachers should be on the same page." Some parents felt there was no need for improvement. Suggestions from parents on improving communication include: "receiving information from the teacher before the next conference," "communication with teachers outside of conference," and the "need to inform parents on an ongoing basis." Teachers also need to create the space for "parents to have the opportunity to ask teachers if they don't understand." For their part, parents need to "inform teachers of their child's needs" and "share history of family," if needed. This also includes the need to listen to teachers and solve problems together, and "pay attention to teachers throughout the year."

Parental involvement/showing concern
Overall, parents felt the need to "get the parents more involved." The methods of involvement included: spend more time in school, volunteer more, an know what your child is doing and what is expected of them. One of the responses was that each parent needs to "pay more attention to [his/her] children, including ways to help them," another added "make education a priority" and "learn about their child's education and how it affects the child and [his/her] life." Parents emphasized that they need to make time for their children and let them know they really care.

Preparation
Parents emphasized the importance of "knowing your questions and concerns going in." Parents should "always be prepared," which includes requesting to see the child's work and communicating with the teacher before the conference. One of the parents suggested that parents need to go in "feeling good about what you are going to discuss."

Showing up
Suggestions by the parents include the advice that parents should "attend the conference, it's important." One couple also noted the importance of "going in as a team." Other suggestions include keeping your appointment and to "be prompt and leave on time."

Summary
While many parents have positive comments to share regarding their conference experience, they also have some concerns and a number of suggestions for parents to consider. Suggestions include the importance of attending and showing concern, being prepared, and keeping the time commitment. The importance of ongoing and effective communication was once again a high priority.

Executive Summary

One hundred twenty parents attended the parent–teacher conferences; of that number 88 were surveyed for this project. The general themes of the findings were communication, scheduling, the school and teachers, the children, and what parents learned from the experience.

While many parents had positive comments to share regarding their conference experience, they also had some concerns and a number of suggestions for teachers to consider. Scheduling and communication issues dominated critical conference feedback, but parents also expressed interest in broadening the parent–teacher interaction to cover a range of issues affecting the lives of children both in and out of school. Some concerns revolved around the length of conferences and the availability of teachers during the year for more frequent communication and progress reports. Suggestions included the importance of attending and showing concern, being prepared, and keeping the time commitment. The importance of ongoing and effective communication was by far the highest priority.

The results were summarized and presented to the community in the following one-page document, produced in both English and Spanish on either side of a single page.

PROJECT SUMMARY

Undertaking the project has proved significant in three regards. First, it has demonstrated that neighborhood organizations like Barrios Juntos are capable of designing and developing a collaborative endeavor involving community members, school and district personnel, and university faculty and students. Second, this project has demonstrated that neighborhood organizations such as Barrios Juntos play a significant

---

Listening to Families at Dominguez Elementary School

The purpose of this project is to improve children's education by improving relationships between parents, children, and teachers.

Members of Barrios Juntos Neighborhood Collective talked with the school principal and teachers about parent–teacher conferences. During the week of March 20, Barrios Juntos interviewed 88 out of 200 parents about their parent–teacher conference experience.

Many parent were generally satisfied with the conference, however they suggested that conferences should be improved in the following ways:

Parents could:
- Attend the conference and be on time; this shows that parents care and are interested.
- Be aware of what your child is doing in school and what is expected of your child.
- Get more involved in your child's classroom—volunteer at school and request to see your child's work.
- Meet with teacher before conference and ask for follow-up meetings.
- Inform teachers of your child's needs.
- Put time and thought into questions to get more out of the conference. Be ready with questions and concerns.
- Show your children you care by making time for them; ask children about their concerns and ways to help.

Teachers could:
- Research and understand more about problems such as dyslexia, as well as hearing and eye tests.
- Keep parents informed on an ongoing basis and especially before conferences.
- Take ideas from families on how to work with children, problem solving, and parents.
- Bring problems up before conferences; parents want to take care of things right away.
- Supply a translator/interpreter for children who need more support understanding directions.
- Provide homework plans so parents can encourage and support child at home.
- Explain more about grading system and ways teacher/school deals with discipline.

---

role in developing and deepening home–school relations through their ability to organize the collection of large numbers of parent surveys. Finally, the project has demonstrated to a neighborhood organization such as Barrios Juntos that through their ability to develop action research agendas, universities have a potentially valuable role in strengthening community-building endeavors in school settings.

DISTRIBUTING FINDINGS

A one-page summary of project findings was distributed to the Dominguez community during the school's annual celebration. It is anticipated that a more detailed report, perhaps based on the documents, will be made available to parents upon request. Findings from the research process to date have also formed the basis of a research class presentation made by university partners, while Barrios Juntos partners have made a presentation to a university Family Literacy class.

ADDENDUM

Since completion of this project, Dominguez School has instituted changes in the way parent–teacher conferences are conducted, including extending the time available for each conference. The principal indicated that school staff were continuing to explore ways to incorporate suggestions from the research project.

---

4. STUDENTS AND TEACHER AS CO-RESEARCHERS: DEVELOPING MULTICULTURAL AWARENESS IN A HIGH SCHOOL CLASS

By Shelia Baldwin

This paper, produced as part of a dissertation study, describes a process by which a high school teacher facilitated a study of the school and local community by a group of her students. It describes the largely ethnographic methods used by students to gather and analyze data, including the innovative use of video. Of particular interest is the way major features identified by students and the teacher were formulated into tables to assist in clarifying information emerging in the study.

INTRODUCTION

This paper reports on ways in which I, as teacher of a multicultural student body in an American Culture Studies class, instituted collaborative, community-based approaches to pedagogy in response to the multicultural realities of my classroom. It reveals how the development of a community of learners through use of participatory decision making and students as researchers enabled students to affirm their cultural identity and make powerful connections between their homes and the school. In the process we were able to engage a curriculum that was more relevant to student's lives, that provided students with opportunity for critical thought in questioning existing school practices, and led them to take positive action in response to the outcomes of their inquiries.

THE GENESIS OF THE AMERICAN CULTURE STUDIES CLASS

My concern for why many high school students appear to lack interest in learning led to the pilot study that preceded the major study. I conducted an informal inquiry with a group of high school student volunteers who were encouraged to do an ethnographic study of their own cultures and the culture of the high school (Baldwin, 1997). The nine students (six seniors, two juniors, and one sophomore) of White, African American, and Hispanic backgrounds were members of the Action Committee, a group that was formed as an answer to the high school's problems with race relations.

The students and I met in the mornings before school several times during the spring semester of 1993 to learn about ethnographic methods and then to discuss observations that they had made in the school setting and in their home settings. The outcome of this inquiry was their recognition of a need for raising student awareness about cultural diversity.

So successful were our efforts that the student ethnographers encouraged me to continue with the inquiry with another group of students the next year (most of this group was graduating) or by offering a course in multicultural awareness. The course, American Culture Studies, became a reality because of the suggestion of the nine students.

Being a part of this study with students acting as ethnographers had a great impact on my teaching philosophy. The subject of the study—an inquiry into school and community culture—was relevant to them. The student ethnographers were interested and committed to this project because they were learning about themselves. They became involved and took ownership. Their desire for this project to be perpetuated through a course or continued study emphasized the importance they placed on it. I realized that inviting students to participate in decisions that affect their learning is motivational and empowering, as was demonstrated by the student ethnographers.

A CONSTRUCTIVIST APPROACH TO AMERICAN CULTURE STUDIES

Raul announced to me one day in our American Culture Studies class, "I can't believe this class is so noisy so early in the morning. Nobody's sleepin'! Everybody's so lively!" He was one of 21 high school students who assembled every morning at 7:25 A.M. for 90 minutes of cultural awareness. Of the 21 sophomores, juniors, and seniors, 14 were African American, 6 girls/8 boys; 4 were Hispanic, 3 girls/1 boy; and three were White, 2 girls/1 boy. Raul's comment is indicative of the high levels of student engagement and reflects their response to the constructivist approach to teaching/learning I had instituted for this class.

In response to the student requests just described, I had formulated an American Culture Studies course the previous semester. After gaining approval for the course outline that I wrote and submitted to the school district curriculum coordinator, the first class was offered as an elective the fall semester of 1994. I introduced the students to the course outline that would serve as a framework. I emphasized that I intended for the course to take a direction based on their own inquiries into and curiosities about cultures.

The course was divided into three-week units: "World," learning about our own heritage and other world cultures; "America," identifying and discussing sociocultural issues that permeate American society; and "Community," exploring our school/community cultures. We began our semester together with community-building activities in order to become better acquainted and more comfortable with each other. Several of the students were well acquainted—some good friends, others unknown to each other. Also, the students cooperatively devised classroom rules in order to ensure a comfortable environment in which everyone's opinion would be respected.

The requirements of the course included a reflective journal in which students wrote about anything that might relate to the course, a book to read that pertained to some aspect of culture, and participation in class discussions. Other activities evolved with the unfolding nature of the curriculum. What happened each day led us in a direction within the framework of the course outline. For example, during the second week of class, one student raised a question about her self-identity, "I'd like to know why I do some things the way I do. Like where'd they come from?" I took that cue to ask them to write down some questions they had about culture. They posed questions about their own unique heritage, cultural traits, or about the American culture: What do some of my features mean? Did my father's family originally come from Mexico? How did a particular culture start? Why do White people think they own America? Why did the pilgrims take America away from the Indians?

Another activity that evolved from a student's question became the creation of a survey about cultural relations. While we were reviewing the course outline, a student asked, "What's this survey?" I told the class that I had intended to give them a pre/postsurvey to determine attitude change, but I couldn't find one and didn't have time to construct

one. Another student suggested, "Why don't we write one and survey the student body?" So, we did. We worked collaboratively, compiling questions that related to our school and community. After it was approved by the principal, the 18-question survey was distributed to approximately 10% of the student body. Because the results came back after the end of the course, 13 volunteers (11 class members and 2 friends) tallied and interpreted the results during two afterschool sessions and had them published in the school newspaper. The results were better than what the students thought they were going to be. "It's not as negative as we thought but there is still too much negative. We need to get to know each other." The action they took was to organize a volleyball tournament for a get-acquainted activity.

Another major project the students selected was to study cultures. The class determined which cultures they would like to study and worked individually or in groups on the culture of their choice and then presented what they learned to the class.

To further our knowledge about different cultures, we invited guest speakers to our class. Our foreign exchange students from Finland and the Slovak Republic informed us about life in their countries. Another guest was a visiting professor from Australia whom they immediately dubbed the "Crocodile Man." Each class member had prepared some questions to ask our visitors. "We got to hear what *really* goes on in their countries and we stop believing only what we hear . . ." The students' attentiveness toward our foreign visitors and toward their classmates' culture project presentations indicated their interest in different countries and cultures.

A field trip, an event they talked about from the beginning, became a reality. We visited an art museum that had a special photography exhibit of the everyday life of African Americans. At another museum, we enjoyed the Imax presentation of *Serengeti* and a live butterfly center. Finally, we experienced lunch at a Chinese/Vietnamese restaurant. Several mentioned that the trip brought them closer together, exemplified in a student's comment, "I basically enjoyed everything, *especially being together.*"

Although the aforementioned were all praised and enjoyed, the highlight of the class was discussion. When I interviewed the students individually about the class, one activity that was mentioned over and over as a favorite was discussion: "We talked about things that we never talk about in other classes."

The discussions stemmed from readings taken from the Anti-Defamation League of B'nai B'rith's *A World of Difference*. They talked openly about societal issues such as alternate lifestyles, prejudice, racism, and discrimination. Students provided stories, personal experiences, and opinions, all of which prompted further discussion. One student commented, "We could go on and on." We never had enough time.

On our last day of class I asked them to interview a classmate whom they didn't get to know well during the semester. After they had completed their interviews with each other, they wrote their personal accounts of the interviews and shared them with their partners. Not only had they learned some things about each other that they didn't know, but they also changed some assumptions they had made. For example, Clifford wrote, "I thought Rosalia was just a quiet person, but the reason she didn't talk a lot is because she doesn't speak English that good." Raul wrote about Bonnie, "I never thought she was this way. Now, I know it doesn't matter who you are, color or background, we are all humans and have feelings and needs." After the sharing, students spread out to other classmates to comment about their interviews or just to visit. It was an appropriate way to close the semester. Instead of saying goodbye, I said, "I'll see you all later!"

The semester passed quickly. None of us were ready for our time together in a most meaningful learning community to be over. Students offered suggestions for continuing what we had started, "How about a Culture Studies II," or "Can we make this a year class?" or "Can I take this again?" Bonnie wrote in her final evaluation of the class, "If this class were a person, it would be an open, talkative, interesting person."

REVIEWING AND EVALUATING THE CLASS: TEACHER AND STUDENTS AS CO-RESEARCHERS

Toward the end of semester I moved toward evaluating the class. In doing so I planned to use the participatory processes that had been central to the operation of the class. It not only fit my current educational philosophy, but was consonant with educational theories of multicultural education, constructivism, and critical pedagogy, which suggest that people learn by being actively involved, by thinking about and being articulate about their learning. I was concerned not only to reflect on my own teaching processes, but to engage my students in exploring the nature and extent of their own learning.

True to the democratic, participatory intent of my pedagogy, therefore, I instituted a collaborative process to evaluate the outcomes of the class. Of the 21 students in the class, 8 to 10 students accepted my invitation to be researchers. The student researchers and I met after school on four occasions and during lunch one day. After socializing over pizza, sandwiches, or spaghetti, and soda, everyone settled down to the task at hand.

Before we began the analysis of the videotapes, I provided the student researchers with Spradley's (1979) nine major dimensions of every social situation as a means for guiding their observations, and then we proceeded. First, they viewed a videotape of some of the class sessions. As they viewed the video, I asked them to write down on their own papers words or phrases that identified what they saw happening in that classroom. From their individually written notes on their observations, they compiled a list of descriptors that a student researcher wrote on a piece of poster paper attached to the chalkboard.

The audiotape analysis proceeded a little differently because the students chose to read the transcription out loud, as though they were reading a play. They verbalized their observations at three different intervals that I recorded directly on the poster paper hanging before them.

Next, they organized the list of descriptors into categories and labeled each category. This process was repeated in each of the four analysis sessions according to which elements they agreed went together. Finally, they placed the categories from each session into a final set of categories that became their key elements that framed the account of their experience (see Table 1).

I identified key features from recurring themes that became evident in the students' analysis, together with my own journal, student journal writings, interviews, and final class evaluations (see Table 2).

CO-RESEARCHERS' PERSPECTIVES AND INTERPRETATIONS

The result of our inquiry reveals the impact of complex human relationships, curricular decisions, and

Table 8.1

Student Researchers' Categories and Key Elements

Communication	Individualism	Feelings	Involvement
Discussion Items	*"Doing Our Own Thang"*	*Emotional Feelings*	*Class Participation*
Different lifestyles	Focusing on camera	Serious, digging	Discussion—lots, good
TG has most to say	Finally settled down and	Own experiences	Interested in visitor—
Interested but afraid to	started reading	Everyone involved	asking questions
comment because of	Took Mrs. B long time to	BO upset	Certain times—all
others' opinions	get us to settle down	Heated—LL, TM, CA,	paying attention
Blurting out	Class liked CW's idea of	TG, JC	Hoodrats paying
Some students silent	cultural dancing	Feelings hurt, quiet	attention with Ernie
Not involved in discussion		Pointing the finger	All getting along
but listening		African American/	
Maintaining an image		White issue	
		Interesting	
Class Coming Together	*Stand Outs*	*Feelings of Loss*	*We Were Serious*
More positive	TG lots to say	Missing people missing	Serious, digging, best
Got to know each other	LL got serious with report	Missing Mrs. B	discussion
better	Those who never got		Storytelling, own
	into class		experiences
	TM and TG "ganging up"		Everyone involved
	on LL about pep rally		Everyone talking
			Hoodrats involved
Communication		*Letting Go*	*Interest*
Communication, flirting		Relief from class	Interest in animals
No fighting, fun all around		Students off task	Awe
Discussion, laughter		Calm—relaxed—chillin'	Involvement
Loud—quiet			Hyperactive
Mixed groups			
Beverly Hills took over			
"ghetto"			
Everyone associating			
true feelings			

pedagogical practices on a learning environment. "Getting to know each other" was mentioned numerous times in reference to different situations. The student researchers recognized the importance of getting acquainted in order to develop cultural understanding, before being able to become a viable learning community. One of the student researchers commented about this as they were categorizing the data during the second session. "We're starting to come together." As we became better acquainted, the learning atmosphere changed. Discussions became

more open and serious. We were able to discuss sensitive issues and share personal experiences.

The students' friendships extended beyond the classroom. They spoke to each other outside of the classroom, which was not common in other classes. One student explained, "When I see people from this class in the hall we speak to each other. I know them. It's not like that in other classes." First impressions of students changed after they got to know each other. A young man told me during his interview, "I would a thought they would offer this course before

Table 8.2
Teacher Researcher's Categories and Key Elements

Emerging Community	Effect of Class Makeup	Curricular Decisions	Pedagogical Practices
Students getting to know each other	African American issues	Evolving nature	Course design and content
Teacher getting to know students	African American/ White issues	Students involved in curricular decisions	Process vs. product
"Sitting with friends"	Subculture issues	Student criteria for good reports	Teacher perspective on student behavior
Varying levels of student involvement		Involvement	Missed opportunities
		• Interest in other countries	Missing Mrs. B
		• Everyone should take this course	

now. . . . Maybe we wouldn't a had all the trouble before. Just being in the class with other kids. Getting to know them. I think differently about people. Everyone should take this course." The students identified a solution to improving cultural relations as getting to know each other. The stress on getting to know other students extended beyond the classroom to the student body after the student researchers analyzed the results of the survey on culture relations. They surmised that the feelings and understanding they developed for each other in a classroom context extended beyond those walls, thus, having a rippling effect. Our recognition of the complexity of human relationships warrants the need for more effort being made to build social communities in our classrooms and in our schools. Providing time in our school day for students to get to know each other is a critical aspect of education in today's world of diversity.

Not only is it important to build understanding among the student body but also among all school personnel. I got to know my students better than any class I have ever taught because I let them bring their lives into the classroom. I learned about their home cultures, families, the dreams their parents have for them, and the respect they have for their families. I developed a greater appreciation for the pride that the students have in their cultural heritage. I learned about their painful experiences. I caught a glimpse of life from their perspective. This experience has affected the way I view my classroom, my students, my school, and my community. My own socialization had caused me to have a naïve, narrow perspective and a "that's the way it is" acceptance. That has changed as

a result of being involved with this class in cultural awareness, taught from a constructivist, critical perspective.

The makeup of the class had an effect on the direction it took. The predominance of African American students in the class steered the discussions. Discussions centered on how negative behavior of some African Americans reflected on the population as a whole, resulting in stereotyping. One student talked about "getting real embarrassed by some of the things that my African American people have been doin' and it upsets me." Another wrote, "One thing that really bothers me is the lack of respect the African American culture has for themselves." The students shared their own experiences with White prejudice. This class offered them an opportunity and a comfortable environment in which to discuss with their peers how they felt. The lived experiences they shared were an acknowledgment of how deeply rooted racism is in our society. The experiences they have had in our school and community reflect the way it is—the failure to discuss racism is problematic (Tatum, 1992).

The students' observations drew attention also to the lack of acceptance by other students and school personnel of students who represented different subcultures such as "kickers," "headbangers," and "skaters." They were becoming more critically aware of the lack of acceptance of difference in our school.

The students in the class were of varying levels of abilities, interests, and motivations. Therefore, my emphasis was on the process of learning about cultural awareness rather than the products, creating a cooperative learning atmosphere rather than a competitive one. I incorporated their perspectives into the operation of the class so that their own explorations and the reality of their community and school became the "content" of the class rather than a fixed content dictated by me. The classroom reality was transformed through their questions, discussions, presentations, reflections, and actions toward themselves as learners and toward each other.

Alternative assessments, such as self-evaluation, group evaluations, and peer evaluations, and performance-based assessments provided serious, reflective assessments of their learning, of the value of different activities, and of the strengths and weaknesses of the course.

CONCLUSION

This class was a new teaching experience for me. I was learning about multiculturalism and how to respond to it. The cultural balance in this class was unique for all of us. When the semester ended, we had become a group of people who were comfortable with each other. It was a community in which everyone had a place. As Freire (1990) discussed, we had created a dialogic community. Through dialogue, we established a climate of trust. Everyone became a partner in learning, serving as both teacher and learner. This is what happened in seven and one-half weeks.

What might have happened if we had had another seven weeks? I think we could have begun examining why some things were happening in the class. For example, we needed to talk about the different relationships in the class, such as with the two groups that existed within the African American students in the class. They had referred to one group as the "sisters" and the "pretty boys" and their seating area as "Beverly Hills." This group consisted of students who were involved in school activities and were academically motivated. The other group, the "Hoodrats" located in "the ghetto," would be described as marginalized students, those who lacked motivation and interest in school. Unfortunately, the significance of these two groups, the former representing conformity and the latter, alienation, was never a point of discussion. Why did some students participate in discussions and others didn't? What kind of community was emerging? We could have explored our feelings of discomfort and what we could do about it. We should have presented our findings of the importance

of building a community of learners and the importance of critical dialogue in classrooms today to our faculty.

The process of theory building, reflection, and action is recursive. Through my critical reflection on my own teaching practices, transformation was the result. The questions I ask continually about accepted practices of learning and teaching come from the theoretical perspectives of multicultural education, constructivism, and critical pedagogy that are reflected in the following description of our class:

> The classroom was a dialogic learning community in which teacher/learner and students/teachers were guided by a negotiated dynamic curriculum whose permeable boundaries accommodated students' inquiries as they explored, discovered, and critically questioned their world. Education was viewed as a democratic, social experience. Participants were actively involved in a cooperative partnership in which all voices were respected and afforded an opportunity to be heard in a collaborative search for understanding.

IMPLICATIONS FOR EDUCATIONAL SETTINGS

My approach to teaching this class was nontraditional. My students and I sought to change existing classroom practices through collaboration and community-based pedagogical processes. The following are suggestions for responding to multiculturalism in educational settings:

1. Build a community of learners through cooperation and collaboration, not competition. We need to recognize the complexity of the classroom as was illuminated in this study. The student researchers emphasized the importance of students getting to know one another. What happens in our classrooms is dependent on pedagogy, class makeup, and curriculum, all of which affect the building of a learning community. A critical focal point in teacher preparation and ongoing inservice for veteran teachers should be classroom dynamics. A positive, cooperative environment will have an effect on the learning that happens.

2. Invite students to participate in the decisions about their learning and their school community. The importance of students having a voice was demonstrated in this study. It was empowering and had an

effect on their interest and motivation. Let's not assume students don't know what they want to know. The curricular framework identified the course content. My students and I collaborated about how to study it and what we do to evaluate what was learned. Allowing students to have a voice will affect the climate in the classroom.

3. Affirm students' cultural identity by making a connection between the knowledge they bring to school and school knowledge. Schools tell children that the knowledge they bring to school is not important. Many of the students we teach have a home culture different from the school culture. What is validated is the White, Western European perspective, the dominant culture. As so many of us come from the same perspective, we take it for granted that "that's the way it is." We need to be more critically aware of our own socialization and how it has shaped our perspective.

4. Make curriculum relevant to students' lives and flexible to fit the diversity of learners. With each new year (new semester), we get new students. Our tendency is to teach content, not students. It is necessary to reevaluate our curriculum with each new group of students to make adjustments. The diversity of classrooms today demands that we be more flexible in order to provide equal educational opportunities.

5. Involve students in critical thought and action. Democracy should be practiced within the walls of our schools. Students should be encouraged to question existing practices and to take action if possible. My students' discovery of the need for students to get better acquainted through their survey led them to take action by organizing a volleyball tournament. Students need to know that they have insights and are a source of valuable information that can make a difference.

6. Support teachers as reflective practitioners. Teachers should be provided opportunities and support to conduct research in their classrooms and schools. This study has demonstrated how research has contributed to my developing educational theory and has informed my practice.

7. Provide teachers with ongoing professional development to help them cope with the changing demographics they are experiencing in their classrooms and schools. Teachers need to know how they might do things differently, but also they need support groups when contemplating and implementing change.

8. Incorporate ways to bring students in the school together in meaningful activities to facilitate getting to know one another.

REFERENCES

Baldwin, S. (1997). High school students participation in action research: An ongoing learning process. In E. Stringer and colleagues (Eds.), *Community-based ethnography: Breaking traditional boundaries of research, teaching, and learning.* Mahwah, NJ: Lawrence Erlbaum Associates.

Freire, P. (1990). *Pedagogy of the oppressed.* New York: Continuum.

Spradley, R. (1979). *The ethnographic interview.* New York: Holt, Rinehart and Winston.

Tatum, B. D. (1992). Talking about race, learning about racism: The application of racial identity development theory in the classroom. *Harvard Educational Review, 62,* 1–24.

5. Creating a Dialogue for the Role of Computers in the Classroom

Shepherd Lutheran School

An Action Research Project by Bill Miller

This study demonstrates how novice researchers can engage in productive studies having real relevance to the schools in which they work. Produced as a requirement of a research methods class, it explores the issue of the use of computers in the school. The study provided the school board with useful information that assisted them to make decisions about the allocation of resources in the school.

SCHOOL HISTORY

Shepherd Lutheran School offers classes K–8 and is located at 3900 Wyoming NE, in what is known as the North East Heights of Albuquerque, New Mexico. Shepherd Lutheran School (SLS) is associated with Shepherd Lutheran Church of the Wisconsin Evangelical Lutheran Synod (WELS), at the same address. SLS was started in 1982 as a two-room school housed in the church building. During the first few years the classrooms had to be disassembled every Sunday morning and reassembled each Sunday afternoon. Over the years more space was created and allocated for the classrooms. In 1994 an ambitious project of constructing a three-classroom building with a library and principal's office was completed. The school now has over 60 students and three full-time teachers with several part-time teachers for various subjects such as music and art. The student body comes from a wide economic distribution of families. There is a much less diverse mix of religious beliefs, being mostly Protestant.

By all accounts the level of caring and instruction are considered exceptional. Parents responded that the moral influence and Christian teachings were a deciding factor in placing their children there. When asked what was important to them, most parents replied, "the Christian education." Features such as small class size and interaction between the different ages are unique to Shepherd Lutheran and recognized as valuable to a child's development. Parents also felt that a good secular education was a consideration. "The secular education is

important and I think that the principal has worked hard to improve the material." A school board member added, "I think the most important thing is offering a quality education." Another parent replied, "I love it, the small class size and the big kids helping little kids." There is a concerted effort to make the students feel like part of a family by involving their families in activities and displaying family photographs on bulletin boards. While there are not the extensive programs of public schools, Shepherd Lutheran offers more than many other parochial schools. Shepherd Lutheran has the ability to change its curriculum much quicker than a larger school. Without exception the teachers are seen as dedicated and hard working. The fact that, "The teachers are approachable and easy to talk to," was stated several times. The students consider the school fun, safe, and remarked on the smallness as a positive influence. Shepherd's school board understands that the tuition costs must be competitive and that a quality education must be offered. Not only must the parents and students be satisfied, but also the teachers are seen as the most important part of the school.

INTERVIEWS CONCERNING THE USE OF COMPUTERS: PARTICIPANT VOICES

Parents' Points of View

Most of the parents spoke of using a computer in their work not just occasionally but all the time. "Today's jobs require them. The sooner the better to start learning so that there is no fear." One parent said, "This is a very serious thing; the future is in computers. I want my children to know how to use computers." More than one parent said, "It should be second nature to them." Some could not imagine their work without a computer. "Kids learn by poking around and by being exposed so they will learn to not be afraid of computers." When asked, "How do you feel about computers in the classroom?" one parent said, "They are a must." All of the parents interviewed were in favor of computers in the classroom, but there were varying degrees of what that involvement should be.

Teachers' Points of View

The teachers, depending on the grade level, had a slightly different response. Comments ranged from "Computers are very important" to "My room would function with or without a computer." One teacher said "There is one computer in my classroom that we use and I wish I had three or four computers so that more children could work at one time." Computers are seen as an important tool that can add to the classroom. "It's like having unlimited knowledge and could be used for research." New and different teaching methods can be explored. One arrangement could be a computer pod dedicated to teaching keyboard skills and word processing, plus classroom computers for research and educational presentations. There is a need to update the SLS resources: "Our current encyclopedia is 10 years old and not very good." Individual classrooms would have computers based upon need. The upper grades might have more machines, numbering anywhere from three per room to one for each student's desk. New teaching materials offer exciting and the most up-to-date knowledge for use in research. The lower grades would have a few computers for the students to use during their free time and if the appropriate software is available, learn some computer-related skills. By having computers in the school, those children that don't have one at home can gain experience. Also, the congregation could have access to the computers at certain times.

School Board Point of View

Members of the school board feel that there are many components to a quality school. The reason for creating a church school was so they could "Integrate Christ-like living into every aspect." At the same time it is recognized that "No matter what other things we stress it doesn't work unless the education component is good." School board members were more skeptical of the value of computers. "The problem with computers is they are used for the wrong reasons." Some good reasons to use a computer would be, "If a student had trouble with penmanship or to use National Geographic material." One member felt that research should be done from a book rather than a

computer and that those sources should come from outside the school. There was some concern about learning a technology that is constantly changing. "It doesn't take very long to learn how to use a computer." However, it was also recognized that "There is a lot to be gained with technical savvy. It's kind of the way we teach science these days; there aren't as many details but the purpose is to develop an interest and keep an awareness."

Students' Point of View

The students liked the smallness of the school and thought that it was harder to get good grades than in public school based on what new transfer students would tell them. They felt that some resources were rather limited, such as playground equipment. When asked about computers most said there was little or no activity with computers now. They indicated that there had been more software in the past. "There is nothing worth doing on the computers anymore. There are only three programs, a painting program that we just use to make funny drawings, an encyclopedia that doesn't have very many pictures, and a writing program." I asked what a computer could be used for and one student said, "To look things up for the dailies." "Do you have enough computers?" I asked, and several said, "We don't need more computers, we need ones that work."

PROBLEMS WITH COMPUTERS

Some of the participants spoke of sources like *High-Tech Heretic* and *Snake Oil Silicon* (Stoll, 1999, 1995), *Fool's Gold* (Cordes & Miller, 1999), and *The Computer Delusion* (Oppenheimer, 1997), but no one had actually read these books. There are some people who have become disillusioned with all the hype about how computers can solve many of education's woes, including a teacher who said, "I have been where it wasn't for the best. We had to teach children how to program a computer and that was a waste of time." There is a backlash from technology programs that promised great gains but failed to deliver. With resources being finite and having to be shared with so many mandatory expenses, computers and the associated upkeep are seen as unnecessary.

What about how quickly computers become obsolete? Are we teaching our children skills that will be of little value in the future? "The children are not interested in reading long clues and directions. They spend their time destroying robots."

Most people thought that some form of the technology will be around for a good while; the keyboard and video screen, for example, have been around for generations. "It's the generic knowledge that is part of the evolution of technology that's important," and "It was the exposure to older technology that paved the way for learning the new."

Several people had stories about how their fathers or coworkers had been afraid of computers and at the very least didn't trust them to handle their business transactions. Each of the groups recognized certain problems that come with computers. People were divided about controlling Internet access. One teacher felt that it was a personal responsibility of the student and teacher as to what was downloaded from the Net. One teacher complained, "The trouble with politicians is that they say they want government out of our lives but then introduce legislation to control what we do." All interviewees felt that some form of restriction should be employed but were divided over whether it should be from the teacher, software, or both. The jury is still out on the most effective method. A recent article in the Sioux Falls, South Dakota, *Argus Leader* reports, "Written policy to keep South Dakota State Library computer users from accessing obscene material seems to work better than electronic filtering software."

There was some concern about relying on the Internet to do research and allowing programs to automatically check and correct for spelling. Turning off features in a word processor would reduce this dependency but also eliminate some of the power of the computer. One teacher said it is "just another tool that if used correctly can be of value." The Internet really does bring the world onto a screen just inches from your face. This could be threatening to some as it is unfiltered and contains many wildly different points of view.

SOLUTIONS

There must be common ground that all the stakeholders feel comfortable with. The parents see computers in the classroom as a natural part of the curriculum. Teachers depending on grade level see value in having the technology available. Students seem unsure of the value of a computer in the classroom. They know how much fun they can be and how to use the available software but in general don't see them as

being valuable in schoolwork. Some recognize that the current machines are very old and slow. The school board is more cautious, being wary of what computers bring into the classroom as well as the added expense.

How to handle the added expense of a new program is perhaps the biggest stumbling block. One teacher felt that "Given a reasonable amount of resources we should have one computer for every three or four students in the classroom." Parents all agreed that it would be reasonable to increase either the registration fee or tuition by $40 per student per year. One parent remarked, "I think it would be worth twice that." Other sources would be required, as $40 per student would bring in about $2000. Some of the expenses such as Internet access would require consistent funding. Donations are a good way to purchase additional items that are a "one-time expense," but cannot be depended upon for a program that hopes to build and maintain a high level of reliability.

One school board member remarked that "more teacher involvement with the school board and maybe even a female school board member" would be desirable. The PTO was also mentioned several times as a possible major player. Another school board member suggested "We need a model and to look down the road because there is no plan or plan to create a plan."

A PLAN TO CREATE A PLAN

A joint plan was created by representatives of all interested parties—parents, teachers, students, school board, and members of the congregation.

REASON AND METHOD

The purpose for conducting this ethnographic research was to produce a qualitative look at how these different groups of participants view the use of computers in the classroom. By recording these voices and weaving them into a report so that each of the groups could hear themselves speak, it is hoped that a discussion will be initiated and action taken to create a clear vision of how Shepherd Lutheran wants to proceed with introducing its students to the technology of today.

During the course of interviewing Shepherd's stakeholders I asked each group to tell me about Shepherd Lutheran School. The questions were intended to get the participants talking about their feelings. Other questions were varied from "Tell me about your classroom" to a more direct "How do you feel about computers in the classroom?" Rather than build a survey and have the results displayed in graphical format, an action research project provides for a qualitative analysis for the facilitator and participants to interpret.

METHODOLOGY OF STUDY

The use of computers in the classroom was not so much in doubt, but rather the extent of use. All of the classrooms currently have computers. There is not a policy in place that all the interested parties can refer too in order to achieve a desired result.

To determine what Shepherd Lutheran School might desire to do about technology in the classroom, they could look at what other schools are doing. Several studies and inventories have been done in similar schools locally and around the country, such as Valine (1995). Rather than site statistics and make comparisons to other schools, SLS can take this opportunity to find out what the various stakeholders desire in their school.

Members from each stakeholder group were interviewed at least once over the course of two months. A second interview with selected participants helped to clarify statements and cover new ground opened up by the first interview. Many of the interviews were conducted in the participants' homes. All of the teacher interviews took place at school either in their classroom or in the administrative office. Several people wanting to be interviewed chose to do so in a public place such as a restaurant because they could do so during a lunch break or felt more comfortable in a neutral setting. Most of the interviews were one hour long except those of the students, which were 15 to 20 minutes. I found that the younger participants required a great deal of interaction to get a response of more than three or four words. I selected four teachers, seven parents, two school board members, and four students. This gave about an equal ratio of participants for three of the four given group sizes. The teachers were overrepresented as I felt they would be impacted the most by any changes in the classroom. My role in this study was to be a facilitator in making the various opinions known to each group. I am not a member of the Shepherd Lutheran Church congregation. My two sons have attended SLS for a combined total of 15 years. For three years I severed as chairman of the Technol-

ogy Committee. It was during this time that I realized that there was a significant difference between what the four groups wanted to do about computers in the classroom.

I used the concept of descriptive questions as formulated in *The Ethnographic Interview* (Spradley, 1979). Stakeholders were asked to engage in dialogue, which required them to reveal feelings rather than facts about their situation. I used what is known as the unstructured schedule interview and the unstructured interview as outlined in *The Research Act* (Denzin, 1970). This allows for a more flexible series of questions that can build on the answers of previous answers. The differences in people interviewed and their backgrounds and roles made it desirable to enter into the interview from different points. Most all of the questions remained consistent in content but the order was changed. In a few situations some questions were not asked or were modified to take advantage of a particular person's knowledge about some aspect that he or she was involved with. The process evolved much like that described in *Action Research* (Stringer, 1999), where there was constant reevaluation and modification to the process. New questions evolved from the interview process. Each phase of the project had an impact on all the others and forced changes to be made all along the way. The processing of information was not nearly as complex as that reported in *Pedagogy of the Oppressed* (Freire, 1974); however, the intent was the same and that was to give a voice to the participants and allow for their experiences to influence the reality their children will be molded by in the school environment.

The sense that I got from this project and the study of several forms of participant research seems to be shared by Guba when he discusses alternative paradigm dialogues in *The Paradigm Dialogue* (Guba, 1990). There is a synthesis of theories that can be made by a newcomer that blurs the boundaries defined by various schools of thought.

All of the interview material was transcribed from hand notes or tape recordings into type-written documents. These notes are available upon request as both raw field notes and transcribed MS Word documents. Answers to like or similar questions from each participant were grouped together and reviewed for division into units of meaning. From these categories and subcategories a narrative was written to give each group of stakeholders a story created and organized by the data (see Appendix).

FINAL MEETING

The final meeting with participants took place on the evening of November 28, 2000, at the Parent Teacher Organization (PTO) meeting. I presented the details of what was required for this study. I asked the participants to put together a puzzle for me, which was well received and required them to work together for a few minutes.

A couple of additional comments were made as follows:

"We as a school board have to be wary of what are known as 'gifts that eat.'" It was explained that money was in short supply and that the school was in no position to commit itself to an expensive program.

A parent came up to me afterward and expressed support for use of computers in the classroom because she had worked for a construction company during the summer, and had noted that "No one at this company knew how to use a computer and we had a terrible time completing the project."

The outcome was to form a committee that would meet early next year to discuss how to formulate a plan that would get Shepherd Lutheran on the road to implementing a modern computer project. For the short term it was agreed to gather the existing computers and create a "computer lab" in the old church building. One person volunteered to contact an electrician to install the required extra electrical circuit.

An indication of the commitment to improving the school was the approval later that evening to spend $6000 on new playground equipment. This showed, at least to me, that while money is scarce there is still the ability to obtain funds and gather the support for big projects. Installation of playground equipment requires a lot of sweat equity on the part of the parents.

REFERENCES

Cordes, C., & Miller, E. (1999). *Fool's gold.*

Denzin, N. K. (1997). *Interpretive ethnography.* Thousand Oaks, CA: Sage.

Freire, P. (1974). *Pedagogy of the oppressed.* New York: Seabury.

Guba, E. G. (1990). *The paradigm dialogue.* Newbury Park, CA: Sage.

Oppenheimer, T. (1997, July). *The computer delusion. The Atlantic Monthly.*

Spradley, J. P. (1979). *The ethnographic interview.* New York: Holt, Rhinehart & Winston.

Stoll, C. (1995). *Silicon snake oil.* New York: Doubleday.

Stoll, C. (1999). *High-tech heretic.* New York: Doubleday.

Stringer, E. T. (1999). *Action research.* Thousand Oaks, CA: Sage.

Valine, D. (1995). *Lutheran school computer technology survey elementary schools.* AAL.

6. DOGGEREL

An Elementary School Children's Research Project

By Michael LaFlamme

This piece was originally produced as a poem by a teacher as a record of a project engaged in by children and teachers in a kindergarten class. It records the way they explored and then developed solutions to a problem experienced by the school and its community. The poem was later modified and put to music.

This is story about children and dogs,
In Ojo Amarillo Elementary
In a town called Fruitland on the Navajo land,
A land where dogs run freely and their hearts are free.
It happened in a school with 300 kids
With freedom to walk around,
A school in a town with 300 dogs
With freedom to roam the ground.

Refrain
They said,
Don't let 'em run loose,
Keep 'em tied up all day,
In a yard where they'll always be found.
Take care of your dog,
Or the dog catcher will,
And she won't live long at the pound.

Every day the dogs roamed over to school,
And waited for the kids at the school front door.
Every day when children walked out of their
    school,
The dogs at the door scared 'em a little bit more.

One day the principle cried, "Dog catcher
Catch these 300 pets."
The next day the children cried for their dogs,
Numbered a few hundred less
The kindergarten brainstormed what they
    could do,
And decided to visit the city dog pound.
The kids asked some questions and they thought
    of a plan,
To care for the dogs who live in their town.
They counted the dogs that were fenced in or
    chained,
They counted the dogs that were stray
They met with a vet with her stuffed dog and cat,
And molded their pets out of clay.
They opened a veterinary clinic in school
And learned how to keep their pets well.
They read all the books that the library had,
And decided it was time to tell.

They wanted to share all the knowledge they had,
And thought that some posters might help dogs
    the most.
They posted them up at the grocery store,
And posted them down at the trading post.
The posters told grown-ups to take care of pets
A message from kids of age five.
They published their research in posters 'round
    town,
To save a few hundred more lives.

7. CLASSROOM CHAOS

By Margo Jones

This study enabled a special education teacher to explore a difficult class situation to which she had been assigned. The purpose of the study was to enable her to understand the nature of the difficulties she experienced. By observing the class systematically and interviewing students she was able to gain greater clarity about the dynamics of the class and the history of the situation. She commences with a poem as a means of evoking an understanding of her experience, then reflects on the information she had accumulated in the course of the study. Much of the account mirrors her interpretation of her own reflections, rather than a description and analysis of events. It might be seen, therefore, as auto-ethnographic.

Entering into a world of yelling and anger,
A place where screaming and noise abound—
I don't feel like staying here for long
My world is spinning, whirling round and round.

There are children in this chaotic place
Have they been like this for long?
How can they stand the fighting and bickering?
The unrest that keeps going on and on and on—
A piece of this and a grain of that—a word said
Here and there
Not much makes sense at the present time.
Is there any one insider or out that cares

By themselves and alone they slowly come
Waiting to listen to strange questions of sorts
Like none they have expected to hear
  Faces that show no happiness, faces that are
    alone.
    Faces that have learned to hide some kind of
      fear . . .

Do they have so much anger?
What has made them like this?
Can it be just one solid reason?
Can it be answered in one quick list?

The major components that seemed to emerge from my analysis of data—observations of the class and student interview—were student anger and frustration, and negative relationships that had existed during the time that the previous teacher and the substitutes had been in charge. Although the students made many negative comments, I do not think that they knew exactly what was causing their discontent. I do know that they all told me they did not like their other teacher and thought she did not like kids. Though most of their anger appeared to be directed toward the previous teacher and the educational assistant, it was carried over to me when I took the position. When interviewed, the students were most definitely unhappy with the classroom situation and did not have any sense of wanting to cooperate with each other or to develop a positive relationship with the teacher or the assistant.

Since the approximate age of the students was 11, I think part of their anger originated from a sense of helplessness and confusion in the classroom situation, as they did not have an established safe atmosphere. The students had many learning difficulties as well as emotional problems, and this factor, combined with many changes in their daily routine, created an even larger sense of frustration and helplessness. Since they did not know who would be there from week to week, or exactly what they would be learning, emotions became more inflamed, and they directed their anger at the teacher and the assistant as a way to vent their unhappiness.

The previous teacher indicated she did not leave because of a wish to leave teaching, but a number of substitutes had been called in, which contributed to a continuing lack of consistency. This factor probably accounted for the children's sense of instability and laid the foundation for insecurity in the environment, and the way they were dealing with the situation that had developed in the classroom. According to the students, there was much vocal activity from the teacher, which appeared from their comments to be focused both toward individual students as well as the class as a whole.

When I arrived in the classroom, I was not prepared for what was taking place. After the first day,

I was convinced that there had been no follow-through on rules, and that whatever had happened previously must have been an absolute disaster. This first impression was also colored by the actions and words of the students and the educational assistant. None of the students had anything good to say about the previous teacher and many were constantly complaining about the educational assistant. The classroom was a total mess! Students were up and down constantly, none raised their hands to speak, and if one tried to tell me something, others were constantly making rude comments. If the educational assistant (EA) tried to intervene, students told her to "shut up," and would not listen to anything she had to say. All I heard for the first few weeks was talking out, rude comments, and students who were complaining, crying, and very disturbed.

After providing some ground rules and trying to establish some kind of relationship with the class, I decided to interview the students in order to find out as much as I could about why there was so much chaos and discontent. Although I saw a difference in the class after I had been there for a few weeks, I wanted to try to find out what was the cause of so much anger and discontent. Even though I did take information from formal interviews as well as informal discussions with students and the EA, I needed to do more interviews after more time had passed. My situation and the dynamics of the class were so "out of wack" that my main time and focus was on working directly with the students, with limited time to work on formal interviews. I was able to gain insight over the next several months, since I stayed until the end of the year. I do not think that the students actually understood clearly why they were so angry, but from their perspective, they appeared to be feeling unsafe and unsure because of the lack of consistency in teachers and in rules. They appeared upset because the previous teacher had told them she did not want to be a teacher any longer, which added to their anger when confronted by numerous substitutes.

When I arrived in late September, they had already established patterns of classroom behavior, perceptions of what constituted teacher effectiveness, and opinions about who should be respected. This was a great "wall" to overcome, but by March, the students gave me a surprise party! I did have some changes in my class roster, but the main contributor to the success of the class was that I stayed and established some sense of respect and relationship with the students. At the end of the year, many asked if I was coming back, and they hoped they would be in my class! I would like to have seen more educational learning accomplished during the year, since the majority of my time and effort went into building trust and security. Formal learning took a "back burner" to creating a safer and more peaceful environment.

8. CLASS EVALUATION: SOMETHING

By Denise Baccadeutre

Written by a teacher as part of a group presentation for a conference, this paper includes the sung rendition of the author's experience of a graduate class. It demonstrates the way performances may powerfully evoke a person's learning experience, though much of the impact is lost in this print version. As a means of evaluation, it provides concrete evidence of the meaning of her learning experience, enabling the audience to understand how learning research enters her inner personal life and her more public professional life. As an evaluation, it focuses on student outcomes rather than instructional processes.

The class assignment at the end of the Qualitative Research semester was to pair off with another person in the class and, using Spradley's questioning techniques, focus on the other person's experience in this class, identify the key or important elements of the other's experience, and put it in a framework to create a presentation—an evocative account, a performance assessment—that would enable the others in the class to understand that person's experience in the class. Elliot Eisner (1999) states, "Despite the lack of a single definition, performance assessment is aimed at moving away from testing practices that require students to select the single correct answer from an array of four or five distractors to a practice that requires students to create evidence through performance that will enable assessors to make valid judgments about 'what they know and can do' in situations that matter."

I teamed with classmate Karen Higgins. She interviewed me and, together, we went back through what I had articulated to her; we bracketed the information. We discovered that the difficulty of the class assignments and my accomplishment of the assigned coursework gave me the confidence to approach and complete further assignments. I shared with her that I had so many insecurities as a woman in my late 40s believing that I had the intellectual ability to achieve at the doctoral level. We discussed the stereotypical views of women our age—they emerged from a period in time when women became teachers, nurses, librarians, or homemakers. Although this assignment occurred years later, there was still tremendous societal and familial pressure as well as personal guilt over leaving family roles and obligations behind and pursuing personal educational growth. It was a constant struggle not to give it up and slide back into the traditional female roles. The construction and understanding of the experience allowed me to make meaning of what was happening to me as I successfully completed each assignment of the class throughout the semester.

As a music educator at the secondary level, I am very aware of the nearly unparalleled ability of music to express and elicit emotional response. I have witnessed this response in my students, parents, and community to musical performance. I have shed tears at the beauty of my students' musical expression. I am also aware that the arts are in constant danger of eradication in the public schools as the current swing of the educational pendulum calls for greater accountability, standardized testing, and rising test scores. With music, with emotional response, measurable outcomes seem incompatible, and therefore must be invalid. Eisner (1999) further offers:

> Each of the forms of representation that exist in our culture—visual forms in art, auditory forms in music, quantitation forms in mathematics, propositional forms in science, choreographic forms in dance, poetic forms in language—are vehicles through which meaning is conceptualized and expressed. A life driven by the pursuit of meaning is enriched when the meanings sought and secured are multiple.

Through the nature of this assignment, I was able to utilize that which was most comfortable to me, a familiar mode of emotional expression that would provide the framework for helping others make meaning of my experience—musical performance.

Qualitative Research Evaluation Presentation: A Vocal Parody on "Nothing" from Chorus Line

Submitted by Denise Baccadutre
December 9, 1999

SOMETHING

When I read my email and learned that Tom Smith was back and was going to teach Qualitative Research, all of a sudden the LLSS class I had enrolled in seemed very uninteresting. So I called Tom up and asked if he thought I was ready for this class. I had discovered that many students in my previous two semesters were much more brilliant than I was and some had taken an academic writing classes. They were surely leaps and bounds ahead of me. Tom kind of snickered and replied, "There's more to qualitative research than writing. Yes, I think you're ready."

In spite of Tom's confidence in my abilities, I had so many insecurities. But pursuing this degree, taking one course a semester, is really the only thing I ever do for myself.

Sing:

Once a week, for myself I would wave goodbye to my students, hit the highway, leave it all behind

Once a week, I would allow myself to feel worthy, myself to feel special, open my mind.

And I dug right down to the bottom of my soul to see what I had inside,

Could I understand what was presented to me? So I tried, I tried . . .

Speak:

And my students were preparing for All-State, and two District Honor Choirs, and the Winter Concert literature had to be taught, and I got a call asking me to be choral president for the state of New Mexico

Sing:

But I was learning something, I was feeling something, and Something was Special to me . . .

Could it be happening that I could interpret what the "other" was telling to me??

Speak:

But I said to myself, "Hey! This is Denise the Insecure fooling herself into believing she understands something."

Sing:

Second month, more advanced and we had to turn in a proposal, focus our research, tell what and why. . . .

Tommie-man, he would say to us, "gotta state the purpose, gotta state the outcome"—I wanted to cry.

But I dug right down to the bottom of my soul to see what I had inside,

Could I represent to him what I wanted to explore—so I tried, I tried . . .

And I wrote something, I envisioned something, and wrote and re-wrote until I was fried.

I turned it in and Tommie liked it and in my mind I felt suddenly glorified.

Speak:

And then I received an email from Tom stating our second draft of our research must be expanded to at least eight pages—I hyperventilated and whispered—Oh my God!!!!!

Sing:

Went to church, praying, Santa Maria, send me guidance, send me guidance, On my knees.

Went to church, praying Santa Maria, help me feel it, help me know it, Pretty Please?

And a voice from down at the bottom of my soul came up to the top of my head.

And a voice from down at the bottom of my soul, here is what it said:

You are something! You can do something! You can do this, you just need to try.

And when you do it, you'll know you're special—just go to the computer, focus your mind and fly . . .

Speak:

Well, flying meant many hours of reading, working on the Internet, working on the computer, and rewriting something to submit that would not be an embarrassment . . .

Sing:

Ernie gave it back to me, and I confess, I hesitantly turned to the back page and nearly cried . . .

Because he wrote "Emerging beautifully, but still some way to go."

REFERENCES

Eisner, E. (1999, May). The uses and limits of performance assessment. [Online]. Available at *http://www.pdkintl.org/kappan/keis9905.htm.*

9. ODE TO DENIZEN

By M. Cathrene Connery

Sometimes a learning journey creates movements in people's lives that cannot be expressed through the linear logic of written prose. This poem provides insight into the complexity of a teacher's transformative experience of a graduate class. In her journal she had written: "It has been a long time since I have had a paradigmatic shift like this in such a profound way . . . like a small earthquake or miniature shock of lightening arousing me from my day-to-day automatic pilot semi-slumber. .".

1st

My
  static
    obscurity
a- stainless- steel- alone
  assigned by
  sharp edged
  numerals,
    bruised
not so funny bones.

2nd

Two
  his
  his / story?
    Tory, hegemonic
  plot of
    dualistic seesaws
    number battles
    power sought.

III.

You /I/ Together
  triads standing strong
    creators
    preservers
    destroyers
    words,
      descriptions,
        songs.

Fourth

We are balanced centers
  body-mind-and-soul
  dance~defined~e~motions~
    sensitivity: understanding::
    affect: growth.

Fifth

The promise of a homecoming
  as we slowly top the rise.
    Smoke of distant fires
      clearing in the skies.
Circles of atonement
  no ethical postponement
    for ours is now the moment,

Sixth.

10. Children's Construction of History: A Quilt

By Ann Claunch

This dissertation study by an elementary school teacher sought ways to improve her teaching of history by understanding how children learned history. She started from the research question "How do 9- and 10-year-olds construct historical time from reading and discussing narrative?" The outcomes of repeated cycles of inquiry were presented pictorially and assembled as a quilt.

SEGMENT 1

I chose to use a visual representation for two reasons: Representing my thoughts with images forced me to sort my thinking into concise statements, and the artistic representation of thought paralleled what I asked elementary students to do in my research. I used the construction of the images as a prewriting activity. In each segment there are two figures and a triangle. The two figures represent my husband and daughter. Committing to a doctoral program is a paradox; it is a selfish act but cannot be completed alone. My husband and my daughter were my "emotional committee," which I found as vital as my academic committee. The triangle in each segment represented my attempt to

continually view my research from three different angles, through the lens of the curriculum, of the teacher, and of the students.

SEGMENT 2

I have never held the view of my mother's generation on limiting women to certain roles, but as I entered graduate school again, I discovered there was a residue of a "woman's place" ingrained in my psyche. As I considered continuing my education, I had internal and external pressures reminding me that embarking on this journey was not a necessity. My daughter was seven and an only child. I struggled with the balance between the roles of student, mother, wife, and teacher. My husband let me torture myself for a time, knowing this is a natural decision-making process for me, until he intervened. He helped me narrow my hesitations and I discovered my primary reservation was our daughter. He opened my mind to a new perspective by stating, "What better mom could you hope to be, than to show your daughter life's possibilities." Thank you John.

SEGMENT 3

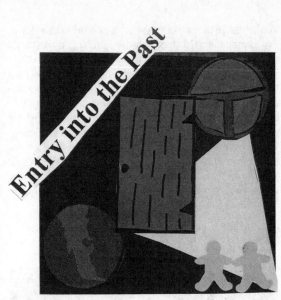

I wanted children to study how history is learned. After teaching for 18 years, I was puzzled about how to teach history to 9- and 10-year-olds. The textbooks and the curriculum seem to present isolated facts and events along a timeline, and it was up to the students to piece together the larger pictures over years. The closer I observed and thought about what was actually being learned when I taught from the textbook, the more I became frustrated. I identified that somehow I must match the facts and the events into a complete story to help children understand history. In order to accomplish this I had to mesh together different elements in teaching: the pedagogy, the curriculum, the content, the resources, and the cognitive development of the students. One of the results of my study began with moving from presenting history deductively—large to small—to more inductively, small to large.

SEGMENT 4

I wanted to provide an entry into the past by moving backwards from the present. I imagined this entry like a curriculum doorway that supported children's experiences and moved them to another place and time. In this segment I attempted to depict a modern globe and compare it to a T-O map of the early twelfth and thirteenth centuries, where there was thought to be only three continents, Africa, Asia, and Europe.

SEGMENT 5

The conceptual plan (Taba, 1969) for my curriculum was my roadmap. I used the conceptual plan to broaden my thinking for a year-long curriculum plan. It also structured the curriculum for the teacher deductively and for the students inductively. As a teacher I knew that in order to bring the big picture of history it needed to be developed through description. Stories invite the reader into a mental picture of the setting. I opted to use narrative rather than textbooks in my teaching of history. I wanted to see if it made a difference. By including different narratives, I wanted to create an entry into the past that was relevant to young historians. I wanted the students to be excited about moving from the present into the world of history. The curriculum, the pedagogy, the resources, and my understanding of cognitive development became the passageway to move students mentally into history. My question evolved, "How do 9- and 10-year-olds construct historical time from reading and discussing narrative?"

SEGMENT 6

History was an interest I developed after my master's degree and 10 years of teaching. I remembered hating the subject in high school because it was reduced to "read these pages, answer the questions, and be prepared for the test on Friday." I learned about skimming and memorizing the bold-print words but very little about the content. The history I remembered was about people. The history that was of interest for me was the narratives that were descriptions of how people lived and everyday life in another time. I began to read and think about children's literature as a way to present history. Knowing that it is important to allow for the voices of history that have traditionally been

silenced, I collected books that looked at history from different perspectives. The quilt piece segment has books about World War II that look at the Japanese as heroes, victims, and aggressors.

SEGMENT 7

I had an idea about how to change the curriculum by using narrative, and I had formulated my question. Next I chose my research setting. After four years out of the classroom, working with novice teachers, I did not want to go back to the isolation of one teacher in a classroom so I decided to team teach. I chose someone I had known for 10 years and had spent the last 4 years teaming with as a supervisor. We knew each other well. I wanted someone who would tell me what they thought quickly without the dance of politeness. We both believed in the constructivist approach to teaching. We found an opening with a principal that was accepting of my research and team teaching. It was a unique setting because the public school was located in an U.S. Air Force Base surrounded by six-foot chain-link fence. Access to the school was through a military gate that required all who entered to show proof of insurance, current registration, and a driver's license. I was interested to see how a traditional military community would react to my "Revisionist" history lessons.

SEGMENT 8

August brought the realities of the classroom and dumped chaos into my research road map. Fissures in my curriculum, my lack of knowledge of the student population, my ability to team with another teacher, and my choice of novels (difficulty level) began to develop. This was not only in teaching history but also in my math, reading, and science classes. Partly this was due to being out of the classroom for four years as a supervisor of novice teachers and partly due to trying to layer my research plan onto students I knew very little about.

convinced that our time as a community of learners would be better spent on concepts children were ready to learn—geography-like mapping skills, continents, and states and capitals. She often questioned me whether 9- and 10-year-olds were too young to learn history. At times I agreed with her but a persistent thought of "How can I present the idea of history better" kept me pursuing my research. The opportunity to articulate my views on teaching and learning were both good and bad. I enjoyed challenging my thinking but it was emotionally draining having to justify and negotiate every decision in the classroom. Looking back, she was key to my research because she always insisted on my articulating "why" I thought what I was teaching was important for children to learn.

SEGMENT 9

Another major chasm in my research was my team teacher. Although we both believed that students learn by constructing knowledge, we had a different opinion about the teacher's role in that learning. I aligned myself with Jerome Bruner, believing that any child can learn any new concept if it is presented in an intellectually honest way. My team teacher held to strong beliefs of not delivering curriculum until it was age appropriate. The agreement was that children constructed their own knowledge, but what became an intellectual battleground was our differing opinions of what opportunities to provide. After meeting our children she was firmly

SEGMENT 10

During the initial part of the year I read many historical narratives as a part of the reading aloud section of the day. I chose to do this in order to help students familiarize themselves with a relatively new genre. I immediately noticed a trend in how students scaffold new historical knowledge. The students used the media as their backboard when explaining unfamiliar information. I documented 24 times in a three-week period where a student referenced something we were reading to a television show or a movie. Popular movies were *Sounder, Gone with the Wind,* Disney's *Pocahontas,* and *Titanic.* I began to wonder what their

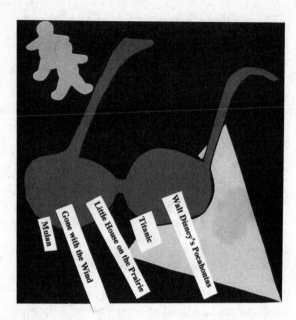

Students had a difficult time in organizing time from past (10 years ago) to long ago (400–500 years ago) and then to the very distant past (1000–2000 years ago). Organization by events, thought processes, and articulation were inconsistent. I began to work with the students on passage of time. The class experimented in developing ways that show passages of time and movement through drawings. I did this because history is tied to chronology.

"mind's eye" was seeing as I read the book *Morning Girl* by Michael Dorris (results are in Segment 17). I began to ask the students to draw as I was reading in an attempt to make comprehension visible.

SEGMENT 12

SEGMENT 11

I wanted to know what knowledge the students had about history, so I asked them to tell me or illustrate the following question; "What is history?" This was prompted by the interest and confusion about the passage of time that I had. The broad categories that I extracted from their responses were: a record of the past, a list of peoples that died a long time ago, and the dinosaurs. I also looked for the binary concepts of what history isn't. The major underlying assumption in the answer to the question was that history happened a long time ago and was not happening now.

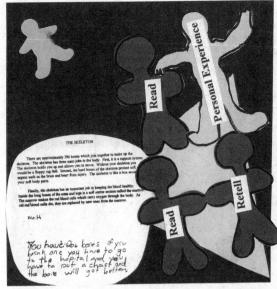

SEGMENT 13

"Listen to the Mustn'ts" is a poem by Shel Silverstein that I read to see how students interpreted texts with multiple meanings and outside the history arena. I knew this was an important mind-set of history since there are always multiple truths with any historical event. I read it aloud and asked the students to think about the poem and then asked the students to read the poem silently. The discussion was opened with "Tell me what you read." The 9- and 10-year-olds went into literal interpretation, and I continued with, "What does this mean to you?" The literal interpretations of the poem by the students continued. Two aspects of teaching were going on that were frustrating. One, I wanted an answer in the abstract and the students were entering into the conversation through the concreteness of personal experiences. The second phenomena was that the open-ended questions I was asking were unsupportive of students that had spent their last years in school believing that reading had a right answer. I needed to listen to what students said, not what I expected them to say. I also needed to scaffold my questions when I wanted to elicit abstract responses.

SEGMENT 14

Another "Aha" happened during a science lesson when I was exploring a teaching strategy known as read and retell. Students would be able to read a

crucial paragraph from the text as many times as they needed to reproduce the paragraph in their own words. This is a common strategy used in working with students learning a second language. It allows students to be comfortable with the text and then use their own words to reconstruct the meaning. I noticed a trend: Students would read the text but when they began to reconstruct the paragraph, it was a mixture of what was said in the text and a connection with personal experience.

SEGMENT 15

Words≠Action? I continued to take note of what students were saying about the novels as I read each aloud. I also increased the expectation of drawing as I read. I teased out another insight. When I was reading a historical novel and began a discussion, many times students were able to discuss the novel coherently. At the same time, when I looked at what they drew, it became evident that there were discrepancies. This segment shows a drawing of Morning Girl, a character in a book by the same name. It is set in the 1490s. The main character is a Taino Indian. Chapter 14 opens with Morning Girl's mother cooking breakfast and discussing the day's events. When a student referred to this part orally she said, "Morning Girl is listening as her mother is talking about gathering berries and getting ready for the winter. Her mother is cooking breakfast."

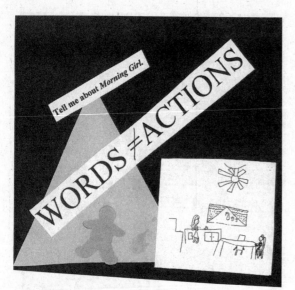

It was at this point that nothing was new in the discovery of how children learned in my research. I knew the information about schema, the importance of relevance in curriculum, the child development theories, and I was proving them over and over in what I was seeing. I had a paradigm shift in my thinking. Instead of validating all the things that 9- and 10-year-olds could not do, I began to question what they could do. I began to watch for the tools they brought to their historical toolbelt of understanding. One of their tools in their toolbelt was drawing. Nearly all students doodled and drew while they were thinking. The example I had on the segment was a typical "Spelling Test." Nine and 10-year-olds used drawing as a way to communicate thought.

The student's drawing of the same scene clearly depicted the kitchen in the present. My next question was, "How does this impact comprehension of history?"

SEGMENT 17

SEGMENT 16

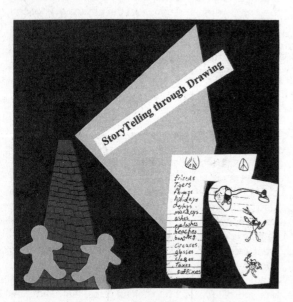

I knew that students understood that there was a passage of time and that certain events came in chronological order. I used this tool of understanding to nudge forward and build a complex, comparative timeline alongside the students as well as at different perspectives in history.

SEGMENT 18

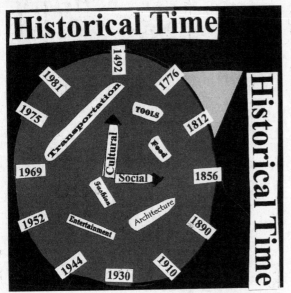

I narrowed what historical time was to the social and cultural aspects of different time periods. I asked the students to concentrate on thinking about the art, the transportation, the architecture, the fashion, the food, and the entertainment of each period we studied. This was a strategy that helped the students to compare their lives to those of another time period.

Online Resources

INTRODUCTION

In the past few years online resources to support action research in schools have proliferated. A reasonably superficial search will uncover a vast array of links that provide educational practitioners with access to resources specifically relevant to their work. By judicious selection, action researchers may link to the courses, project descriptions, organizations, resources, listservs, and/or papers most suited to their purposes.

ONLINE WEB SEARCHES

Web searches may be conducted to acquire understanding of action research processes, to acquire data relevant to a particular topic or issue, or to extend a literature review. The Educational Resources Information Center (ERIC) provides a comprehensive database for educational literature, but a broader search may be made using any of the standard search engines, such as Yahoo!, Altavista, and so on. Google Academic is a particularly good source.

To conduct an online Web search, researchers should:

- **Carefully define the topic.** A succinct definition of a topic aids clarity and precision. It ensures you get the type of information you require. A description that is too general or lengthy will not give sufficient focus to the search.
- **Identify key terms.** Key terms identify the type of information required. Select two or three terms that define the nature of the topic. If you were searching for information about the use of phonics in teaching reading, you might use the terms "teaching," "reading," and "phonics."
- **Log on to search function.** Log on to the ERIC website (*http://www.accesseric.og*) and click on "Search ERIC Database"; or log on to a search engine (by clicking on to the "search" icon, then selecting the desired search engine).
- **Enter key terms.** Enter previously identified key terms.

- **Refine the search.** Often an initial search will not provide appropriate sources. It may identify many sources only peripherally related to the topic investigated, or fail to identify an adequate body of resources. The search may be refined by changing the key terms, or by adding another term that locates the topic more precisely. For example, the terms, "teaching," "elementary," and "phonics" may be substituted for the previous key terms. It might also be possible to refine the search by identifying the years to be searched or the type of publication to be included in the search.
- **Evaluate sources.** Web searches may identify a large array of material, some of which is of questionable value. Researchers should evaluate the quality of material to ensure its adequacy or appropriateness to the study in which they are involved.

USEFUL WEBSITES

The sites listed in the next section provide but a small sample of websites giving information about action research. There are some limitations to these materials, insofar as even new sites go temporarily offline, and some become superseded. In some instances those authoring the sites have no resources to update the information and the sites become outdated. Those limitations aside, however, there is a wide range of resources having the potential to greatly enrich an action research project by providing links to practitioners with similar professional or educational interests.

The following categories differentiate between types of sites, but these are not mutually exclusive, since some sites are linked to others or link to similar sources. A brief search, however, will provide researchers with an understanding of the range of sites relevant to their purposes and contexts. A rather simple but effective method of identifying action research sites is to enter "Action Research Schools" as the descriptor in a search engine and review the sites presented. More focused searches using more specific descriptors will reveal sites with more relevant information.

GENERAL WEBSITE RESOURCES

These websites are multidimensional sites, each providing access or links to a broad range of topics and resources related to action research. They include literature, links, lessons, resources, papers, publications, and descriptions of projects.

AR Expeditions—Action Research Journal: An online professional journal promoting dialogue between members of the action research community. It includes articles describing action research projects as well as strategies for conducting action research. It also hosts an online dialogue about issues in action research. (*http://www.montana.edu/arexpeditions/index.php*)

Action Research Resources: The site provides an online journal, access to an online course, useful papers, and other general resources. (*http://www.scu.edu.au/schools/gcm/ar/arhome.html*)

Action Research at Queen's University: Provides excellent links to programs, conferences, sites, resources, publications, and student and faculty reports related to action research. (*http://educ.queensu.ca/~ar*)

Action Research Page: A wide range of action research resources, including papers, links, and so on., from the University of Colorado at Denver School of Education. (*http://www.cudenver.edu/~mryder/itc/act_res.html*)

ACTION RESEARCH RESOURCES

Websites in this section provide more specific resources for those engaged in action research studies.

Action Research International—Online Journal: A refereed online journal of action research. Edited by Bob Dick. (*http://www.scu.edu.au/schools/gcm/ar/ari/arihome.html*)

Jack Whitehead's Home Page: A particularly comprehensive website that offers a wide range of resources especially pertinent to schools and education. Information includes many examples of action research theses, and links to other home pages. (*http://www2.bath.ac.uk/~edsajw/home.html*)

Research for Action (RFA): A Philadelphia-based nonprofit organization engaged in educational research and reform to improve educational opportunities and outcomes for all students. A rich range of resources. (*http://www.researchforaction.org/index.html*)

AROW—Action Research Open Web: Action Research Open Web provides open access to research, education, projects, and reports. (*http://www2.fhs.usyd.edu.au/arow/*)

CARE: This UK action research site located at the University of East Anglia focuses particularly on education and offers a variety of resources, as well as links to other websites. (*http://www. uea.ac.uk/care/*)

ACTION RESEARCH GUIDELINES AND METHODOLOGY

These sites provide specific guidance to those wishing to extend their knowledge of and skills in action research methods.

Areol: Areol is "action research and evaluation online," a 14-week introductory course offered by email each semester as a public service by the graduate college of management at Southern Cross University. (*http://www.scu.edu.au/schools/gcm/ar/arhome.html*)

A Beginner's Guide to Action Research: A very useful and comprehensive guide to action research from Bob Dick. (*http://ousd.k12.ca.us/netday/links/Action_Research/begin_guide_action_research*)

Action Research Methodology: An overview of the methodological approach of action research. (*http://www.web.net/~robrien/papers/arfinal.html*)

Classroom Action Research Overview: Assists the teacher to find out what's happening in his or her classroom and to use that information to make wise decisions. Website by Gwynn Mettetal, Division of Education, Indiana University. (*http://www.iusb.edu/~gmetteta/Classroom_Action_Research.html*)

Action Research: This INFED website explores the development of different traditions of action research and provides an introductory guide to the literature. (*http://www.infed.org/research/b-actres.htm*)

TEACHER RESEARCHER RESOURCES

These sites are very specifically oriented toward the teacher researcher. They provide a rich range of resources and descriptions of school-based teacher-research projects.

Teacher Action Research—EdChange Multicultural Pavilion: A teacher action research resource particularly relevant to equity and multicultural education. (*http://www.edchange.org/multicultural/tar.html*)

Teacher Action Research: The action research "Teachers as Researchers" program is a successful program started in the 1999–2000 school year. The program awards teachers a stipend for research projects conducted in their schools. (*http://www.tec.leon.k12.fl.us/gi/action_research.htm*)

Action Research: This teacher research program provides a variety of useful resources for teacher researchers. (*http://www.rochesterteachercenter.com/teacher research.htm*)

Classroom Action Research Overview: A useful resource for novice teacher researchers. (*http://www.iusb.edu/~gmetteta/Classroom_Action_Research.html*)

Teacher Research (Action Research Resources): An interesting list of magazine and journal articles. Some of the articles are presented with the full text available online. (*http://ucerc.edu/teacherresearch/teacherresearch.html*)

Classroom Action Research: A comprehensive overview of procedures for classroom action research. An excellent resource. (*http://www.madison.k12.wi.us/sod/car/carhome-page.html*)

Action Research Network: The Action Research Network is a tool that enables researchers (teachers) to share their research and view the findings of others. It provides an online template that helps researchers record information about various aspects of their research. (*http://actionresearch.altec.org/*)

TEACHER EDUCATION

This section provide sites relevant to teacher education. It includes discussions and examples of teacher education portfolios, and the use of action research in student teaching.

Teacher Education: ERIC citations for portfolios in teacher education. (*http://ericae.net/infoguide/PORT_TE.txt*)

ACTION RESEARCH IN SCHOOLS

Action Research: A general introduction to action research in schools, sponsored by a state education agency. (*http://education.qld.gov.au/students/advocacy/equity/gender-sch/action/action.html*)

An Action Research Approach to Curriculum Development: Action research is used in contexts where an understanding of complex social situations has been sought in order to improve the quality of education. (*http//:informationr.net/ir/1-1/paper2.html*)

School Renewal: This site describes how a group of schools uses action research for purposes of school renewal. (*http://www.fau.edu/coe/sfcel/browsch.htm*)

COMMUNITY EDUCATION

Informal, Adult and Community Education: A select, annotated bibliography covering the nature and use of action research within informal education, adult education, and community education. (*http://www.infed.org/research/b-actres.htm*)

LISTS, ORGANIZATIONS, AND GROUPS

Centre for Action Research in Professional Practice: Presents approaches to action research that integrate action, reflection, and collaboration. (*http://www.bath.ac.uk/carpp/*)

Action Learning and Action Research Association: An international network providing conferences, a journal, and website resources. (*http://www.alarpm.org.au*)

AR Special Interest Group: Action Research Special Interest Group of the American Educational Research Association. (*http://www.coe.westga.edu/arsig/*)

Collaborative Action Research Network: This website provides a variety of resources in education, health, and welfare. (*http://www.did.stu.mmu.ac.uk/carn/*)

Action Research Network, Ireland: Provides links to a network of action research contacts in Ireland. (*http://www.iol.ie/~rayo/AR_Web/index.html*)

PAPERS AND JOURNAL ARTICLES

Action Research: Papers and abstracts of classroom action research in schools in Madison, Wisconsin. (*http://www.madison.k12.wi.us/sod/car/carabstractintro.html*)

Action Research Suggested Readings On-line: A list of suggested action research readings identified by the Pathways to Learning in co-operation with the National Network of Regional Educational Laboratories. (*http://www.ncrel.org/sdrs/areas/issues/envrnmnt/drugfree/sa3act.htm*)

Action Research Page: Provides a diverse selection of action research resources, including papers, links, and so on. (*http://www.cudenver.edu/~mryder/itc/act_res.html*)

Teacher Enhancement: Science: Teacher action research helps improve schools. Provides access to nine papers included in the publication resulting from a teacher enhancement program for middle school science teachers in Georgia and Florida. The program concentrated on helping science teachers find ways to solve some common problems. (*http://www.middleweb.com/SERVEreport.html*)

Social Movement: "Action Research and Social Movement: A Challenge for Policy Research," by Stephen Kemmis, Deakin University—Geelong. (*http://olam.ed.asu.edu/epaa/v1n1.html*)

REFERENCES

Altheide, D., & Johnson, J. (1998). Criteria for assessing interpretive validity in qualitative research. In N. K. Denzin & Y. S. Lincoln (Eds.), *Collecting and interpreting qualitative materials*. Thousand Oaks, CA: Sage.

Anderson, G., Herr, K., & Nihlen, A. (1994). *Studying your own school: An educator's guide to qualitative research*. Thousand Oaks, CA: Corwin.

Arhar, J., Holly, M. L., & Kasten, W. C. (2000). *Action research for teachers: Traveling the yellow brick road*. Upper Saddle River, NJ: Prentice Hall.

Armstrong, F. (2004). *Action research for inclusive education*. Routledge Falmer. Abingdon, UK.

Astin, A., Banta, T., Cross, P., El-Khawas, E., Ewell, P., Hutchings, P., Marchese, T., McClenney, K., Mentkowski, M., Miller, M., Moran, E. T., & Wright, B. (1996). *Principles of good practice for assessing student learning*. American Association of Higher Education. Washington, DC. Routledge Falmer. Abingdon, UK.

Atkinson, P. (1992). *Understanding ethnographic texts*. Newbury Park, CA: Sage.

Atweh, B., Weeks, P., & Kemmis, S. (2005). *Action research in practice: Partnerships for social justice in education*. New York: Routledge.

Baldwin, S. (1997). High school students' participation in action research: An ongoing learning process. In E. Stringer & colleagues (Eds.), *Community-based ethnography: Breaking traditional boundaries of research, teaching and learning*. Mahwah, NJ: Lawrence Erlbaum.

Barbour, S., & J. Kitzinger (Eds.). (1998). *Developing focus group research: Politics, theory and practice*. Thousand Oaks, CA: Sage.

Bell, J. (1993). *Doing your research project: A guide for first-time researchers in education and social science*. Buckingham: Open University Press.

Berge, B., & Ve, H. (2000). *Action research for gender equity*. Buckingham, UK: Open University Press.

Berger, P., Berger, B., & Kellner, H. (1973). *The homeless mind: Modernization and consciousness*. New York: Random House.

Berger, P., & Luckmann, T. (1967). *The social construction of reality: A treatise in the sociology of knowledge*. Anchor. Garden City, NY.

Block, P. (1990). *The empowered manager: Positive political skills at work*. San Francisco: Jossey Bass.

Bogdan, R., & Biklen, S. (1992). *Qualitative research for education*. Boston: Allyn & Bacon.

Bray, J. L., Lee, J., Smith, L., & Yorks, L. (Eds.). (2000). *Collaborative inquiry in practice: Action, reflection, and making meaning*. Thousand Oaks, CA: Sage.

Brown, A., & Dowling, P. (1998). *Doing research/reading research. A mode of interrogation for education*. London: Falmer.

Brown, T. & Jones, L. (2002). *Action research and postmodernism: Congruence and critique*. Open University Press/McGraw-Hill. Maidenhead, UK.

Burnaford, G. E., Fischer, J., & Hobson, D. (Eds.) (2001). *Teachers doing research: The power of action through inquiry* (2nd ed.). Mahwah, NJ: Lawrence Erlbaum Associates.

Burns, A. (1999). *Collaborative action research for English language teachers*. Cambridge, UK: Cambridge University Press.

Calhoun, E. (1994). *How to use action research in the self-renewing school*. Alexandria, VA: Association for Supervision and Curriculum Development.

Chirban, J. (1996). *Interviewing in depth: The interactive-relational approach*. Thousand Oaks, CA: Sage.

Christiansen, H., Goulet, L., Krentz, C., & Maeers, M. (Eds.). (1997). *Recreating relationships: Collaboration and educational reform*. Albany: SUNY Press.

Christensen, L. (1997). Philosophical and pedagogical development: An ethnographic process. In E. Stringer and colleagues, *Community-based ethnography: Breaking traditional boundaries of research, teaching and learning.* Mahwah, NJ: Lawrence Erlbaum.

Claunch, A. (2000). *Understanding teaching history.* Unpublished paper. Albuquerque: University of New Mexico.

Coghlan, D., & Brannick, T. (2004). *Doing action research in your own organization* (2nd ed.). Thousand Oaks, CA: Sage.

Connelly, F., & Clandinin, D.J. (Eds.). (1999). *Shaping a professional identity: Stories of educational practice.* New York: Teachers College Press.

Connery, C. (2003). *Sociocultural semiotic texts of emerging biliterates in non-academic settings.* Ph.D. dissertation. Albuquerque: University of New Mexico.

Cook, T., & Campbell, D. (1979). *Quasi-experimentation: Design and analysis for field settings.* Chicago, IL: Rand McNally.

Creswell, J. (2002). *Educational research: Planning, conducting and evaluating quantitative and qualitative research* (2nd ed.). Upper Saddle River, NJ: Merrill/Prentice Hall.

Darling-Hammond, L., & McLauglin, M. (1995). Policies that support professional development in an era of reform. *Phi Delta Kappan, 76*(8), 597–604.

De Laine, M. (2000). *Fieldwork, participation and practice: Ethics and dilemmas in qualitative research.* Thousand Oaks, CA: Sage.

De Marrais, K. B. (Ed.). (1998). *Inside stories: Qualitative research reflections.* Mahwah, NJ: Lawrence Erlbaum Associates.

Denzin, N. K. (1989a). *Interpretive biography.* Thousand Oaks, CA: Sage.

Denzin, N. K. (1989b). *Interpretive interactionism.* Newbury Park, CA: Sage.

Denzin, N. K. (1997). *Interpretive ethnography.* Thousand Oaks, CA: Sage.

Denzin, N. K., & Lincoln, Y. S. (Eds.). (1998b). *The landscape of qualitative research: Theories and issues.* Thousand Oaks, CA: Sage.

Denzin, N. K., & Lincoln, Y. S. (Eds.). (2005). *Handbook of qualitative research* (3rd ed.). Thousand Oaks, CA: Sage.

Dewey, J. (1916/1966). *Democracy in education.* New York: Macmillan.

Dewey, J. (1930). From absolutism to experimentalism. In G. Adams & W. Montgomery (Eds.), *Contemporary American philosophy* (pp. 13–27). New York: Macmillan.

Edwards, C., Gandini, L., & Forman, G. (1993). *The hundred languages of children: The Reggio Amelia approach—advanced reflections.* Greenwich, CT: Ablex.

Fals-Borda, O., & Rahman, M. (1991). *Action and knowledge: Breaking the monopoly with participatory action research.* New York: Apex.

Feiman-Nemser, S. (2000). *From preparation to practice: Designing a continuum to strengthen and sustain teaching.* Unpublished manuscript. Michigan State University.

Fine, G., & Sandstrom, K. (1988). *Knowing children: Participant observation with minors.* Thousand Oaks, CA: Sage.

Fink, A. (1995). *The survey handbook.* Thousand Oaks, CA: Sage.

Gay, L., Mills, G., & Airasian, P. (2006). *Educational research: Competencies for analysis and applications.* Upper Saddle River, NJ: Merrill/Prentice Hall.

Genat, W. (2006). *Aboriginal health workers: Primary health care at the Margins.* Perth, West Australia: University of Western Australia Press.

Glanz, J. (2003). *Action research: An educational leader's guide to school improvement* (2nd ed.). Christopher Gordon Publishers.

Goodenough, W. (1971). *Culture, language and society.* Reading, MA: Addison-Wesley.

Graue, M., & Walsh, D. (1998). *Studying children in context: Theories, methods, and ethics.* Thousand Oaks, CA: Sage.

Greenbaum, T. (Ed.). (2000). *Moderating focus groups: A practical guide for group facilitation.* Thousand Oaks, CA: Sage.

Greig, A., & Taylor, J. (1998). *Doing research with children.* Thousand Oaks, CA: Sage.

Guba, E., & Lincoln, Y. (1989). *Fourth-generation evaluation.* Newbury Park, CA: Sage.

Haraway, D. (1988). Situated knowledges: The science question in feminism and the privilege of partial perspective. *Feminist Studies, 14*(3), 575–599.

Hawley, W., & Valli, L. (1999). The essentials of effective professional development: A new consensus. In L. Darling-Hammond & G. Sykes (Eds.), *Teaching as the learning profession: A handbook of policy and practice.* San Francisco: Jossey-Bass.

Heath, S. B. (1983). *Ways with words: Language, life and work in communities and classrooms.* Cambridge University Press.

Helm, J. (1999, March). Projects: Exploring children's interests. *Scholastic Early Childhood Today.*

Henderson, J., Hawthorne, R., & Stollenwerk, D. (2000). *Transformative curriculum leadership.* (2nd ed.). Upper Saddle River, NJ: Merrill/Prentice Hall.

Hollingsworth, S. (Ed.). (1997) *International action research: A casebook for educational reform.* London: Falmer.

Holly, M., Arhar, J., & Kasten, W. (2004). *Action research for teachers: Travelling the yellow brick road* (2nd ed.). Upper Saddle River, NJ: Prentice Hall.

Holstein, J., & Gubrium, J. (1995). *The active interview.* Thousand Oaks, CA: Sage.

Horowitz, I. (1970). Sociological snoopers and journalistic moralizers. *Transaction, 7,* 4–8.

Huffman, J. (1997). *Beyond TQM: Tools and techniques for high performance improvement*. Sunnyvale, CA: Lanchester Press.

Johnson, A. (2002). *What every teacher should know about action research*. Boston, MA: Allyn & Bacon.

Johnson, A. (2007). *A short guide to action research* (3rd ed.). Boston, MA: Allyn & Bacon.

Johnson, B. (2001). Toward a new classification of nonexperimental quantitative research. *Educational Researcher*, 30(2).

Keck, L. (2000). *Children's experience of art in the classroom*. Unpublished paper. Albuquerque: University of New Mexico.

Kelly, A., & Sewell, S. (1988). *With head, heart, and hand*. Brisbane, Australia: Boolarong.

Kemmis, S., & McTaggart, R. (1988). *The action research planner*. Geelong, Australia: Deakin University Press.

Koshy, V. (2005). *Action research for improving practice: A practical guide*. London: Paul Chapman/Sage.

Krueger, R. (1994). *Focus groups: A practical guide for applied research* (2nd ed.). Thousand Oaks, CA: Sage.

Krueger, R. (1997a). *Moderating focus groups*. Thousand Oaks, CA: Sage.

Krueger, R. (1997b). *Developing questions for focus groups*. Thousand Oaks, CA: Sage.

Krueger, R., & Casey, M. A. (2000). *Focus groups: A practical guide for applied research* (3rd ed.). Thousand Oaks, CA: Sage.

Kvale, S. (1996). *Interviews: An introduction to qualitative research interviewing*. Thousand Oaks, CA: Sage.

Lather, P. (1993). Fertile obsession: Validity after poststructuralism. *Sociological Quarterly*, 35.

Lewin, G., & Lewin, K. (1942). Democracy and the school. *Understanding the Child*, 10, 7–11.

Lewin, K. (1938). Experiments on autocratic and democratic principles. *Social Frontier*, 4, 316–319.

Lewin, K. (1946). Action research and minority problems. *Journal of Social Issues*, 2(4), 34–46.

Lewin, K. (1948). *Resolving social conflicts*. New York: Harper.

Lincoln, Y., & Guba, E. (1985). *Naturalistic inquiry*. Beverley Hills, CA: Sage.

Little, J. (1993). Teacher professional development in a climate of educational reform. *Educational Evaluation and Policy Analysis*, 15, 129–151.

Malaguzzi, L. (1995). *The fountains: The unheard voice of children*. Reggio Amelia, Italy: Reggio Children.

Malinowsky, B. (1961). *Argonauts of the West Pacific: An account of native enterprise and adventure in the archipelagoes of Melanesian New Guinea*. New York: E. P. Dutton. (Original work published 1922.)

Marcus, G. (1998). *Ethnography through thick and thin*. Princeton, NJ: Princeton University Press.

Marshall, C., & Rossman, G. (1999). *Designing qualitative research* (3rd ed.). Thousand Oaks, CA: Sage.

McCaleb, S. (1997). *Building communities of learners: A collaboration among teachers, students, families and community*. Mahwah, NJ: Lawrence Erlbaum.

McCracken, G. (1988). *The long interview*. Thousand Oaks, CA: Sage.

McDiarmid, G. (1994). *Realizing new learnings for all students: A framework for professional development of Kentucky teachers*. East Lansing, MI: National Center for Research on Teaching.

McEwan, P. (2000). The potential impact of large-scale voucher programs. *Review of Educational Research*, 70(2).

McLean, J., Herman, J.L., & Herman J.J. (2005). *Improving education through action research: A guide for administrators and teachers* (Roadmaps to success). Thousand Oaks, CA: Corwin Press.

McNiff, J., & Whitehead, J. (2006). *Action research for teachers–A practical guide*. Abingdon, UK: David Fulton Publishers.

McTaggart, R. (Ed.). (1997). *Participatory action research: International contexts and consequences*. Albany: SUNY Press.

Mead, G. (1934). *Mind, self and society*. Chicago: University of Chicago Press.

Meerdink, J. (1999, February). Driving a car for the first time: Teachers, caregivers and a child-driven approach. In *Early Childhood Matters: The Bulletin of the Bernard Van Leer Foundation*, No. 91.

Merriam-Webster Online Dictionary. (2001). Available online at http://www.m-w.com.

Mertler, C. (2005). *Action research: Teachers as researchers in the classroom*. Thousand Oaks, CA: Sage.

Meyers, E., & Rust, F. (2003). *Taking action with teacher research*. Heinemann. Portsmouth, NH.

Milgram, S. (1963). Behavioral study of obedience. *Journal of Abnormal and Social Psychology*, 67, 371–378.

Mills, G. (2007). *Action research: A guide for the teacher researcher* (3rd ed.). Upper Saddle River, NJ: Merrill/Prentice Hall.

Morgan, D. (1997a). *Planning focus groups*. Thousand Oaks, CA: Sage.

Morgan, D. (1997b). *The focus group guidebook*. Thousand Oaks, CA: Sage.

Morgan, D., & Krueger, R. (1997). *The focus group kit: Volumes 1–6*. Thousand Oaks, CA: Sage.

National Board for Professional Teaching Standards. (1994). *What teachers should know and be able to do*. Detroit: Author.

National Commission on Teaching and America's Future. (1996). *What matters most: Teaching for America's future*. New York: National Commission on Teaching and America's Future.

Noffke, S. (1997). Professional, personal and political dimensions of action research. *Review of Educational Research, 22*. Washington, DC: AERA.

Oleson, V. (1998). Feminisms and models of qualitative research. In N. Denzin & Y. Lincoln (Eds.), *The landscape of qualitative research*. Thousand Oaks, CA: Sage.

Oleson, V. (2005). Early millennial feminist qualitative research. In N. Denzin & Y. Lincoln (Eds.), *Handbook of qualitative research*. Thousand Oaks, CA: Sage.

Oliva, P. (2001). *Developing the curriculum* (5th ed.). New York: Longman.

Oppenheim, A. (1966). *Questionnaire design and attitude measurement*. London: Heinemann.

Pedraza, P., & Rivera, M. (2005). *Latino education: An agenda for community action research*. Lawrence Erlbaum Associates.

Petty, R., (1997). Everything is different now: Surviving ethnographic research. In E. Stringer & colleagues (Eds.), *Community-based research*. Mahwah, NJ: Lawrence Erlbaum.

Pratiss, J. (Ed.). (1985). *Reflections: The anthropological muse*. Washington, DC: American Anthropological Association.

Punch, M. (1994). Politics and ethics in qualitative research. In N. Denzin & Y. Lincoln (Eds.), *Handbook of qualitative research*. Thousand Oaks, CA: Sage.

Reason, P., & Bradbury, H. (2001). *Handbook of action research*. Thousand Oaks, CA: Sage.

Reason, P. & H. Bradbury (2007). *Handbook of Action Research* (2nd ed.). Thousand Oaks, CA: Sage.

Rorty, R. (1989). *Contigiency, irony, and solidarity*. Cambridge, UK: Cambridge University Press.

Rossi, P. (1997, September). Having an experience in five acts: Multiple literacies through young children's opera. *Language Arts, 74*.

Rubin, H., & Rubin, I. (1995). *Qualitative interviewing: The art of hearing data*. Thousand Oaks, CA: Sage.

Sagor, R. (2000). *Guiding school improvement with action research*. ASCD.

Schouten, D., & Watling, R. (1997). *Media action projects: A model for integrating video in project-based education, training and community development*. Nottingham, UK: University of Nottingham Urban Programme Research Group.

Scriven, M. (1981a). *The logic of evaluation*. Inverness, CA: Edgepress.

Scriven, M. (1981b). Summative teacher evaluation. In J. Millan (Ed.), *Handbook of teacher evaluation*. Beverley Hills, CA: Sage.

Selekman, M. (1997). *Solution-focused therapy with children*. New York: Guilford Press.

Silverman, D. (2000). *Doing qualitative research. A practical handbook*. Thousand Oaks, CA: Sage.

Somekh, B. (2005). *Action research (Doing qualitative research in educational settings)*. Open University Press/McGraw-Hill Maidenhead, UK.

Spradley, J. (1979a). *The ethnographic interview*. New York: Holt, Rinehart & Winston.

Spradley, J. (1979b). *Participant observation*. New York: Holt, Rinehart & Winston.

Spradley, J., & McCurdy, D. (1972). Prospect Heights, IL: Waveland Press.

Stake, R. (2005). Qualitative case studies. In N. Denzin & Y. Lincoln (Eds.), *Handbook of qualitative research* (3rd ed.). Thousand Oaks, CA: Sage.

Stein, M., Smith, M., & Silver, E. (1999, Fall). The development of professional developers: Learning to assist teachers in new settings in new ways. *Harvard Educational Review, 69*(3). Fall.

Stringer, E. (2007). This is so democratic: Action research and policy development in East Timor. In P. Reason & H. Bradbury (Eds.), *Handbook of action research*. Thousand Oaks, CA: Sage.

Stringer, E., & colleagues. (1997) (2001). *Community-based research: Breaking traditional boundaries of research, teaching, and learning*. Mahwah, NJ: Lawrence Erlbaum.

Stringer, E., & Genat, W. (1998, January). The *double helix of action research*. Unpublished paper. Qualitative Research in Education Conference, Athens, Georgia.

Sykes, J. (2002). *Action research: A practical guide for transforming your school library*. Libraries Unlimited. Portsmouth, NH.

Tennant, G. (2001). *Six sigma: SPC and TQM in manufacturing and services*. Gower Publishing.

Tomai, D. (2003). *Action research for educators*. Scarecrow Education.

Trinh, T. (1991). *When the moon waxes red: Representation, gender and cultural politics*. New York: Routledge.

Tyler, R. (1949). *Basic principles of curriculum and instruction*. Chicago: University of Chicago Press.

Van Manen, M. (1979). The phenomenology of pedagogic observation. *Canadian Journal of Education, 4*(1), 5–16.

Van Manen, M. (1982). Phenomenological pedagogy. *Curriculum Inquiry, 12*(3), 283–299.

Van Manen, M. (1984). Practising phenomenological writing. *Phenomenology and Pedagogy, 2*(1), 36–39.

Van Manen, M. (1988). The relation between research and pedagogy. In W. F. Pinar (Ed.), *Contemporary curriculum discourses* (pp. 437–452). Scottsdale, AZ: Gorsuch Scarisbrick.

Van Manen, M. (1990). *Researching lived experience: Human science for an action sensitive pedagogy.* London, Ontario: Althouse Press.

Wadsworth, Y. (1997). *Everyday evaluation on the run* (2nd ed.). St. Leonards, NSW: Allen and Unwin.

Wallace, M. (1998). *Action research for language teachers.* Cambridge, UK: Cambridge University Press.

Weis, L., & Fine, M. (2000). *Speed bumps: A student-friendly guide to qualitative research.* New York: Teachers College Press.

Wiggington, E. (1985). *Sometimes a shining moment: The Foxfire experience.* Garden City, NY: Doubleday.

Wolcott, H. (1994). *Transforming qualitative data: Description, analysis and interpretation.* Thousand Oaks, CA: Sage.

Youngman, M. (1982). Designing and analyzing questionnaires. In J. Bell (Ed.), *Conducting small-scale investigations in educational management.* London: Harper & Row.

INDEX